Dialogues with Master

Talking with Leaders of the Past

Dedication

"The Guys"

Celestial Voices' Books

The trilogy, *Dialogues with Masters of the Spirit World* contains a set of soul interviews with the following titles:

Talking with Leaders of the Past.
Famous people, all born in the nineteenth century

Talking with Twentieth-Century Women, and
Talking with Twentieth-Century Men
Celebrities in many fields of life, all born in the last century.

Our latest book of soul interviews is:

How I Died (and what I did next)
Unknown souls from all over the world tell their fascinating stories of how they transitioned through death and went Home.

For full details of our current offering, please go to

www.CelestialVoicesInc.com

Talking
with Leaders
of the Past

A Book of Spiritual Interviews

Arranged by
Peter Watson Jenkins

Channeled by
Toni Ann Winninger

Celestial Voices, Inc.

Talking with Leaders of the Past

Cover design by Robert Buzek Designs Inc., Lake Zurich, Illinois

Published by Celestial Voices, Inc.
13354 W. Heiden Circle, Lake Bluff, IL 60044

Library of Congress Control Number: 2007907531

ISBN: 978-0-9798917-2-4

FIRST EDITION (revised)

Contents

Introduction

Working with Spirits

These days, large numbers of people are openly examining the spiritual issues of daily life, and are reviewing their personal philosophy and spirituality. This book aims to provide fresh ideas to inform that search for truth about the meaning and purpose of our human existence.

Compiling this material involved Toni Ann Winninger in psychically channeling from the *Other Side* the vibrational thoughts of a wonderful group of Masters of the Spirit World (*the Masters*), with whom she interacts daily. With their help, she made contact with fifteen leading individuals of the nineteenth and twentieth centuries (*the Leaders*), who dwell currently in the spiritual realm, which they usually call *Home*.

This group of Ascended Masters includes wise souls who became spiritually enlightened while still in physical form, and a number of mature advisors who previously incarnated on planet Earth but who have finished doing so. There are also souls in the group who chose never to incarnate, whom people sometimes describe as *angels*. Our group of Masters tells us that these celestial beings are involved in counseling incarnated souls on planet Earth.

In addition to the large core group of Masters were fifteen individual Leaders, named in the table of contents, with whom we were encouraged to speak. When these souls were last in physical form, each was a leading figure in some part of human society. We were not told what degree of spiritual enlightenment these individual souls may have attained at this stage, but they were made available to us with the Masters' enthusiastic agreement.

Interviews of the Masters and Leaders were conducted by Peter Watson Jenkins. In making his choice of topics, he aimed to cover issues of interest and concern to a wide audience. He conducted the dialogues fully aware that, being just a layman, he had only a little background in the historical or academic disciplines involved in the study of each personality.

Toni channeled the thoughts transmitted from Home by the Masters and Leaders as faithfully as possible. She has a great facility at channeling and is exceptionally accurate. She is painstakingly aware of the need to suppress all interference from her own mind that might influence the meaning of the messages transmitted from Home. She is justly proud of her skill in cutting off her own thoughts during each interview by maintaining a self-imposed regimen of strict mental control. Scholars might prefer more extended discussions than are given here, but contacts with Home are necessarily short, not because of any restriction by the souls involved, but because of the limitations of the channeler's body. This book has no academic pretensions, however; we just saw that our task was to get to the point with dispatch in order to meet the practical needs of psychic contact and communication.

How accurate is channeling? Certainly anyone who does *not* question whether those we interviewed can possibly be who we say they are must be lacking in curiosity! As authors we know full well that we are inviting controversy and risking criticism by asserting that those with whom we have spoken are neither imposters nor figments of our imagination. Based on our experience of regular but ever-critical contacts with the Masters, however, it is our sincere judgment that all those interviewed in this book are genuinely who they say they are, or to be more accurate, who they *used* to be when last in human form. Back again in the spiritual environment, these souls are only as much the named person interviewed as they are any other individual whom they have been during their series of personal incarnations over a multitude of lives.

We publish these interviews with both of us wholly sure—in the language of the law, "beyond a reasonable doubt"—that those we interviewed truly are the people whom we have sought. We are convinced of this mostly by the subtle differences of their energy, tone, style, and use of language—and also because Toni had no prior knowledge of some of the people with whom Peter spoke. Nevertheless, we are very aware that it is quite impossible for us to offer any *absolute* proof about those whom we interviewed here. We also appreciate that even daring to ask people beyond the grave for their opinion may not appeal to everyone's sensitivities—a sensitivity that frequent bursts of loving laughter from back Home has long dispelled within us.

If you are among the skeptics, we respect your view and commend the Masters' words to you for their fascinating content. After all, it is neither impossible nor ridiculous for the curious to ask, "If these people really are who they say they are, what might they want to tell us now?" We believe absolutely in the authenticity of these interviews, but should you prefer to read this book as a work of fiction, enjoy it—it is thought provoking.

It was fascinating to observe many shifts and even some clear reversals of personal opinion that have followed the earthly death of the Leaders whom we contacted, and whose words are this transcript. Above all, we want to tell you how the Masters, who have made this volume possible, always appeared to us as being happy, modest, and full of love. It has been a delight to work with them, and so we affectionately dedicate this volume to "The Guys," as we call them, with our grateful thanks.

Toni Ann Winninger works daily with clients who are helped by this ever-changing, friendly, fun-loving group of spirits. She is very careful in her preparation for sessions with them to request that "only those beings who are in and of the Light," and who come "for the highest and greatest good," will enter into the discussion. As a channel, Toni is involved in a very specific contact with this spirit group. Unlike mediums who choose to work with discarnate souls who have not yet returned Home, Toni has dedicated her contact to be with only the most advanced spiritual sources available, those who will give wise counsel to her many clients who come seeking growth in spiritual knowledge and wisdom, and psycho-spiritual health.

Channeling is as much an art as a science. Although most ideas transmitted by the Masters come in thought forms similar to language, some are given as metaphors, frequently in picture form, necessitating that the channel herself find appropriate words. Having worked for some time in this way, Toni usually can make a close approximate interpretation. So, as you read our conversations, be aware of the problem of having too narrow a reliance on the precise words of every statement—although each line we have written has been carefully double-checked for accuracy with the souls involved. Coming from the Masters and the Leaders are wise words and vital information, not legalistic formulas which should be interpreted literally and strictly.

We need to understand that the Masters work under different conditions. They live in the timeless, genderless, non-judgmental, and unconditionally loving Home environment, where the concept of our free will dominates many conversations, and where ego trips are noticeably absent. This brings a refreshing flavor to every discussion. Spirits have little ability to be accurate about issues based on earth-time, however, so it is no good asking them for future winning Lotto numbers (we tried!) because they cannot (or, in love, will not) tell you on which day the game is played. More importantly, if any of our questions can even remotely be answered with the words, "You have freedom of choice," they will be! Finally, although their answers are very helpful, the Masters seldom initiate conversation. Their role is to answer, if they are able, whatever we ask sincerely, so we must always do the asking. Anything else and they might risk violating the strict free-will rule.

One thing must not be missing from this statement of our relationship. We stress that the whole experience of working with the Masters is shot through with their kindness and immense sense of fun. They all laugh freely! We remember their greeting us one day when we had dodged the raindrops to get from our cars to the office. Toni opened her psychic channel to them and immediately enjoyed a ham group recital of Gene Kelly's dance from *Singing in the Rain*, replete with lampposts and unfurled umbrellas.

If some of the discussions we have in this book ramble a little, they may have been drawn from more than one session. Together, however, they comprise a powerful comment on how we should view and live our life, and how we may get to know that help is always available for our physical and emotional healing.

The Spirits and this Book

Over the years spent working with the Masters, we have become aware that this unique contact provides us with exceptional information and enlightenment about the nature of spiritual life. Wanting to deepen our understanding of the process of reincarnation, we began to grill the Masters on their views. In the early discussions, not recorded in this book, we compared our existing knowledge with theirs, only to find that they frequently did not agree with many of the so-called "informed" views put forward by contemporary past-life regression, reincarnation, and New-Age gurus whose work we mentioned to them.

That was the starting point. So, wanting to have a firm and accurate basis for our own ideas about reincarnation, we decided to formalize the dialogue. Parts of these early conversations are recorded in the first chapter. Then we went on to health issues, where we found that the Masters had a very specific viewpoint on the nature of human disease and healing methods, which we knew would cause great controversy when published. Consequently the chapter on health was taken out of this book and now provides the basis of our first publication: *Healing with the Universe, Meditation, and Prayer.* Our agenda thus simplified, we were free in this book to concentrate on observing and analyzing the many aspects of human reincarnation.

In thinking of ways to expand the discussion of reincarnation, both sides agreed with the idea that having dialogues with a number of recently incarnated spirits would add muscle to the book. This enhanced our reincarnation studies and brought the spice of personal discovery to the proceedings. Working with leaders of the past gave us a new set of options. We could ask now if the historical record of their life is correct, and if the soul—now back Home with a clearer and more balanced vision of the past life—had had any personal change of heart since its physical death. We got much more than we bargained for! Many corrections, even reversals of opinion came to light, and some explanations and elaborations given us were much more radical than we ever anticipated.

The main burden of coming up with a list of names of potential subjects fell to Peter, although he is sure that his intuition was stimulated by the Masters themselves. We made a practical decision that all our subjects should have been born in the nineteenth century, giving a small measure of distance from our present time. Actual physical contact had taken place with only one subject: Peter had spoken at a peace rally also addressed by Lord Bertrand Russell, and they had talked together very briefly. Peter had also been in a student audience at Bristol University where Sir Winston Churchill, recently turned eighty, was the featured speaker. The selection of leading individuals was hard to make. With help we chose fifteen (more might have been too many), and left lots of good people out.

To start with, we picked five men of contrasting religious and philosophical beliefs: Dwight Moody, the popular Protestant evangelist; John XXIII, the Roman Catholic reformist pope; Bertrand Russell, the agnostic philosopher; the aesthete and playwright Oscar Wilde; and William James, philosopher, psychologist, and author of *Varieties of Religious Experience*.

There followed a trio of leading ladies, Margaret Sanger's humble birth contrasting powerfully with the privileged background of Florence Nightingale and Eleanor Roosevelt. Each was involved in working for the betterment and emancipation of women. Their styles of serving the community were sharply different, but their honored place in history is secure.

The theme of empire was the basis for the choice of Andrew Carnegie (industrial empire), Winston Churchill (British Empire), and Mahatma Gandhi (the overthrow of British rule). We had not given any great thought to including Adolf Hitler (Nazi Germany's Third Reich), but the Masters strongly wanted us to consider him and, with no little trepidation on our part, his name was eventually added to the list.

To round out the Dialogues on a scientific note we selected three intellectual giants: Charles Darwin, Carl G. Jung, and Albert Einstein, whose major contributions to science have clearly changed forever our understanding of the nature of human evolution, human psychology, and the physical laws of the universe.

We have no pretensions concerning the briefly sketched biographies and the series of questions and comments Peter employed in the dialogues. We do not claim to be scholars of these quite different fifteen historical lives, and our dialogues delved only a small amount into the religious, philosophical, sociological, or scientific issues of each subject's past life. It is vital to add that during and after the interview each soul was given an opportunity to correct and add to the record, and all of them did so both modestly and helpfully.

We discovered that many of the Leaders have changed their opinions and broadened the basis of their knowledge since going Home. Some human opinions, which are mere speculation, are seen quite differently by the truth-centered community of souls at Home. Back in this atmosphere souls express little concern for personal reputation, so their once-cherished beliefs may be freely abandoned. Examples are Margaret Sanger's outright rejection of eugenics, and the qualifications Gandhi now places on vegetarianism. Of import are radical reassessments in the thinking of John XXIII, Russell, James, Darwin, Jung, and Einstein.

There is no hidden agenda in this book, just the authors' desire to get to the core of the secular issues of human reincarnation. But, like T. S. Eliot in *Little Gidding* (1942), during the course of our discussions we rediscovered the enigmatic truth that:

> *We shall not cease from exploration*
> *And the end of all our exploring*
> *Will be to arrive where we started*
> *And know the place for the first time.*

In a nutshell, we are transmitting ideas and concepts of significance from master spirits who live in that dimension from whence every reader of this book has come, and whither, in due course, every reader will return. The Masters have chosen this time of deep trouble and chaos in our earthly society to make their views plain through us (as they have done through other chosen writers). To our mind it is as challenging a set of opinions as any humanity has ever met. Although we remain essentially their messengers, we thought it right to draw our own conclusions of the blueprint of the world view they have presented. These comments we have shared with them, and we have gratefully received their broad approval.

Peter Watson Jenkins
Toni Ann Winninger

Special Terms Defined

(Cross-references are marked *)

Advisors: Souls who are given the task of advising incarnated souls.

Akashic Records: An energetic* library containing a record of all the knowledge* and wisdom* that has been gained through the experiences that souls* have had upon planet Earth. Each soul has its own record of what has transpired throughout each of its incarnations*. The library contains records of everything undertaken by all the souls who have spent time on Earth.

Angel: A human term for a celestial being who, after being separated from Source*, acts as a guide* to those upon Earth, but may or may not at some later time choose to experience a physical shell*.

Ascended Masters: Souls* who have incarnated* and have completed all their lessons, allowing them to come into full enlightenment* of their true nature. These souls no longer need to return to Earth for additional learning. They may choose to return if they wish to teach and mentor other souls in human form.

Contracts: Voluntary agreements that souls* make with other souls while at Home* to ensure that they will have the right Earth situation to help them experience the physical lessons they desire.

Council: A group of guides* who help souls* decide what lessons they wish to experience, and who help them make the best use of the lessons they have learned.

Creator: See, Source.

Dimension: A waveband or stratum of vibrational energy. Planet Earth is at the third dimension. Home* is at the fifth and higher dimensions.

Discarnate: A soul* who clings to the physical because it wants to continue with its past life. This soul/body image remains connected to Earth and contacts or haunts those who remain, until it chooses to return Home*.

Ego: A function of the physical mind that employs judgment* and measures how people perceive themselves. It is a template for the soul* to operate in society so that it may learn lessons and gain wisdom. It is a compilation of human belief systems deemed necessary for a person to exist in their physical body

Energy, Energetic: (1) The basic component of all that exists. (2) Non-physical vibration of a dimension* higher than Earth's, used by the spirit world to communicate.

Enlightenment, Enlightened: The state existing when an incarnate soul* comes to full awareness of the fact that it is an immortal soul and recalls all the implications of its essence*, who it is and what it can do.

Essence: The reality of who you are: a part of the eternal God-Force*.

Freedom of Choice: A universal law that says all souls* have the ultimate right to decide exactly what they are going to do while incarnate*. It extends to all aspects of living, from the choice of biological parents, to the lessons* they will learn, and the manner and time of their physical death.

God: See, Source.

God-Force: See, Source. Sometimes meaning "all souls*."

Guide: A non-physical soul* who makes itself available to help incarnate* souls use their freedom of choice.*

Heaven: See Home. Also, a state of mind on Earth.

Hell: A state of mind on Earth.

Higher Self: That portion of the incarnate* soul* that may be accessed to gain information.

Home: Not a physical place but an energetic* dimension* of unconditional love and of conscious connection with Source*. It is where each soul* works with its guides* and council*. Every soul who is not incarnated* is consciously within the dimension of Home.

Incarnate: A soul* who has gone down to planet Earth and is now in a physical body.

Judgment: A state of mind existing only in Earth's physical third dimension*. In the duality and polarity of the planet, everything has an opposite. Human beings grade all other people by an impression of where they feel the others exist on a personal, ethical, or religious scale of "good" and "bad."

Karma: A term which relates to the effects of an action taken by human beings. Many people use it to explain away what they consider bad experiences that happen to them. This is inaccurate in its application to human experience. The accurate view is solely the energetic* effect of the action taken.

Knowledge: Awareness of facts and principles but not necessarily of how to use or apply them in living.

Lessons: The various pre-planned experiences that a soul* has while incarnate* that allow it to gain wisdom*.

Masters: See, Ascended Masters.

Reincarnation: The process the soul* uses to experience more lessons to obtain wisdom*. After completing one incarnation*, the soul returns Home* to assess its experiences and to determine what else it wishes to learn. It then reincarnates by entering into a new physical body in order to have further experiences.

Shell: The living physical structure inhabited by a soul*. No human or animal body can live without some connection to Source*.

Soul Mate: Another soul* who came into being at the same time. There are groups of individual souls, usually numbering 144 in each group. Generally these are the souls with whom you choose to make your most important contracts* prior to incarnation*.

Souls: Individualized pieces of energy* split off by and from Source*, in order to have unique experiences outside the perfect. They are all particles of Source, so each and every soul is also Source. All souls are equal regardless of the human shell* they have chosen to inhabit.

Source: The point of origin of all that is known by human beings, and of all that exists. It is the energy* of unconditional love, the highest vibrational energy* anywhere, and is found in everything.

The Source makes no judgments* and does not reward or punish souls*.

Supreme Being: See, Source.

Transition: The movement of a soul* from life in the body to life at Home*. Physical death.

Wisdom: Awareness of the facts and principles of spiritual life with understanding of how to apply them in living.

Notes

In the book, questions and comments by Peter Watson Jenkins are printed *in italic script*. Toni Winninger's channeled replies, are printed in roman script. Editorial comment is in square brackets.

Some Leaders used the male pronoun inclusively. English usage has changed only recently, and we decided, so as to retain the historical overtones of an individual's speech, not to adjust the record to be gender neutral (as both of us would prefer).

In the commentaries following individual dialogues, Toni portrays what the energetic feel of the conversation was like. Then Peter reviews its content and comments on selected issues.

"Without a body the soul is in the realm of unconditional love, and it doesn't have the opportunity to experience anything else."

The Masters
On Reincarnation

The Incarnation Process

Please explain the process of incarnation. I understand that a soul, who is a distinct being, comes into relationship with a body, a physical organism that becomes enlivened by the presence of that soul.

Correct.

How is it done?

The soul is a spark of light which is a fragment of the Creator. It is an energy able to inhabit many different things. When a soul chooses to experience something it must have the vehicle of a body, a living organism, to do so. It determines, with its council of advisors, what it wishes to experience within the life-span of that living vehicle. It then chooses the parentage for that vehicle, who will allow it to be placed into an appropriate situation to experience whatever it has decided to experience.

So, should the soul want to experience grief, it chooses parents who are going to die, or a family in which there is going to be a physical loss. Therefore it chooses to inhabit the cellular division, the fetus, that occurs from the union of those two parents. The soul generally does not inhabit the growing organism until it is near to birth, but it remains close, monitoring what is going on, to ensure that the circumstances being set up are those which it had anticipated, and which it wants to experience. Sometimes, because of the freedom of choice of the parents, the situation may change; there may be a stillbirth, or some anomaly, so that which is delivered does not need the soul.

Can a human being exist without a soul?
Although a soul may not choose to fully enter a fetus until it is being born, it has to make a connection in order for the fetus to be viable.

When the fetus starts kicking, does that indicate the soul has entered it?
Yes. There only has to be a connection. [*Toni: They are showing me fine strands between the soul and the fetus.*] That's how the soul can travel outside the fetus and still maintain the viability of the "host". The host in this sense is the body that the soul has chosen to inhabit. This happens even within an adult host—it has to have at least some contact with the soul. At the moment of conception there is a determination made by each soul that that unique fetus is in fact the chosen one. That's not a connection but an energetic acknowledgment. The soul is aware of the act of conception, but this is not a specific connection. The soul may, in fact, be acting in cooperation with the biological parents to give the urge for the conception at a moment of its choosing. It also determines whether it wants to be male or female.

How does the soul actually inhabit the physical body: is it by an interface at the cellular level, or at the level of the DNA?
It goes into the fetus and brings knowledge of its DNA and its prior experiences—not the DNA strands which have been identified on Earth, but additional strands with which you are unfamiliar. It enters into everything, like a liquid totally saturating a piece of material. It becomes everything that is within the body. In the same way the light—the energy of the soul—comes in contact with the body and can be completely absorbed. In addition to having a connection with that body, the soul can also project out through the ether.

Then the memories of the soul are downloaded progressively. The soul is still free while the fetus, whose DNA is gradually being filled up, is becoming a storehouse of the knowledge and experience that the soul has had in its prior lives. Ultimately, this part of the physical memory bank is stored in the DNA. Contained within the DNA of the host are all of the soul's memories and lessons, including whatever is desired to be accomplished in this particular incarnation.

At what point does the total connection take place—if it is, in fact, total?

There is no set format. There are instances, with less mature souls in particular, where they enter the fetus almost at the point of conception and remain there. The more experienced souls "watch the cake baking" but don't become a part of it until it is ready to be consumed—or in this case, delivered. These souls will spend their time elsewhere, saying goodbye to their friends, for example. There is also a small part of the soul left at Home, but the majority of the energy is put into the learning experience.

For the baby to live apart from the mother, the soul must be inside. The idea is incorrect that the fetus may be delivered and ten minutes later the soul would inhabit it, because within that ten minutes the shell (body) would die. It is rare that the connection between soul and fetus ever takes place after birth. Incorrect readings of this process come from the physical host's faulty memory, not from the facts. It takes a while for the host to be acclimated to the energy of the soul, and to be aware of the point when the two united, which accounts for the occasional incorrect perspective.

How is it that all the people we have sought to interview for this book have not returned to Earth?

There are various reasons. Some of them have not come back because they are acting as guides for people now in similar incarnations. Others are still going through their life-reviews, comparing and contrasting what they learned with what is going on now. Some have chosen not to enter the chaos which is on Earth at present—we can choose to come when we want to.

Soul Groups

Dr. Ian Stevenson's research shows some souls going back into their immediate biological families, and others back into the extended family of the tribe. How common is that compared with people coming back more randomly, not to the family but to other situations?

It depends completely upon the contracts which were made within the soul group. You continually reincarnate with a fairly small number of peers. Within your group are up to 144 souls. Most souls have a close soul group of about 24. If you make very involved contracts within your soul group, it is possible that if you *transition* (die) but have agreed to more complicated contracts, you will have to come back to complete the rest of the contracts. This is particularly true of grandparents who have started things with grandchildren and then come back, perhaps as siblings or cousins.

This appears to happen in the Tlingit tribe in Alaska.

There is a very closely intertwined soul group there.

How much does the culture of the tribe influence the soul group?

Not at all. If no complicated contract necessitating your coming back into the same close-knit group, has been made you have no reason to come into that group. Most people choose to have differing experiences: you might be a native American Indian, then an African, then a white in the United States or in Europe, so you get a varied experience. Then you would make contracts with others among your soul mates who are not occupied within the initial close group.

Why do so many souls appear to make contracts?

For a number of different reasons. One is that a lot of souls want to prove something that they can best get by having contracts. This is secondary to their choosing to experience such things as prejudice, or lack of self-esteem, so severely that it results in their not being functional. In some situations [*Toni: the Masters are showing groups in Africa where so many are starving*], there's a richness of life (besides the hunger) that a lot of souls want to experience. So there are all kinds of reasons in these choices.

Gender

When is gender decided upon?

The decision concerning gender is made before the joining of egg and sperm.

How about differences of sexual orientation and trans-sexuality?

Those are all lessons which the soul wishes to experience.

So sexual orientation is the lesson?

Yes.

How does it come about? Is it that the soul is now wanting to be the other sex?

That's only how it is manifested. The soul wishes to experience ambivalence, prejudice, and self-worth issues generally. It goes further than that in their ability to clearly feel themselves in the physicality of the body. In feeling the physicality of the body, souls begin to re-feel their own essence.

Primarily, souls come down to learn lessons, and then, while in the process of learning or after having learned those lessons, to recall the essence of who they are. So people who are going through an apparent conflict between whatever their physical body shows everyone else and whatever their inner feelings may be, are actually leaning toward connecting with who each of them is as a soul, as opposed to who they are as a physical being.

Is a gay male truly in a male body with an emotional desire to be a female?

It is other than that. It is that they are able to tap into their emotional core, which is sexless. They choose to experience what it is that makes them feel better in a human body, which are the

17

emotions and the energy of the female aspects of themselves. Because society says that makes them female, they identify strongly with that gender, which makes them feel so good that then they choose to be female, or to play the female role while remaining in the male body.

Can homosexuals be talked out of their attitude by society?
If they choose not to continue to grow, experience, and learn lessons, yes, they can. But in that case they wall themselves off and fail to continue to grow and to mature.

So a gay's not a hard-wired female in a male body, but a soul tapping into its female nature more than its male nature, and who happens to be in a male body?
Yes.

Soul and Body
Describe the relationship between the soul and the body.
The soul connects with the body to experience physicality. Without a body the soul is in the realm of unconditional love, and it doesn't have the opportunity to experience anything else. It cannot experience anger, sorrow, or joy of any kind—other than the joy of unconditional love. It can't experience particular kinds of love, such as a child's love; it can only experience the vastness of being in the presence of unconditional love. So it has to have physicality in order to experience any of the physical emotions that we have on Earth.

There is an in-between body—depending upon your perspective. The in-between body can be thought of as the prior lessons that the soul has experienced in other bodies. That is primarily a physical state rather than an etheric one, so in that regard you can say that it is a physicality that isn't totally of the soul (which is etheric). Truthfully, there is no real division; it's akin to a physical body growing from childhood into adulthood— the adult isn't different from the child but is just a different aspect of the child. The experience of the child is still there. Such is the way that its experience of past lives remains within the soul itself.

In our discussion, C. G. Jung told me that when we tap into a past life we find the one with which we have the greatest energetic connection, which is most likely to be our own past life. We download our own experiences into the DNA but sometimes happen to draw from a greater database. Where is that database?

That database is everywhere. It's in the collective energy where everything is interconnected. So the experience of one soul is the experience of all—but not precisely the same, because you can know the experience of running a four-minute mile, but if you haven't actually done it physically, you don't have the experience of the exertion that it takes. If you observe it occurring, you have the experience that it can be done and the effort needed to do it, so in one sense you do have an experience of it, but in another sense, you don't. You could tap into the greater database and draw on it to discover what you need to know for the physical experience of it.

Does each cell's DNA have a holographic impression of everything, including an impression of the whole of the body?

Yes—and of the Creator.

So the current idea that there is an interface between the body and the soul is ephemeral? It's a question of who is doing the looking?

Yes, and at what depth.

There's a lot being said about our having many bodies: physical, etheric, astral, and so on. I'm getting the feeling it's all nonsense!

Yes. It is all a matter of perception, and the reality that the spirit creates at the moment of that perception.

If going into the body involves downloading experiences into the DNA, what happens at death?

The soul has kept all of the downloaded information. It's like when you buy a new computer. If you have all of your files already on one computer, you have to download them into the new computer in order for them to be easily accessible. But you can still retain the original files.

So when the soul leaves the body, it leaves the DNA to rot?

Yes, but it doesn't make any difference because there's an exact copy. Everything is transferred, with periodic updates. Only copies are involved in the DNA.

Sometimes we can carry negative ideas from one life to the next. Are they stored in the general database?

All ideas are energy. Energy is how the DNA imprint is conveyed. If, as we pass from a physical life to the non-physical, then back to the physical, there is something that is still firing—an emotion such as hatred or jealousy which hasn't been dealt with, hasn't dissipated, and that lesson isn't learned—that emotion carries over into the next body, and if not dealt with there, it is carried over to a subsequent human lifetime. If you eventually go back and correct it at the point of origin, it cuts the connections to the subsequent lifetimes. You've changed the database; you've erased what's there and rewritten the program.

Past-Life Regression

That is like my client whose bad experience in one past life was resolved, and that positively affected another past life and also her current life.

Yes, you changed the master database. It's how past-life regression therapy works.

Does such a change in the master database relate to the absence of time in the spiritual realm, where everything co-exists—so if you change one part it will have a ripple effect on the experiences of the soul?

The master database is in the Akashic (celestial) records. Once you have experienced something, you cannot un-experience it. So, regardless of where in your linear time you may have had the experience, it becomes the experience of the soul in all of its manifestations.

So, what is the effect of the rewriting or reframing of the past-life experience in hypnosis?

We make a distinction between the two different types of possible action. If you only rewrite the experience, changing the script without the person learning the lesson, the energy of that lesson will still be there. But if you totally reframe it, in terms of feeling that it was wrong, or feeling that you can understand fully now, then the change becomes permanent.

The change is permanent, but the original experience is still etched in the record?

It's as if you have a person who has learned just the rudiments of a foreign language. They will always have those basic skills. If they then go and take an immersion course and really understand the language, and think the language, and have it become part of them, afterwards they don't have to go back to the rudiments. It's a learning experience that's now part of them.

Is it like a proofreader's copy, all marked up?

Yes, one does not erase the other, but it matures and improves it and lets you feel it more.

So reframing experiences is a very effective way of dealing with problem areas.

Yes. It is the whole basis of a therapeutic past-life regression.

One issue for me is interference. When a soul goes back into the interlife (i.e., life between incarnations), it is given an opportunity to erase problems that are still sparking away. But it doesn't always choose to do so.

It doesn't have to do it. It always has freedom of choice.

Would the therapist be interfering with that freedom in such a situation?

Has the person come to you for their problem? Has the person come to you to deal with their life-lessons, to get to know themselves, so they can move ahead in this lifetime? That is not interference. If you were to go out to a group of people to brainwash them against their will, it would be interference, but it wouldn't be successful because it is only with their intention that they can clean things up. If you put them into the therapeutic situation and they choose not to deal with forgiveness, not to get rid of their fear, or not to learn the particular lesson, then they are still not going to learn it because it is their intention that controls what happens.

Commentary

Peter: These words of the Masters were recorded over several sessions. We had made no current plan for a book when asking for this description of incarnation, but what they say here covers a lot of questions that people frequently raise concerning the topic. Many of these themes are also picked up in our dialogues with the Leaders.

What the Masters say about human sexuality will be novel for many readers. When our souls are about to incarnate on Earth we choose our parents, decide which sex we will be, and are quite loosely attached to the fetus until, usually, soon before the baby's birth. Then, when the downloading of vital information into the DNA of the fetus is complete, we make the little "shell" our temporary habitation until just before or at the moment of physical death. No human body survives outside of the womb without an indwelling soul.

The most controversial section of this dialogue will probably be the Masters' views on homosexuality. This issue comes up in dialogues with several Leaders, and all of these spirits sharply contradict those judgments made by homophobes and their innocent followers in our current worldwide human society.

"The man known as the Lord Jesus Christ in the Bible and by me, while in physical form, is an energy which is of the most intense, beautiful, totally giving, totally loving energy within all of creation."

Dwight L. Moody
1837-1899

Biographical Note

Dwight Lyman Moody was born in 1837 at Northfield, Massachusetts, the seventh of nine children. His bricklayer father died when Dwight was very young. Because of the family's poverty, he left school after the fifth grade and went to Boston to sell shoes in his uncle's store. There he attended Sunday school classes and, at eighteen, became a Christian. He moved to Chicago, still selling shoes and working hard to amass a personal fortune. Then he began to feel that God had called him to help the poor, and to establish a Christian mission in the Chicago slums. In the fall of 1858 he started his own Sunday School in an abandoned freight car, later moving it to a vacant bar. The little community quickly grew into a church. Now, sure that his future lay with evangelism, Moody left the shoe business to concentrate on social work and preaching the gospel among the city's poor, immigrant workers. In 1861 he became a city missionary for the YMCA. The next year, at the age of 23, he met and married Emma Revell (19), one of the mission's Sunday school teachers. The couple reared three children, a girl and two boys.

In 1863, he raised enough money to erect the 1,500-seat Illinois Street Church, which opened the following year with only twelve members. This was the beginning of what is now called the

Moody Memorial Church. He preached there until a pastor was called in 1866. Moody was a tireless evangelist, distributing tracts and holding daily prayer meetings. He also helped to erect America's first Y.M.C.A. building. Moody refused to fight in the American Civil War, but used his connections in the YMCA and the United States Christian Commission to bring the Bible to the Union troops, visiting the battlefields nine times. In 1867 he held his first revival campaign in Philadelphia. At an 1870 Y.M.C.A. convention in Indianapolis, he met Ira A. Sankey. Greatly impressed with his singing, Moody persuaded him to join the Chicago mission's staff.

In October 1871 Moody's mission church, the YMCA, and the parsonage were all destroyed in the Great Chicago Fire. He visited New York in a fundraising effort to rebuild the church, and while there he sensed a divine presence strongly calling him. Returning to Chicago, he preached the gospel with renewed zeal and rebuilt the church with twice the seating capacity.

In 1873 Dwight Moody and Ira Sankey were invited to take the gospel to Britain. They held small rallies in the north of England, then in Newcastle and the industrial North of England. Their efforts were rewarded with thousands of converts, and their popularity increased greatly. After two very productive years working as evangelists in the British Isles, Moody returned to America with an international reputation. He strove to perfect his evangelistic techniques and his campaign's administrative model. Eventually, over 100 million people attended Sankey and Moody's gospel campaigns in Europe and America, and their hymnbook proved a best seller. In one single day in 1893, over 130,000 people attended evangelistic meetings in Chicago, coordinated by Moody.

Bible training for working people was one means of enlarging the outreach of his inner-city evangelism. Moody saw dedication to the cause, rather than great talent, as central. He established two schools for girls and boys and, in 1880, created summer Bible conferences at his Northfield, Massachusetts, home to foster biblical fundamentalism and foreign missions. In 1886 he founded what was later called the Moody Bible Institute. Following this came the Moody Press, which used "Gospel wagons" to sell affordable evangelical Christian literature nationwide.

Dwight Moody continued to work immensely hard as an evangelist right up to the time of his death at his Northfield farm in 1899 at 62 years of age.

The Dialogue

Bible and Belief

You were a child in a poor family.

Not in the value of life, but only in those benefits that could be provided to us by money.

Your father's affiliation was Unitarian; was your mother also a Unitarian?

My mother's family moved a lot, and it was whatever church was convenient for them to attend throughout her youth.

When you joined in the Chicago YMCA Bible studies, was that a break with your family tradition?

My mother was always reading the Bible to us. The YMCA Bible study was a way of learning the ideas and the interpretation of others beyond the mixture that my mother had picked up along the way.

Your early life was spent selling shoes, first with your uncle in Boston and later when you went to Chicago. You had a large ambition to create a pile of wealth. Do you feel that drive, that ambition, helped you in the development and organization of your evangelistic work, in which you were so successful as a pioneer?

Yes, it did. My uncle and my thirst for money—based upon how god-like money sometimes seemed to us within the family— established within me the drive to go toward an end and put all of my effort into it. It propelled me forward until I could attain what I sought. It established a work ethic that was a model for others to make something out of their lives. When it seemed as if I wasn't able to get through to people and increase the importance of my word throughout the community, it enabled me to know that you don't get anywhere until after you have put in substantial effort. When I first came to Chicago, I thought I was going to be as successful as I had been working with my uncle, but I had to start from scratch there and build up my business. When I heard the Word, and it became a part of me, I knew it was important to get it across. I knew I had to start from the bottom again and build up.

You heard the Word of God in the YMCA Bible classes?
    That was where the first echoes began.

You said once, "A man ought to live so that everybody knows he is a Christian, and most of all, his family ought to know." And you also said, "I have had more trouble with myself than with any other man." Will you comment, please.
    All people in physical form should live by the tenets of Christianity and should know that you should "Do unto others as you would have them do unto you," that "It is better to give than to receive." These are the basic principles of religion. In the beginning I had more problems with myself because of the allure of money, which was able to provide for me what I did not have as I was growing up. I looked upon money as some kind of demon: it was something that could lure you in and promise to provide you with everything you could possibly imagine, and yet provided you with nothing that took care of your soul and your growth. It was a constant battle in the beginning to realize that money should not be put before God, and should not be put before our Christian principles.

Evangelism
That sort of temptation does not come only with money; it also comes with power. In your work with Ira Sankey, something like a hundred million people heard you. Wasn't a power issue involved there?

[laughs] I cannot deny that it felt good to be able to influence others, and I did have to be very conscious of the fact that I was not promoting myself—although in the beginning it was like selling shoes: you promote yourself in order to bring the clientele back. It was a little bit of a battle to realize that all I was doing was being a messenger of the Word, and being a director of the way in which people could improve their lives by connecting to God, and connecting to the unity of a group of people who all have the same beliefs and principles and live their lives in the same manner.

There were some outstanding developments of evangelistic techniques in the movement you created. On one occasion you wanted to ensure people came to Sunday worship rather than going to the Great Chicago Fair. So you organized 130,000 people to attend your meetings. That must have taken a lot of organizational clout. Did you see yourself as an organizational genius?

I don't think that I thought of it in those terms. I thought of it more as being somewhat of a savior of the people. I was taking them out of the poverty mode that they were in, and enriching their lives—not in a monetary way but in a spiritual way. I was giving them something that was long-lasting, that permeated every aspect of their being. As to that time with the Fair, it was very easy to let them know the Fair was something put together by other people to benefit those other people, and that visitors got nothing more than a little bit of eye-candy out of it, whereas in coming to the service they got a connection with their Savior, with their God, with the people of the community—something to enrich their lives and to transport into every aspect of their lives. It would take them beyond the little time that the Fair was going on, and provide them with a pathway.

I understand a big change started in Wall Street, when you were seeking financial help for the YMCA and your own church. You turned a spiritual corner at that point.

I began to realize that this wasn't just another business venture. Unfortunately, I had started it as a business thinking I could turn from having a "product" into providing something of which I didn't have to keep an inventory. That I could go with my wits, and that I could go with my understanding. I had always been able to persuade people with my words. It was as if, one day, the context of what I was saying, and the heart-connection that I was attempting to establish with the people, clicked in for *me*, and I felt the power of the Lord coming in. I felt the energy of spreading that power to others and how, by magnifying it, the power became all the more intense for all of us, including myself.

Was this on one occasion, or was it a whole series of experiences for you?

It was a series for me. Various other people felt it when they reached the point where they opened up to the message. They no longer chose to specify that they only wanted to be with the Lord on Sunday; they began to know that this was a way of life, that this was a way to connect with God and with their souls as they traveled through life towards eternity.

The Bible and Truth

The Bible was of enormous importance in your message. You said, "The Bible will keep you from sin, or sin will keep you from the Bible. We can stand affliction better than we can prosperity, for in prosperity we forget God." In your thinking now, is the Bible still as central to the life of the Christian as it was?

For people in human bodies, yes. The people who were my first "sheep" were those who had nothing. They had ideals, most of which had been crushed. They needed something they could look to as the ultimate answer, the ultimate hope, and they looked primarily in times of trouble. When they were making money they had to be reminded to go back to the Bible, because it became tedious for them when they could go off, make money and purchase things with it. That was why it was so important to get them into that habit of coming to the services and of going to the Bible study groups. Then they could know how important it was to have a set of rules by which they could become Christians, the best people possible.

Are you putting all this in the past tense, or was it the Channel?
No, that was me! [laughs]

You said, "Sin will keep you from the Bible." What about people who know the Bible, have read the Bible, but do not live by the Bible? Are they being kept from it by sin? Do you still hold that view of sin?
I think the mentality of society has shifted. It is not as true now as it was then. I still feel that sin, as I defined it, was anything that was not completely within the Christian principle—that could be drinking, gambling, and the things of the flesh—anything that kept people from the tenets of the Bible. As it exists today, society has a different mentality, a different inbuilt experience. Now people have a front-line experience of what is good and evil provided to them by the news media. We did not have that interchange in my time. It was at the point where the people had to be led by the hand, and they had to be given a book of rules, which was the Bible. Anything which kept them from adhering to that was sin, even if it was laziness, or some of the other major sins.

So you made a black-and-white statement to help their self-discipline?
It was what they needed because they had no discipline.

But people don't need that today because they have a wider view of what life is like?
Yes.

Is the Bible no longer to be seen as the Word of God?
The energy of the Bible is the word of God. Each little word was chosen for each edition of the Bible by the compilers and is not necessarily a true account of the Word as it was given. It was put into a form which provided the action that was thought necessary by the compilers.

There is some evidence that parts of the Bible have been deliberately left out.

Certainly, I know that now; I did not know it when I was in physical form.

Bible Omissions

What part of the original teaching of the Bible is most missing from it these days?

Reincarnation, and the soul's journey through life.

Is there a misunderstanding about the place of women in society because of the Bible's teaching?

Yes. Here again, the Bible was shifted to comply with what those who ordered the compilations wished the energy set-up to be vis-à-vis men and women. It was always men who asked for Bibles to be compiled or translated. They had the idea that women were less than they. This was at a time when there were very few women who were allowed to have any degree of literacy, so it played into what everyone currently thought, when women were considered to be mere chattels rather than people who should have rights as well as duties.

So the teaching about the nature of marital relationships is flawed for that reason?

Yes.

What about the teaching concerning homosexuality?

That is also flawed.

The Bible and the Word of God

Some Bible teachers have considerable influence in today's Christian church. Should they be listened to?

By those people who are drawn to their message—they are drawn because they are at a stage where they need the message which is being taught, as all of my flock were drawn to me because they needed my message. With my message they were able to grow and become as enlightened as they could, within their intellectual, mental, and physical limitations.

So for these people today, the Bible is still...
Very critical.

...the Word of God?
The Word of God, and very critical, too.

The Word in a broad sense. Despite the Bible's missing reincarnation, despite its distorting the place of women in society, despite incorrect teaching about women, homosexuality, and maybe one or two other things, it still represents the Word of God?
The energy of the Word of God is there, and it represents the how-to manual for people to go through life, because this is what they need at this stage of their becoming mature.

Can you explain to me what you mean by the phrase "The Word of God"?
That is more your term than mine at this point. I now use "the energy of the Word of God," which is unconditional love. That permeates everything. If it is allowed to be felt, it can be said in any language, in any set of words, and it <u>will</u> be felt. The words themselves are immaterial; it is the energy behind the words that is important.

Jesus and Heaven
You said this once: "A rule I have had for years is to treat the Lord Jesus Christ as a personal friend. His is not a creed, a mere doctrine, but it is He Himself we have."
The man known as the Lord Jesus Christ in the Bible and by me, while in physical form, is an energy which is of the most intense, beautiful, totally giving, totally loving energy within all of creation. It is an energy which, once you open to it, becomes a part of you. It joins with you and allows you to feel the unconditional love which is God the Creator and all of the universe. In accepting that unconditional love it is as if I become a twin with that energy—then it and I are inseparable.

You once said, "We talk about heaven being so far away. It is within speaking distance to those who belong there. Heaven is a prepared place for a prepared people." How do you prepare?

You prepare by going in and connecting with the energy. It was a bit presumptuous of me to say it was a place so far away, when I am now here, there, and everywhere. It is heaven to be in this unconditional love. I could have been in it on Earth in physical form, had I opened up to the suggestion and not put it as something that was so far away to be attained. That, again, was what was necessary to shape the lives of those who came under my tutelage.

In fairness to you now, you once said, "It is within speaking distance to those who belong."

But to speak is not to feel, and I now know that feeling is important. I could speak of it but not accept it. So I quibble with my own terminology! The idea was somewhat right, but very narrow in its application. If one were but to reach out to the unconditional love that is heaven, it is within reach. To speak of it without believing in it, accepting it, and surrendering to it, does not get one to that place of ecstasy which is heaven.

A lot of people would like to ask you what heaven is like.

In a sensory sense it is everything you could possibly want. It is being enwrapped in unconditional love, support, companionship, comfort—everything that you could possibly envision. It is not for most a physical place, where people walk around in bodies. Those who transition generally keep some form of their body until they acclimate. Those of us who travel around a lot, experiencing and sampling, simply go with energy. We are totally connected with all of the other energy.

Have you met with Jesus?

Oh! Of course. He is an energy of a higher order than most of those whom I meet. He has the knowledge and the wisdom of all that has gone into what is called "the spirit, the connection of all the souls." Of course He has knowledge of some of the negative experiments on the Earth, and some of the negativity, such as the means of his passing while he was incarnated as Jesus. He envisions and holds only that purest energy of the Creator, without flaws, without negativity. It is an inspiration to be within his energy.

The Bible and the Christian Church call Jesus "The Son of God." How should we understand this description?

All souls are children of God; all those incarnated as males are sons of God; all those incarnated in a female body are daughters of God. The Creator is within all of us. When Jesus was on the Earth and in the Bible, it was at a time when people did not recognize the divinity that was within them. There had to be some torch which brought them to an understanding to the beginning of spirituality. This spirit was coming down to show the way to people in physicality to get in touch with their souls and to get in touch with the God-Force while in physical form, but no one would believe that was possible if he were not designated as The Son of God.

Are there others like Jesus, or is he unique?

There are others like him. Some of them you know as the archangels. He is on a high plateau with those. There is a cadre of souls who were in physical form, who were able to bring their enlightenment, their knowledge of their soul, into their physical bodies and ascend with all of that knowledge intact. What we call the Ascended Masters. They are of a vibration almost as intense.

Satan and Hell

Do you have experience of the devil? I'm sure you mentioned him while you were on Earth.

I have experience of the devil in two forms: I have experience within Earth's dimension of the devil, where there is all the negativity that can possibly exist—hatred, inhumanity to others. This I have experienced on Earth, and on Earth, this energy is called the devil. Secondly, I know the core of this energy which derives from the source of all energy, which is the Creator, is of God.

So Satan is a fallen angel?
  Satan is not a fallen angel. Satan is an angel who, at the request of God, became negativity, so that souls might experience the intensity of the love of God. Without an example of love's antithesis there is no true feeling within the physical of that magnificence. The energy of that negativity does not exist past the physical dimension.

So there's no such place as hell?
  Only on Earth.

But there is a spiritual being who is called Lucifer or Satan?
  He has many names. There is an energy that has been created by him, yes.

With a regiment of minor devils, or is this a myth?
  The energy has spread out into others so that they can tempt more people to experience this negativity—a large number of people. It would be very unlikely that there was only one soul who had to have so great a reach as to establish contact with a vast number of people. So there are, as you say, a regiment of others who have volunteered to help.

You make it seem as if this is a deliberate work done by God to give people on Earth—and only Earth—experience of negativity in all its forms.
  Yes. It is only here on Earth.

Will that negativity ever be conquered?
  Negativity will cease to be needed if the Earth ceases to be a cauldron of experience for souls.

Where do people go who fear they will go to hell?

When they leave their body they will go to a number of different places. They will go into the unconditional love which they typify as heaven; they will go into a neutral locality because they do not allow themselves to accept heaven; they will go into a place of torment, carrying the energies of their Earth experience with them. This is torment that they hold onto and which they refuse to release. Each soul chooses its own destination, based upon the wisdom it has attained while incarnate.

Will they ever be saved from that torment?

The choice is theirs: there are spirits who will help them. They can also become what you call "discarnate souls" or "ghosts," when they refuse to let go of the Earth plane, even though they are no longer in physical form.

You preached that even the worst of sinners would be redeemed through the power of Jesus' blood. Is this not the case?

Yes, the potential is always there. But it is up to them. They cannot be dragged out of the form they choose to be in.

You said "They cannot"—are you limiting the power of God to do this?

No. I am marveling at the Intelligence that says each person has the right to choose. That is what gives them their individuality.

Evangelicals Today

Looking at the modern evangelical Christian movement, particularly in America, do you feel they are doing a good job, or do they need to change in any particular direction?

They are still providing for the people what they need.

Is the involvement of the movement in politics a good thing?

I never particularly cared for politicians while on Earth. I cannot say whether the involvement is good or bad because I have prejudices in that regard, which still haunt me despite the unconditional love in which I am living.

So you're going to come back as a politician!
I don't know. It's not beyond possibility.

Thank you so much, Dwight Moody.
You are welcome. I am glad to provide what little I can for your book.

Commentary

Toni: At times I felt as though I were in the front row within a revival tent; Moody's energy was mesmerizing! It was almost as if we interviewed two personalities. The first was Moody the historian, almost dispassionately recounting his work and accomplishments, causing Peter to ask at one point if use of the past tense came from him or me. The second showed us the eternal soul who saw the potential to use the Bible in the training of less mature souls who needed rules and guidance to complete their physical experience.

Peter: It is clear that Dwight Moody has changed some ideas and has made a reappraisal of his life as an evangelist. But he remains proud of his achievements, and he believes that there are many people today who need to live by the rules that the Bible and evangelistic Christianity can provide for the successful ordering of their lives and the enlargement of their expression of faith in God.

The drive to make money, first by selling shoes and then by selling the gospel, was a stepping stone in Moody's life toward a more mature, deeply and sincerely felt spiritual presentation of the gospel. This was good work which, he now feels, did not lead him astray in search of ungodly power. It was much-needed work within a society with limited horizons, and he would gladly do it all again.

That being said, there are differences in his view now from Home. Moody sees God the Creator, and Jesus Christ, in terms of pure and unconditionally loving energy. He does not speak the language of judgment. Hell is a state of mind for those who intend to endure it. There is no hell outside the Earth's dimension. The devil, call him what you will, is the loyal servant of the Creator, assigned the task of causing negativity to exist on Earth as the foil for the brilliance of the divine light of unconditional and accepting love.

The Bible resonates with this former fundamentalist preacher in a new way. He still sees it as the medium which carries the Word of God, but it is the energy of the Creator speaking through its pages which makes it so. It is the total impact of the book that is the key to its usefulness, not the precise detail of its contents. The ancient Bible, he asserts, does have omissions, such as reincarnation, and it has flaws, such as its teaching on women's place in society, on marriage, and on social acceptance of homosexuality. The Bible is much more a tool by which people may be helped, and much less a rule book, the ignoring of whose edicts would lead a person into giving way to sin.

This was a strong spirit conversing with us, but one without any self-importance and possessing a genuine desire to be of help to those spirits still in human form. Dwight Moody has not abandoned his evangel, because ordinary people need to understand right and wrong, but he also knows that society has moved on and has less need of the Good Book than did the poor immigrant workers of Chicago among whom he worked so tirelessly and so very successfully at the end of the nineteenth century.

Talking with Leaders of the Past

"Revelations signal a time of change.
It is something that is occurring on the planet at the present time."

Pope John XXIII
1881-1963

Biographical Note

Angelo Giuseppe Roncalli was born in Sotto il Monte, Italy, on 25 November 1881, the fourth child in the large family of a sharecropper. He was ordained priest in 1904. During World War I, he served in the Italian medical corps and as a military chaplain. He rose quickly in the ranks of the priesthood after 1921 when Pope Benedict XV appointed him the Italian president of The Society for the Propagation of the Faith. He became a bishop in 1925, and ten years later was appointed Apostolic Delegate, first to Turkey and Greece, and then, in 1944, to Paris. Bishop Roncalli used his position to help the underground resistance save thousands of refugees in Europe. In 1953, he became the Cardinal Patriarch of Venice.

In 1958, at the age of 76, Cardinal Roncalli was elected Pope. After his predecessor's long pontificate, the cardinals chose an older man who, on the grounds of age, they thought would be a "stop-gap" pope. What the Church fathers did not anticipate was that Pope John's warmth, kindness, and modestly expressed radicalism would generate major change. Less than ninety years after the first Vatican Council, which had promoted the controversial doctrine of papal infallibility, he surprised everyone by calling an ecumenical council to achieve the *aggiornamento* or renewal of the Roman Church. From Vatican II came major changes in the liturgy and in ecumenism that radically changed Roman Catholicism.

Pope John's historic mission was fired by a desire to endow the Christian faith with "a new Pentecost," a renewed spirit. It was aimed not only at bringing the mother church of Christendom into closer touch with the modern world, but also at ending the divisions that had adversely affected the Christian message for centuries. Before the Council's work was completed, however, in 1963, Angelo Roncalli, Pope John XXIII, died of cancer at 81 years of age.

The Dialogue

Vatican II

By launching a reforming council to make the Catholic Church sine macula et ruga *(without spot or wrinkle), you set out to adapt the church's life to changes in science, economics, morals, and politics in today's world, and to show that the goal of Christian unity can be reached. How do you view your reforming work now?*

It was handicapped by the tenets of the church itself. There was still the desire for the Church to control the people (which is the main purpose behind most religions). Our reforms were intended to instruct the people in the precepts we believe are the best. My desire was to modernize—not quite going into democracy, as most modern societies are at this time, but into a format in which there was more input from the different nationalities throughout the world. There was resistance from a number of people in the hierarchy who believed in the political structure within the church. I am very proud of the work that was done, because it did take the majority of the church from the twelfth century into about the eighteenth century. [chuckles]

The Vatican II Council discussed subjects ranging from church unity to mass media. The council approved liturgical reforms that enabled bishops to allow parts of the Mass to be said in the language of their own country, and opened the way to decentralization. How do you view the effect of these changes now?

It was multi-faceted. For a large majority of the younger people it was very well received because it was a thing they could understand, a thing they could grow with, and a thing in which they could have an input—such as allowing guitars at various services, and things of that kind. It gave a flexibility to a society where Sunday was no longer a day just to worship, so it gave the people an opportunity to be able to worship on Saturday evenings or Sundays to fit their busy schedule.

For the older people it was a bad idea because they had been brought up in the mysticism associated with the Latin liturgy, and with all its pomp and circumstance. To them it was as much attending a sacred ritual as it was attending a service wherein they knew exactly what was going on. We lost a lot of the older people because they craved that mystery and did not want to go back to a learning process, to learn what the liturgy was really all about.

It was helpful in non-English-speaking lands, such as the Spanish-speaking countries, because they always had more mysticism. There always was a sense of awe and mystery around their church—the saints, the angels, and biblical characters. That was not true of English-speaking areas, such as the United States and Canada. There were some problems in Europe with the switch-over because, again, the pomp was no longer there. In particular, at the time when it occurred, Germanic areas still possessed a very regimented mentality, and to go from a regimented service into a free-form service left them confused and adrift.

The newer, younger people coming up were able for the first time to get a feeling for this. It was no longer just going to their catechism classes and learning to memorize things, memorizing the Latin liturgy without knowing what was behind it. They were enabled to feel the words of the services and to learn first-hand what they meant. It became for them something that was alive, something of their generation, rather than an ancient thing that they were expected to accept without knowing what it was that they were accepting.

Is there still room for both the mysterious and the intimate to co-exist in Catholic theology and worship?

They have to, for the church to grow and be successful. There has to be a communion of people within themselves, growing, helping themselves, being one with those who would teach them, the priest and the nuns and the lay clergy; but at the same time they must feel that connection with the God-Force outside of them, who cannot be touched, cannot be held. So they have to be able to marry the two aspects of the religion, the Divinity that is within as well as the Divinity that is without.

Vatican II dealt with the two sources of revelation recognized by the Catholic Church: scripture and oral tradition. Part of that tradition includes the idea of the pope as the successor of St. Peter and the final interpreter of the Christian faith. How do you see sources of revelation now, and is the Roman Church really, as you declared, "the pillar and ground of the truth"?

[laughs] As much as people in my generation or anyone raised in the church, I felt to my very core that the Roman Catholic Church was the one, true church. I accepted that Peter was the one who kept the church together, and that any person who was to have that distinction as pope was the successor of Peter. The succession was never meant to be in a physical lineage, but rather in title. As I have now come to know, Peter was only one of many who were the founders of the basic element which grew into Roman Catholicism. Revelations signal a time of change. It is something that is occurring on the planet at the present time. It is a shifting in the consciousness of the soul within its human body. It is occurring now. The end time is the end of the complete duality of the human body, the raising of the physical into connection with the soul, and the reuniting with the other souls.

The written and oral sources currently on the planet were modified throughout the centuries to say what those in power at the time wanted them to say—particularly, going back to the time of when the Bible was put together, when the "lost" books were lost to the common people. There are several copies of the lost books, in different languages, in the basement of the Vatican. Parts of them have been leaked out recently.

Most of the writings that are in what is now the Bible accepted by the Catholic church, were put together by the popes to give a hell-and-damnation scenario. So if the common person did not come to church, did not do what the church wanted them to do, they were damned. It was a control issue. I saw that, somewhat, while in physical form, but I did not see a way in which it could be overcome. That was why my intention with Vatican II was to take some of the power out of the hands of the clergy and give it to the people, to form a type of relationship in which people could come together and—with the guidance of the clergy, but not under the dictatorship of the clergy—realize their spiritual connections.

Was teaching about reincarnation effectively put down by the hierarchy in earlier days?

Undoubtedly, and there are many, many such references in the lost books of the Bible. That was something that Constantine and the others simply could not allow to exist, because then they could not justify their dictatorship over the people, and because the people would say, "We don't have to go to them because we can just leave this life and come back to a better life." The Church wanted to have it hanging over the heads of the people so that, if they did not do exactly what the clergy said, they would be damned to eternal hellfire. This was one of the issues they felt that they must control, so no reincarnation!

Vatican II also considered the nature of the church, seeking more tolerant Catholic positions on church-state relations, religious freedom, and the tempering of hierarchical authority by giving the laity a bigger role in the church. One significant omission was reconsideration of the clergy as a celibate and male institution. Is there room for change?

Absolutely! But it does not appear that there will be change within your lifetime. Any change from the currently accepted order, such as relaxation of the celibacy rule or the bringing in of female priests (or priestesses, I guess), would take away from all of the traditional, so closely held-onto tenets of the older religious, the current cardinals and bishops. It would be a shock to their system that they could not accommodate, were things to change so drastically, but it must change for the Catholic church to exist in the future.

So, without such change the church won't exist?
The church will not exist without that change. There will be pockets, but there will not be a global Roman Catholic church without the change, which will not occur until some of the older cardinals give up their power.

Social Issues

In your Encyclical on Christianity and Social Progress, Mater Et Magistra, *you said: "Though the Church's first care must be for souls, how she can sanctify them and make them share in the gifts of heaven, she concerns herself too with the exigencies of man's daily life, with his livelihood and education, and his general, temporal welfare and prosperity." Does the involvement of the Church in the lives of her people really assist them to make spiritual and ethical decisions for themselves?*

No. What it does is that it takes away their power. It programs them, and if they live by the programming, they do accomplish ethical and spiritual tasks. If they follow the tenets without *feeling* them, they are simply robots going along. This harkens back to the flavor of the church throughout the centuries. In early days, the only people within the hierarchy of the church were the rich who could afford to be landowners, and could afford to have clergy who took care of and controlled the thinking and everyday life of the peasants through the church doctrines.

There has always been a feeling within the church, therefore, that the church has a quasi-responsibility to all human beings, to nurture them, take care of them, educate them, because they have no means of their own—which is simply not the case. Nowadays, the church can only help to direct the spiritual growth of people. The church must get out of the mindset that it still has to micro-manage, compute, and regulate every facet of people's lives.

Does the church's strong emphasis on social issues, such as abortion and divorce, represent a balanced view of the social teaching of Jesus?

No. The teachings of Jesus were that people would feel their connection with their soul on the planet, to experience things to bring them more into love, the unconditional love of God the Creator. There are certain things that must be experienced for that to occur.

My feeling on abortion (and I believed it up until my transition) was that the soul enters the cells that become the fetus, at the time of conception. I now know that is not true. The soul chooses its time of entry, and sometimes goes in and out of the fetus before it becomes a viable human. I have also had my memory refreshed, that sometimes an abortion is a lesson that must be borne by the woman so that she may learn some of the various issues which she came down to the planet to learn. Abortion is not the killing of a soul, because the soul can never be killed. The soul never dies; it goes on, and it may not even be in that bundle of cells that is growing, and it won't be there at the time of an abortion.

Don't those who proclaim the sanctity of life have a valid point about cruelty to the unborn, and about the casual way abortion is sometimes treated? Isn't the idea of the sanctity of life—in the light of abortion and of life-support issues—of merit?

The cruelty you mention would be cruelty only if the soul were in the body. If a person has a growth within their body, a cancerous tumor, is it cruel to remove that tumor? That tumor has no soul; it has no connection to the spiritual, except while it is in the body when there is a stream of consciousness of the energy of the soul within it. But at the time of its removal it does not contain a soul. The same thing is true of a fetus; it does not contain a soul at the time of the abortion or the removal, so, therefore, it cannot be an issue of cruelty.

45

What about someone on a life-support system?

With most human bodies on life-support, the soul has just a tenuous connection to the body. In most cases it is out of the body, enjoying itself elsewhere. [chuckles] It is just maintaining a thread-contact to the body, because without its being connected to it at all, the life of the body ceases to exist—the point of physical death, as it is known on the planet. Most people who are in a vegetative state are not in that state for their own growth, because in the process of getting to the vegetative state they have learned the lessons that they should. They are in that vegetative state to provide lessons for those who are connected to them—family, caregivers, caretakers, hospital administrators, the clergy (for them to discuss the theological implications of where that soul is!)—but the souls themselves are not trapped within the bodies. A soul does not have to stay anywhere it does not choose, and is not tied to the consciousness of the body.

Also, what of the church's attitude toward divorce?

The church's attitude toward divorce had a lot to do with the fact that most divorces, throughout the ages, were sought by women who no longer chose to be victimized by their husband. The church hierarchy was male, and men did not want to be deprived of their *possessions*. It is also interconnected with the church's teaching that intercourse is only for procreation purposes. This took out of the mix that it's (1) an animal response, and (2) the truth that, when done as a sacred act, it honors the souls who are involved. It is just another step along the process of being human. Divorce is very much akin to when a woman leaves the house of her parents, being either under her own control or the control of a man. It is like a job where you can learn as much as you can from the job, and then out-grow the job and must move on.

My questions on abortion and divorce were related to the social teaching of Jesus. Would you like to say anything more about his social teaching?

Very little has carried forward from the social teaching of Jesus in the written form you have now on the planet. His teaching was that, in all things, we should honor the soul, we should honor the Creator—the Creator outside of us and inside of us. He did not take a stand on issues of marriage, divorce, abortion. He talked and taught solely about our being in unconditional love in all circumstances with those around us. At the same time, he was battling the religious precepts in which he was raised, the traditions of a man at that time, that he had to be married in order to be successful. He was not tied down by these conditions because he came from his soul level, and on the soul level such things as marriage certificates have no import.

Two more questions on social issues of the day. What is the best way for the church to resolve the pedophile priest problem?

The best way for them to resolve the problem is to be completely open about the fact that it exists, and to take responsibility for the truth that had the policy on celibacy not been so stringent (with the typical human animal having needs and desires), if it had been more realistic, it would not have forced a number of priests, as it did, to follow what they thought was a "safe way." In their studies they were constantly told "you may not have sex with a woman, you may not have sex with a woman, you may not have sex with a woman." To some of them that modified into "I can relieve myself with a boy." It was a way that existed with a number of the early bishops and cardinals, so there was a template of semi-accepted behavior, at least back in the thirteenth to seventeenth centuries. In order to come out of this, the church must open the closets, hang out their linen, and acknowledge that their precepts are somewhat a cause for this phenomenon's evolution.

Religious Conflicts

In view of conflicts in the Middle East, how do you feel about attitudes taken by the adherents of Christianity, Judaism, and Islam, toward these conflicts?

The conflicts have all occurred in the minds of the combatants because of religion—either because they felt it was dictated or accepted by their religion, or because, in their opinion, it maintained the purity of their religion. This is another example of how through the centuries religions have tried to be the law, the controlling force within groups of people. In that situation, the leaders of those religions feel their power and seek to increase the fanaticism of their devotees, so they may feel and relish that power. It has happened within Catholicism, and this is why it is changing, why the various Vatican councils concurred in the hope that we would defuse some of this intensity that we see now with Islam and other religions—that has reached the point of justifying their need to be on top, to suppress other religions, and to say that they are the only true believers of the Creator. It is the human frailty of those at the head of the various sects, who have become divorced from true feelings for their spiritual side, and who have grown into the belief that this is the true way to go.

There is going to be much more bloodshed before there is any realization of the dysfunction occurring within these religions. It is also because the people who become fanatics are the ones who have been oppressed within their homelands, oppressed by the poverty in which they have grown up, and they see their religion offering them insights, offering them power, offering them revenge. Over and over again they will quote "an eye for an eye," and although that was not what was meant by that phrase, they use it as a rallying cry.

In light of what you have just said, what is your view of the man or woman who chooses to be a secular humanist in this generation?

The term Secular Humanist is mostly defined by each individual; there is no commonality. They all have beliefs and understandings that fit in with what has brought each one of them to secular humanism. I would prefer to call the majority of them *Spiritualists*, in that, across the board, they seek to bring all that they deal with into the unconditional love that they experience on the soul level. They seek to understand themselves, not their physical selves but their internal selves—that part which is their soul, and that part which is of their previous lives—and to discover what they can bring to this existence on the planet. Within this search they follow only the beliefs that resonate with their soul, which is their secular part. They are definitely humanists because they believe in the universal love of all souls, even if they do not agree on all the actions souls should take in human situations.

Thank you, Angelo Roncalli, for your helpful observations.
Thank you.

Commentary

Toni: The former Pontiff came in with the feel of a protective, benevolent, rich uncle—his richness not monetary but rather emotional and clarifying. He seemed to "bounce" the current Church hierarchy lovingly on his knee while chastising them. His strong desire to raise them above their erroneous politics and belief systems into an experience of unconditional love within their souls was compelling. It was a very rich experience for the channeler, being able to feel the intensity existing in such a magnificent soul who, though back Home, continues to monitor that which it began on Earth. Pope John XXIII brought a lot of energy, the desire to discuss, and good humor to the dialogue. More than once he burst out laughing. His energy spilled out in a torrent of words. Perhaps it was a memory of his former Italian zest for life.

Peter: Souls at Home are not really concerned with their continuing human reputation, as we soon discovered; however, the old reformer is still chock full of the desire for change. Proud of his work in Vatican II, nevertheless he remained critical of bishops who continue to cling tenaciously to politically correct, though dated, responses to change. This was a recurring theme in our dialogue with Roncalli.

The former pontiff appeared gracious toward those—mostly elderly people and European diehards—who had experienced genuine difficulty with the sweeping liturgical changes brought about by Vatican II. He recognized the different flavors of Catholic spirituality within many areas of the worldwide church. He felt that modernization would lead young people to have a more acceptable experience of worship, which could lead them toward a deepening understanding of their life and faith. Well-balanced change was always necessary for the church to grow and be successful. In what followed, the Pope might be critical of the church, but his passion for its success was expressed powerfully and rang true.

Then we came to some qualifications, difficulties, and outright denials of Catholic tradition. The Church was not founded on St. Peter, because there were many founders of the church. The Bible was a document carefully selected and controlled by the hierarchy, who had suppressed alternative scriptures in the past. They had retained the variant manuscripts, but suppressed such views as reincarnation, which historically they held to be a danger to good church discipline.

The comments in which the former Pope roundly denounced the clergy celibacy rule were more cutting. Here, and in his answer later on the pedophile priest scandal, he simply chastised the church for its organizational flaws. Recognizing that the pace of change would be slow, and conservative and older cardinals would have to die before real change could ever happen, he sadly predicted that if radical change did not come, the church would lose its worldwide outreach and come to exist only in isolated pockets of adherence.

On the issue of abortion he really appeared to pull the rug out from under the Roman Catholic church's current teaching. The soul of a child does not actually enter the embryonic cells at conception and, anyway, it would not be trapped or killed by an abortion. So removal of a fetus is no more grave a procedure than removal of a tumor. Abortion may well exist to teach both parents and society a lesson, but there is no cruelty to the unborn involved in the procedure. In a similar approach to the issue of when doctors, relatives, and priests may sanction the termination of life support, he acknowledged that by that time the soul has largely vacated the body, maintaining only a thread of connection.

Regarding the termination of marriage, he looked briefly at divorcing women's frequent need to move to safer ground. He clearly did not support the church's ban on divorce, which was linked to the ancient traditions of male dominance and to the church's faulty understanding of the role of sex in marriage.

Criticism of Catholicism was more implied than spoken over the issue of conflict in the Middle East. Religions generally were seen as complicit in war, with the leaders of all religions using the devotion of their adherents to the faith as a means of power play. Such was his hostility toward traditional religions that we added a question on how he evaluated the role of secular humanists. This group received one of his warmest appraisals, as he called most of them "Spiritualists" and described them as following a worthy spiritual path.

There is no nonsense in this former pontiff, but his criticisms are clearly made for the betterment of the Roman Catholic church, its growth, its modernization, and the future deepening in its understanding of the needs of human beings and the ways of God.

"Now that I have been connected back to the Source, I know I am immortal. I would not be in a position to speak with you today if I were not immortal."

Bertrand Russell

1872-1970

Biographical Note

Bertrand Russell was born in Wales in 1872, but orphaned at the age of three and brought up by his grandmother. He was taught by tutors, and became fluent in French and German. At Trinity College, Cambridge, he obtained a First Class degree with distinction in philosophy. The next year, aged seventeen, he married Alys Pearsall Smith, an American Quaker, The couple stayed together until 1902, when he began to have numerous affairs.

In 1895 he was elected a fellow of his college but instead of academic work he chose diplomacy and briefly worked as an attaché at the British embassy at Paris. His first published work, *German Social Democracy*, appeared in 1896 when he also began teaching political science at the London School of Economics. He was elected in 1908 as a Fellow of the Royal Society. In 1910 Russell published his first important book, the first volume of *The Principles of Mathematics*, and he worked with Alfred Whitehead to develop ideas relating to mathematical logic. That year he was appointed lecturer at Trinity College, Cambridge.

When the first World War broke out, he took an active part in the *No Conscription Fellowship*, for which his college deprived him of his lectureship in 1916. Offered a U.S. post at Harvard University, he was refused a passport, and in 1918 he was sentenced to six months' imprisonment for a pacifist article. In Brixton jail he wrote *Introduction to Mathematical Philosophy*.

Russell paid a short visit to Russia in 1920 to study the conditions under Bolshevism, which left him cold. Dora Black, his companion on the trip, had supported his crusade against conscription. They went on to China where he lectured on philosophy at Peking University. On their return to London the couple married, and a son was born shortly afterward. In 1927 they opened a school for young children in a five-year radical educational experiment. Russell split with Dora after she had given birth to two children by an American journalist, and he began a relationship with Patricia Spence, who had previously been his children's governess and was one of his undergraduate students. They married in 1936 and had one son, but the marriage was not a happy one.

In 1938 he went to the U.S.A. and taught at UCLA and many leading American universities. In 1940, in a famous court case, his right to teach philosophy at the City College of New York was terminated on the grounds that his radical views on morality rendered him unfit. Instead, he lectured widely, and his popular *History of Western Philosophy*, published in 1945, was based on these lectures. Returning home, he again started teaching at Trinity College, Cambridge, and became well known as a journalist and broadcaster.

The last two decades of his life were spent in campaigning for nuclear disarmanent, peace in Vietnam, many socialist social reform causes, and other issues of personal freedom. In 1952, freed from his unhappy marriage with Patricia, he married his fouirth wife, Edith Finch, whom he had known for many years and who eventually out-lived him. Russell's written work covered philosophical and mathematical concepts, psychology, education, socialism and social reform, agnosticism, mysticism and logic, morality, peace issues, the concept of meaning and truth, the history of western philosophy, human knowledge and authority, and much more. The Nobel Prize for Literature was awarded him in 1950. Bertrand Russell died in Penrhyndeudraeth, Wales, at 97 years of age.

The Dialogue

Agnostic, Atheist, and Believer

As the basis for our discussion I picked your essay "What is an Agnostic", in which you showed the difference between agnostic and atheist viewpoints. How do you feel now about your comment: "An agnostic thinks it's impossible to know the truth in matters such as God, and the future life, in which religions are concerned"?

It was presumptuous of me to categorize the thinking of all souls because of the descriptive title with which they chose to associate. Knowing the truth about God on Earth is one thing so involved with human emotions that most people do not speak their heart to others. Now I see that God is not as I had envisioned when in human form. God is not as my perception was, or for that matter other people's perception—this supreme gentleman in a white beard and cloak who has ultimate power over everything upon the Earth. The idea of ultimate power was what chafed upon my thinking that such a being existed, because it seemed to remove from the thought process any option of another kind of person.

You also said you thought there were insufficient grounds for the affirmation or denial of the person of God.

That was me giving other people a chance to make their own free choices.

You also wrote: "As an agnostic does not accept any authority in the sense in which religious people do, it holds that a man should hold out a question of conduct for himself." Do you see God affecting our conduct?

Yes, the way that Man chooses to use God. The various religions each portray their god in such a way as to establish the rules and regulations of the age, to be followed by their group of people. In that regard, the laws are established for the behavior of the person in society as part of a religious organization. I cannot follow such unbendable restrictions. God does not dictate each facet of a man's life. Man experiences life on Earth in order to exercise his freedom of choice, not to be dictated to. If he chooses to belong to an organized religion, he gives a part of himself to the organization for the membership.

So the idea that God is on our side in war is something you would not follow?

Correct. The idea must be explored to the extent of the ideology of the causative actions of conflict, and to personify a cause as being right or wrong is to obviate the fact that there is a common basis between all of us.

Quote: "The agnostic is not as certain as some are of what is good and what is evil."

Only because he has no written format to rely upon. The Christian, the Muslim, have scriptures to rely upon for their thinking. The agnostic has no pattern within which to change or modify his behavior to conform to the group in which he lives.

Good and Evil

The ideas of good and evil raise issues about punishment, about heaven and hell. How do you view the idea of hell from your perspective now?

Hell is what we create for ourselves upon the planet. It does not exist otherwise. Heaven, as it is thought of by the religious organizations' authorities, also does not exist. It is not a prize to be conveyed only to those people who comport themselves with the regularities of the religion. It is a term that relates to a prize that does not exist. It is better to say that where we are in our pure form is in the presence of all that exists, from the Source to the last to be broken from the Source. And it is all equality and love; it is the essential energy of all that exists: it has no opposites, it has no polarities, it has no dualities, as found in body form. It is just a place where we return in our naked condition, where all are the same.

Does that mean evil does not exist where you are now?

You cannot do evil in soul form. You can in human form, but only so far as humans judge. The great equalizer in the human form is the judgment that the majority in society feels is correct against what the individual chooses to experience.

Can we not do good on Earth?
A relative term, determined within the judgment scenario. Some people, most particularly within the religions, consider good as dictating a certain behavior. For example, when the Chinese bound the feet of women it was "good" in that it showed beauty, yet it was death to the mobility of the person. So the good is only from your perspective.

What of the Golden Rule and the teaching of Jesus that we should love our enemies: do they not lead in a particular direction of goodness?
Again, goodness is a relative term. In Earth's dimension it is to stamp down chaos. "Love your enemies" was said because if you do so you cannot think of retaliating against them. That does not make a distinction between loving the essence of them (their souls), and not reacting to the physicality of what they do.

Listening to you, it feels as though good and evil don't matter as much as we think they do!
Not where I am.

Well then, what does matter?
What matters in the soul's perspective is the richness of the experience of the lessons it learned while in physical form. In physical form, what matters is that you experience lessons, whether they are humanly considered to be good or evil, so you can take that energy back to add to the richness of the experiences of all the souls.

The Source

What is the nature of God? Do you know anything more about God now?

It is a term that, with the machinations I went through on Earth, is laughable. There is not "a" being—it is a part, the Origin, the Source, the connective Force, of all that exists.

You do acknowledge there is a Source?

I cannot help but feel it because it is a part of me and I of it.

You are talking about all that exists. Modern physics is striving to find "a theory about everything." Is there an Everything about which physics can find a theory?

Not in its present Earth-bound form. They can get a little further if they open to it through their feelings—if they throw out the playbook, if they throw out the bibles, if they throw out the dogmatic predictions, and openly observe and feel what is going on around them. But it's a conundrum. They cannot achieve a steady, reproducible result even with that, because each soul inputs a different perspective.

A question of relativity—who is doing the looking?

Yes, who is doing the looking and how deeply they are looking and connecting.

In your book, you wrote that the agnostic does not think he is divinely inspired by the Bible because the book is early history and legend, no more exactly true than Homer. He thinks its moral teaching sometimes good and sometimes bad. What is your view now?

About the same.

Can an agnostic be a Christian?

Yes, if by "Christian" you refer, as I do, to raising oneself to the level at which an individual soul is able to connect itself to other souls, to feel and to exchange experiences within that level of energy. Then the agnostic is definitely a Christian, but not as one who is part of those people who elevate Jesus of Nazareth as the Savior.

What about Jesus' actual teaching? Are you aware of that teaching in its original form?

It's not as you understand it. His purpose on Earth was to show people the way to connect to their soul, to the Source, while still in physical body. His purpose was not to come down and to atone for sins, because there are no sins but those that exist in Earth's dimension. It's the same as the commonly held views of heaven and hell.

In your book you said you gave a definition of the word "soul" as "something non-material which exists through a person's life, or even...through all future time." You thought agnostics would not believe that a man has a soul; what do you think now?

I know I am my soul. The rhetoric that I used at that time was of the human body. It denied that there was a purpose or a connection that organized religions had for a free-thinking man, in which category I classified myself. To be a free-thinking man, I had to be what I defined as "agnostic." My only concept, while in physical form, of anything other than physical form came through organized religion. I could not accept it because it did not feel right; it did not vibrate with me that there was a heaven and a hell, and predestination from this Supreme Being. Now that I have been connected back to the Source, I know I am immortal. I would not be in a position to speak with you today if I were not immortal.

When you were very young your father died and willed that you should be brought up as an agnostic, but then your grandmother brought you up strictly as a Christian. How do you view that experience these days?

It was the groundwork for my writings that were to shake the foundations of people who were ready to explore what they really thought. It created a conflict within me of what was right and what was wrong. By creating a conflict, it created a search.

59

Is there anything good in religion these days, or it is it all a mistake?

It is needed by some of the spirits on the planet, because without it there would be chaos. However, it is also being used as an excuse to create chaos by the less-mature spirits who are trying hard to create their own world, without realizing that they have the ability within them to do so. They don't have to structure it out of the materials of others, but can create their own.

Religion has a comforting purpose for those who cannot feel their self, who cannot get in touch with their soul side. It is also a good diagram of what <u>not</u> to do, for people who are in contact with their souls—some religions proclaim the exact opposite of what life is like on the other side. If a person goes into their feelings of what's going on, it's like having a neon sign showing them what is the actuality in the soul, rather than the make-believe role that is played on Earth to give experiences that will help the soul to mature.

Bertrand Russell, you are still stirring things up a lot. Thank you so much for being with us.

[he bows] My pleasure.

Commentary

Bertrand Russell was the only spirit with whom either author had been in physical contact. In the 1960s, Peter, then in charge of a peace movement, spoke at a rally for peace in Vietnam, in Trafalgar Square, London. He helped to warm up the crowd for Bertrand Russell, a highly popular speaker, featured at the event. The two men exchanged pleasantries as they climbed a ladder onto the plinth of Nelson's Monument to address the peaceniks.

Toni: I felt throughout the channeling as if Russell were still there addressing the crowd in Trafalgar Square. But now his words are based on his actual experiences at Home, and they came across humbly, with sincerity, and with a conviction that the dialogues should be heard and understood by the people they reached. He also felt like a rabble rouser who wanted to get people out of their complacency and into their feeling heart.

Peter: It was significant to hear the formerly agnostic Russell say, "I know I am my soul," and, "I would not be in a position to speak with you today if I were not immortal." It was also a major change for him to assert that the Source "is a part of me and I of it." But if the faithful will cheer his new spiritual certainty, their rejoicing may be muted by his incisive comments on the Christian religion.

Russell's childhood gave him a dislike of church authority, and in this he has not changed. The church is wrong about heaven and hell, which do not exist except as a description of the state of mind people may have here on Earth. Good and evil are not how people on planet Earth perceive them to be. There is a relativism in his viewpoint which people will only find acceptable when they are fully convinced that his vantage point at Home gives him a perspective of the truth that human beings just don't have.

We chose the grounds for our dialogue, which, in terms of Russell's wide-ranging and voluminous output, reasonably matched our need for focus and brevity. Having done so, we found the old antagonist of Christian dogma still sniping amiably at the inadequacies of monotheistic religion, and treating us to exciting vistas of the very different kind of world in which he now lives happily. Russell's incisive philosophical understanding was always, quite disarmingly, couched in remarkably simple English. We had an enlightened philosopher Russell here at his best, with the same economy and clarity of response.

"It is not what the eye perceives but what the soul perceives
that defines beauty."

Oscar Wilde
1854-1900

Biographical Note

Oscar Fingal O'Flahertie Wilde was born in 1854, one of three
children of a prominent Dublin surgeon and his wife, a writer and
revolutionary thinker who cultivated an artistic and intellectual
elite at her weekly Salons. Oscar attended these gatherings from a
young age and learned to emulate his mother's witty style of
speech and love of paradox. He was educated at Ireland's high-
class Portora Royal School, where he received a classical
education and learned to become a snob. The middle-class Wilde
family worked strenuously to achieve their upper-class ambitions,
but their drive "to get on" was severely challenged when his
father fell from prominence, both financially and socially, in a
scandal.

In 1871 Wilde went to Trinity College, Dublin, where he was
awarded many prizes for his scholarship, and where he studied
classics and aesthetic theory. After Trinity, he entered Oxford
University, where John Ruskin taught him moral medievalism,
and Walter Pater inspired him with Renaissance aestheticism. His
Greek studies led him to embrace the concept of homosexuality,
which became of growing importance, although (perforce) he
remained outwardly heterosexual. He considered Roman
Catholicism, attracted by the church's ritual and strong aesthetic
appeal, but even a private audience with the Pope, arranged by
friends, failed to convince him to join the church. Irish

superstition was recounted in Oscar's stories. His eccentricity in dress, well-honed witticisms, and academic prowess all combined to proclaim his brilliance, and made him a rising star even in advance of his literary accomplishments. The first of these, written in his last year at Oxford, was the prize-winning poem *Ravenna* (1878). He moved to Chelsea where his widowed mother then lived; fell in love and was jilted; lectured in America on aesthetics; promoted Art Nouveau there and in Paris; and, in 1884, married Constance Lloyd who bore him two sons in the next two years. The marriage was a truly disastrous one, with Wilde at odds with his wife and largely ignoring his sons. For a while he edited *Woman's World* and wrote *The Happy Prince* (1888) and children's stories, but domesticity was short-lived, and he moved into his most creative period, which was to last a mere seven years.

The exquisite wit and social satire in his dramas marked him out as a literary genius. The best known plays were: *Lady Windermere's Fan* (1892), *A Woman of No Importance* (1893), *An Ideal Husband* (1895), and *The Importance of Being Earnest* (1895). There were Socratic dialogues, other plays, short stories, and, more darkly, his only novel, *The Picture of Dorian Gray* (1891), a sad portrait of vanity and depravity. Like the book itself, his comment "There is no such thing as a moral or immoral book" was controversial. Its homoerotic implications were considered quite immoral by his contemporaries, and presaged his eventual downfall.

Wilde's homosexual affair with Lord Alfred (Bosie) Douglas, a young Oxford undergraduate, triggered his disgrace. Wilde's libel action against Bosie's father, Lord Queensberry (of boxing fame), turned sour when Wilde's passionate letters to the young man and his list of male child prostitutes surfaced. He withdrew his case, but eventually was convicted in 1895 for gross indecency and sentenced to two years' hard labor. On his release from prison he wrote *The Ballad of Reading Goal* (1898), but he was quite finished as a writer. Ostracized by former associates, and penniless, Oscar Wilde wandered through Europe for three years and died of meningitis in a cheap Paris hotel in 1900, at 46 years of age.

The Dialogue

When we began the conversation, he was quite his old self:
How are you, Oscar?
Charming!

Early Days

In The Nihilists *your character Vera says, "Life is much too important a thing ever to talk seriously about it." Was it your experience as a boy in your mother's Salon that taught you the art of talking and writing wittily about serious matters?*

When I was a boy I had the pleasure of making contact with my spirit guides. At one point they were my main companions, and they taught me not to take physical life seriously. They taught me that it was very important to experience what was going on, but not to be controlled by what was going on. This brought about wit and humor, in trying to get others to enjoy life in the way that I was enjoying it.

You said "when I was a boy;" did you lose contact with your guides after that period?

I never lost total contact with them, but in all of the interactions I had with the myriad of people who came into my life, they got put on the shelf for a while. I became more humanized and into dealing with things of the flesh.

Would you call yourself psychically precocious as a boy?

It depends on your definition. Was I connected to the spiritual aspects of myself? Yes I was. Psychically, could I predict things, and was I clairvoyant, clairsentient? No.

Your mother was a writer; was she also psychic?

She was, to some degree, a channeler. When she set herself into "the mode" as she would call it, she was able to call upon records of things that she had experienced previously, and re-work them into whatever she was writing. She was very acutely aware of my energy, and psychically connected to me, so that she always knew exactly where I was and what I was about. It sometimes put a damper on my youthful enthusiasm. [chuckles]

Did your two siblings share your abilities?
No, they were the ordinary bland variety.

You were the "Indigo child"?
It wasn't called "Indigo" then. It wasn't of the same energy of the Indigos who come in now. I was very near to the veil and able to cross over. I also did a fair amount of what is now called Astral Projection, where I visited other areas and other lifetimes.

But you did not make specific use of that experience in your writing, did you?
I considered it as research, and did not copy anything that was there. I tried to make things my own and apply them to what I saw in the physical, going on around me, although I now realize a lot of what I wrote had been experienced in other lifetimes.

In the physical, you and your mother were obsessed with social status.
Yes, frightfully, and it was everything to me at that time. How I was thought of, where I could go, where I would be invited. The benefits of being in with the "In Crowd" were very, very important to me. I began to see myself in the eyes of others, and I chose only to look to the highest segments of society.

Was the collapse of your father's position a severe blow?
It was traumatic. It was as if everything that had been worked for, everything that had been built up, was suddenly erased with a huge eraser. It took away all the connections. We became *persona non grata* to a lot of those people with whom we had worked so hard to ingratiate ourselves. I was devastated!

Then your mother fled to Chelsea (in London).

Yes, she did. It was just too much of an embarrassment, as she would say, for her to remain in Dublin with all those who knew the truth of what had happened.

Love and Marriage

In An Ideal Husband *you wrote, "To love oneself is the beginning of a life-long romance." You had a lot of academic and literary accomplishments, but did you love yourself?*

To the degree that I could—it was not as I love myself now. To love the soul, to be in unconditional love of yourself and everything you do is the ideal for human beings. I did not achieve that on Earth, but I had the feeling that this is how a person truly loves. One can only love another person to the extent that one can love oneself, otherwise what one offers to a relationship is either to vacuum love away from the other person, or to offer something which is less than perfect.

As you talked, I was remembering that bon mot *from* Lady Windermere's Fan*: "It takes a thoroughly good woman to do a thoroughly stupid thing." Was your marriage to Constance a self-loving one?*

[laughs] It was a very pleasurable one at times. It was, at the time, the thing to do for the appearances. We were not as compatible as we could have been.

That's a little bit of an understatement! One of your biographers wrote: "a horrendous marriage."

I'm trying now to think of the good lessons we learned from each other. One of the lessons we learned was that we could not live with each other, but at the time, there were all of the constraints of society upon us. It was very ill-advised, but I was currently trying to play the romantic, and I thought I could shape the relationship into a palatable one at least.

She remained constant to you, to the end?

Yes.

In fact, you said on one occasion that both your wife and mother visited you in jail before they died. Historians have doubted the literal truth of that remark. Was there a psychic visiting?

With my mother, yes. My wife actually did come. On one occasion I got the sense that it was just to gloat. Finally, I had got myself into a position where she believed I belonged.

Success

You should put that last remark in a play! Talking about plays— looking at your life as a whole as Oscar Wilde, what was the most satisfying moment of your career?

In the way I lived my life. Most of the time it was the moment I was living in. I was all about physical sensations, physical feelings, the way I interacted with people, the way they interacted with me. I got as much experience out of the successes as I did out of the abysmal failures, such as my marriage. It was as if I were a tactile being in a room that was loaded with everything from smooth steel to fluffy wool. I went though life feeling these different experiences, and in the moment each experience was the highlight of my consciousness.

So it was not a particular play, but every play had its moment.

Every play—both those which were performed and those which were my day-to-day life.

Beauty and Soul

One aspect of your life, certainly at Oxford, was your delight in beauty, whether of the Pre-Raphaelites, or the ritual of the mass, or the beauty of nature. At times you seem to have been more taken with beauty than with content, asserting once that if there was an afterlife you should like to return as a flower, utterly without soul but entirely beautiful. How do you view your feelings now?

Beauty, if it is taken as unconditional love, is the ultimate. It is not what the eye perceives but what the soul perceives that defines beauty. I was very much of the eye-variety while I was on Earth. It started for me when our place in society amongst the rich and privileged was very important. They chose only that which was appealing to the eye, and I got into that mindset. But I got much more from beauty, much more from the flower; I got much more from the painting, from the statue—I got the feeling of the energy of the soul who has created the non-living things, and I felt the energy of the living things. That to me was beauty. I was just unaware at the time of everything I was perceiving. Now to me everything that exists is beauty.

How do you view Keats' line, "Beauty is truth, truth, beauty—that is all ye know on Earth and all ye need to know"?

That is of the Earth—I have a view now from above. I have a view from within. I have a view from without. I have a view from space. I have a view from the magma of the Earth. All is beauty because all has purpose, all has conviction, all has a life of its own, yet interconnected with all that is. Keats was right in terms of the human view, but he was far short of the energy of the soul.

So you would not "return as a flower, utterly without soul"?

Definitely not. I could not exist without a soul in any form.

In your novel The Picture of Dorian Gray *you wrote, "Nowadays all the married men live like bachelors and all the bachelors live like married men." How much of that story was autobiographical, and how much prescient?*

I took examples from my own life, from the lives of my associates, from the dreams we all had of what we construed to be freedom-without-consequence. I wrote of the angst that could be placed upon a person totally tied up with constraints. There is a way by which people can free themselves of all restrictions, by putting themselves into another dimension.

There is much more to the book than appears. I have a much different feeling of it now. I realize that I was writing of how the person, as a soul, can have a human experience and live it as a soul in another dimension, without all of the complications, the societal beliefs, and that duality which is the human condition. I did not fully grasp what the energy was and what the emotions were that I was experiencing, and which put the book into me. I now know that a person can take their physical infirmities, aging, falling down, and can place them aside and simply live the life of the soul to whatever extent they choose.

Sexuality

There were conflicts during your life over sexuality. I have two more quotes: from The Duchess of Padua, *"We are each our own devil, and we make this world our hell," and from* An Ideal Husband, *"Life is never fair...and perhaps it is a good thing for most of us that it is not." Which is the better evaluation of your affair with Bosie, and your incarceration in Reading jail for the crime of gross indecency?*

Nil desperandum! [Despair nothing!] I was simply following my physical energies, my physical needs that I felt unable to ignore. Because they were so strong I found it to be very unjust that I was condemned for them, but that was because I did not fit into the little cubby-hole which was expected of each proper gentleman. We were also a bit glib about the whole situation, and uncaring of the consequences.

You were a married man with two sons who were born in quick succession after your marriage. Was your homosexuality, especially your liaison with young male prostitutes, a selfish disregard of morality, or—as some have suggested—a search for self-identity? Did you, like Dorian, attempt to live without a soul?

It is very difficult now totally to comprehend everything I did when in physical form. It is so different from the way I feel now. I was tormented by physical needs, which, after the birth of my children, were not relieved by my wife. At first I thought I would go by way of the prostitute, as did many at that time. But then I discovered the beauty of the young male body. The first encounter was actually a seduction of me.

At Oxford?
Yes.

Did the homosexual seduction predate marriage to Constance?

It did, but it was an embarrassment to me and something I tried to hide until I found that the common way of man and woman would not work for me. I tried to blot out the feelings I had had in the first encounter, and to make them disappear, by becoming normal within the realm of sexual relations. When I was denied those experiences, at first I did get enough release to be satisfied in the marriage. But after the second child, Constance, not wanting any more children, forbade me her bed. Then in my sadness, as I went out wandering, I was reacquainted with beauty. Constance became for me the epitome of the hag—that person from whose constant pecking one wants to free oneself. I found relief in the gentleness of beings who wanted to share—young male prostitutes—who did not wish to control, did not wish to peck, did not wish to direct, and who wished only to have money in exchange for pleasuring.

What part does morality play in that drama?

That was where I convinced myself that I was cutting myself off from my soul, and without the soul I surmised I did not have to worry about condemnation or repercussions. I was simply going to live in the physical form and not have to worry about anything beyond.

You are describing your sexuality as having such force that you could not control it except by taking up homosexuality. It wasn't a confusion; it was your deliberate choice.

It was a choice, a physical drive, and an obsession with me. It came at a time when I was totally inexperienced, and led by another to feel the release, to feel physical closeness to another being without other agendas (the pressures of taking care of the house, providing for the servants). It was just the act itself. When I was forbidden Constance's bed, and needed release, had I gone to another woman I felt that I would still have had those same female pressures—a family/no family. I found instead in males a companionship, a camaraderie, all wrapped round the ability for sexual release—but with no ties.

In this generation on Earth, there is a point of view expressed strongly by critics that seems to support what you are saying—that homosexuality is a deliberate choice and you can be talked out of it. How do you view that attitude?

I have two opinions of what you have just said. I believe that in most cases it is a deliberate choice in the present age, the choice of how to experience closeness and sexual relationships. I do not feel it is something people can be talked out of, if their sense of self, if their ability to sense love and vibration within a close personal relationship is attuned to one of the same sex. There still is a choice to participate in that relationship, because everything on Earth is "freedom of choice." People can either follow the urges they have or deny them, but they cannot be talked out of their urges. It has to be their own choice whether or not to follow up on the urge to partake in a physical encounter.

Concerned and loving people are very troubled by the thought of those being forced to take part in prostitution, whether male or female, and they say it should be discouraged or banned. What is your view?

Prostitution is one of the oldest professions, and for some, it is their occupation, their way of life, a thing they have chosen to do, although others are forced into it by circumstances. For the person who is not ready to settle down, or is not ready for responsibility, it is a way to find release, to be serviced, if you would, without attachments. It reminds me of a bull at stud, taken from farm to farm for the purpose of providing the best sperm. That's not to say prostitution has to do with reproduction, but it is just a service that's being performed. It takes a lot of pressure off different relationships, where one party in that relationship does not choose to have sexual relations, or is incapable of performing, yet the energy is so strong in the other partner that they have to find some way to release it.

Are you saying that you lost sight of your soul, otherwise you would not have pursued your sexuality as you did?

I lost contact with the feel of my self-love and soul. I was not totally disconnected from the soul because I was experiencing soul lessons during that period. There is a difference between consciously working on the growth of the soul, and unconsciously having experiences for the soul to mature.

So you didn't try, like Dorian, to live without a soul?
I did not allow myself to dwell upon what, at that time, was considered the moral consequences of my actions. To me, that was akin to living without a soul.

Even though as a child you knew what the soul was?
Correct. I let myself have selective memory to justify my activities.

Looking back from where you are now, do you regret the Bosie affair, or did you learn from it?
I don't regret anything that I experienced. Everything provided lessons.

What was the nature of the Bosie affair lesson?
First, if you are in human form and in society, you must be conscious of societal rules and regulations. Second, no man anywhere in physical form lives on an island alone, and is unaffected by others. There are consequences when you choose to go beyond accepted behavior, if you remain within society. For a while I thought that as I had chosen to separate myself from what I considered moral repercussions for what I was doing, that that would create around me an island where I could exist, do as I chose, and not impact others or be impacted by them. My largest lesson was that I could not.

You died in 1900. Have you incarnated since?
No.

Counting Chickens

Shortly before your death you wrote in a letter, "People who count their chickens before they are hatched, act very wisely, because chickens run about so absurdly that it is impossible to count them accurately." Humanity seems to be facing innumerable moral and physical challenges at this time. As you look at the Earth now, which chickens should we be counting most carefully?

We should be counting most carefully the chickens that are most prolific, chickens who are creating their own little belief systems, their own little worlds that are contrary to the norm of society and that have a negative impact, in Earth terms, upon other people.

OK, name them!

To clump them together I would say the terrorists, the fundamentalists, the dictators of the world, those who feel they have total control or "should" have total control over the planet.

What should we do about them? How do we rise up and throw them out?

The main thing you can do is to go beyond them in your spiritual forms. Don't give them power over you, because they use fear, which gives your power to them to control you. If you do not fear them, if you do not do as they say, they have no control over you. Now you may say that means you will have to leave the physical because they may kill you, and if that is true then so be it, but your spirit still is the winner in the end.

Oscar Wilde, thank you for your time and your thoughts.

It has been my pleasure. I hope my experiences on the planet will not have people think that I am not a spiritual person at this time. I am my spiritual self at this moment; I just forgot my true self while on the planet.

The Masters' Comment

Masters, In view of your remarks about homosexuality, will you comment on Oscar's remark that he was thwarted in his heterosexuality and, having an excess of sexual drive, he was driven into homosexuality. It was not a sexual confusion, or soul searching, but a deliberate choice.

Oscar Wilde was a bisexual, not a true homosexual, in that particular human incarnation. He engaged in and was able to get his physical release within both forms of sexuality. It was opportunity that directed where he went. His feelings and convictions were of what to him was more pleasurable and safer. He was a man who feared being dominated by anyone. Part of the domination he felt came through anything female, so it was then his choice to express his sexuality primarily with males. It was not confusion but a life lesson that he was experiencing; it was a conscious choice. The majority of those in human form who are homosexual are dealing with energies, coming from within them from their soul, which make them resonate only with souls who are physically in the same sexual body as they are.

So bisexuality is a different type of experience?
In most cases.

What about transsexuality?
Transsexuality is a state of internal confusion so pervasive that the person cannot resonate with the body they are in. They go through a series of life-lessons—several incarnations or a number of life-lessons within one lifetime, such as: they are born male, they are raised male, although their feelings are always feminine to the extent that they are not satisfied with being a male acting in a feminine relationship with another male. Their feelings are so strong that they have to become physically female themselves in order to feel as they should feel. So there is a difference.

How do you view homophobia?
A homophobe is a person who is aware of both masculine and feminine energies within themselves and fears that they may be different from their friends because of the yearnings or the sensations they have. It is normal for a person to be able to sense

all such feelings. Because they may feel a strong pull toward someone of the same sex, they rebel against it to the extent that they become raving condemners...

Of "girly-men"?
Yes, of girly-men.

Commentary

Toni: Oscar had the feel of an ancient child. He was petulant, indifferent to criticism, took no responsibility for his actions, and dismissed his life as Oscar Wilde as just one more experience for the soul. His ancient quality came through as he talked about the journey of the soul that he feels he now understands. Yet the sense came across that truly he has not resolved the lessons that presented themselves to him while on Earth, and that he will be back to complete them. I have the sense that he has not wholly completed reviewing his experiences in the life of Oscar Wilde with his spirit guides, which is why he was somewhat serious and contemplative, and also why he has not reincarnated before now.

Peter: I was intrigued by the nature of the soul-drama into which the dialogue developed. It almost had the feel of a stage play! Oscar Wilde claimed that as a child he was psychically advanced and well aware of his own soul, and that his mother's psychic gifts were also advanced, but insight and brilliance were not adequate to save him from ultimate disaster. First, his mother's exceptionally powerful psychic oversight caused the ultra-sensitive boy to be forever nervous of female control. Second, his snobbish drive to succeed, while it brought him great public acclaim, made him indifferent to the boundaries of decency. Third, fuelled by thoughts of brilliance and beauty, and powered by the thirsty engines of his bisexuality, he dared to push his writing and his sexuality to ever new limits, always relishing the hedonism of the Now.

All this Oscar made plain to us, as he looked back on his life, in a series of answers and observations that were polished and quite witty at times. Unlike some souls with whom we have made contact, he offered a re-evaluation of his career, but very little expression of regret or distancing. We wondered, as he glossed over such issues as his use of juvenile male prostitutes and, indeed, expressed his whole attitude toward the dynamics of sexual urges, if his statement "I let myself have selective memory to justify my activities" might not still be true for his soul today. But we must equally recall that Oscar Wilde's eternal spirit may well belong to that group who (like ourselves) have not yet completed the lessons that life on Earth is designed to teach.

We called in the Masters, who have completed their life lessons and who speak to us as a consensus group. They identified Wilde as being a natural bisexual human, and therefore different energetically from the true homosexual, whose soul-searching they had already carefully outlined for us in Chapter One.

Although thoughts coming through the channel Toni from the Other Side tend to be filtered somewhat by her own pattern of speech, Wilde's style of speaking came through quite clearly. We loved his comment on Constance's prison visit, "Finally I had got myself into a position where she believed I belonged," and those, neatly put, about marriage, "One can only love another person to the extent that one can love oneself," and concerning beauty, "It is not what the eye perceives but what the soul perceives that defines beauty." The interview has a distinctive quality of speech, although it was too serious in tone to allow much Wilde wit.

Talking with Leaders of the Past

"God is not a separate, independent being, as religions would have you believe, but we—each soul, each creation, each part of creation—have the force within us to create and to manifest."

William James
1842-1910

Biographical Note

William James was born in 1842 into a wealthy, intellectual, and deeply religious Swedenborgian family living in New York City. His early education was from gifted private tutors, and schools for the privileged in Europe as well as America. His higher education began in Geneva, where he proved himself to be fluent in five languages. He also became a keen naturalist and showed talent for art. After working in a studio as an apprentice, he transferred to Harvard University in 1861 to study science and mathematics, and in 1865 went on a scientific expedition up the Amazon.

James suffered at this time from a host of physical ailments, becoming severely depressed and even suicidal. These troubles caused him to seek a cure in Germany for over a year, during which time he began publishing reviews for literary magazines. Back at Harvard he switched majors to chemistry and medicine, earning his MD in 1869. He never practiced medicine, but, as he put it, "drifted into psychology and philosophy."

After a brief time teaching anatomy and physiology in the medical school, James began his lifetime career of teaching at Harvard University, where in 1876 he established the first experimental psychology laboratory in America. This led eventually to professorial positions in philosophy as well as in psychology.

In 1878 William James married Alice Howe Gibbens. The couple had four sons and one daughter. Family life helped settle him both physically and psychologically, and the couple raised their children in an environment of intellectual freedom.

James was an original and pragmatic thinker in the fields of physiology, psychology, and philosophy. His *Principles of Psychology* (1890) cemented his reputation as the leading American psychologist of his day, and he was the first American to recognize the work of Sigmund Freud. He forged a national reputation in philosophy with his book *The Will to Believe and other Essays in Popular Philosophy* (1897), venturing into the realms of religious belief, the importance of genius, and psychical research. From this sprang his concept of pragmatism, in which he saw humans as essentially practical beings whose minds aided them in adapting to the world around them.

While in Europe convalescing from a painful heart condition, James delivered the Gifford Lectures at Edinburgh University, published as *The Varieties of Religious Experience* in 1902. They focused on "man's religious constitution," and he discussed people's appetite for religion and the satisfaction we gain through philosophy.

After his retirement from Harvard University in 1907, James published *Pragmatism* (1907). This treatise ensured his reputation as a leading American philosopher and psychologist. He was sure that pragmatism would help to secure the status of philosophy by drawing it closer to its scientific origins. The pragmatic method aiming to discover the truth of an idea by determining its agreement with reality, whether concrete or abstract, was for him the philosophy for the future.

In *A Pluralistic Universe* (1909), James explored the possibility of a "science of religion," sensing that the metaphysical world of religious experience was a real human phenomenon, although inaccessible to conventional science. This book and *The Meaning of Truth* (1909) were received with hostility by many academics, including the young philosopher Bertrand Russell. James was also derided for an account, published in the *Proceedings of the American for Psychical Research*, with verbatim records of the conversation in which he had contacted the spirit of Richard Hodgson, who had been a personal friend.

Cardiac pain increasingly afflicted him. He sailed to Europe for treatment, which proved unsuccessful. Back in his Chocorua, New Hampshire, home, William James died in 1910, at 68 years of age.

The Dialogue

Karma

I'm concerned by people's use of the term "karma." Recently, I have called the experience "consequence." When we have ideas that are right or wrong, consequences flow from them and from any action that follows. It's not so much what we do but how we feel and think that causes the consequences in our lives. Is there a better way of stating karma that is not misleading?

Our language is so imperfect that one word, such as *karma*, takes on a multitude of meanings as it is translated and played out from one group of people to another group of people. The karma that we know about best is from the Eastern philosophies, wherein is stated that the karmic effect determines everything you do in your next lifetime—which is phooey! Your use of the term "consequence" more readily portrays what the energetic action is; however, some linguists find it a very harsh word because it doesn't give room for variations.

Is there a better word?

No—but you have to be very clear that consequence is not a firm noun but rather an action word.

Is it basically true that consequence flows from our thoughts and feelings rather than our actions?

The consequence flows from the entire experience of the soul's attempting to learn its Earth lessons in order to attain spiritual wisdom.

Take Hitler: what was the most important, his deeds or his intentions?

Hitler came down to Earth to experience a number of things, including extremes of hatred, and to experience going from the situation of being belittled and misunderstood to that of becoming a dominating dictator. These were all lessons he came to learn. His intention within the lessons was to do the best in each situation that he could. When he was in the realm of pure hatred his intent was to hate everything, so in that example it was intent that caused consequences. He also had the unenviable position, for humans, of being a teacher of many people around him.

If anyone has the intent to learn a lesson to the best of their ability, it is no different if they are a Hitler or a healer—if it is done with the intent of learning. What does happen within a soul when it goes through an intense experience, as he did, is that there is residual energy from uncompleted lessons, which remains in the soul, so that in the next lifetime there is a fight to rid the self of those energies, which are the consequences.

Have I identified the central point?

Yes. The central point is that within a consequence, if you choose, the next lesson can be experienced, expanded, or controlled.

Is "experience" another word to use when talking about Karma?

It's another way of putting it, but what better describes experience is the word "Dharma," which is the reclamation of all experiences. It varies from the Akashic records in the distinction that the Akashic records are the compilation of all of the souls' histories in creation, while dharma is the particular experiences of an individual soul.

I suppose there's an experiential element in "consequence," as well.

Consequence is very narrow because it only indicates a response to something; it does not represent an incompletion of something, as I said before. I'm well aware that people will use the word karma as it is defined within their own belief systems. Anything that I say as to my beliefs on karma will only impact things that I have already said. It still will not rid people of their "eye for an eye" mentality of karma. The only other thing I find amusing with different definitions of karma is in the eastern philosophies, where they believe karma results in a person's coming back as a lesser living being if they have done something wrong. People become cockroaches only if they choose to!

You had your tongue in your cheek when you said that, didn't you? People shouldn't think that William James said they could come back as cockroaches?
Not at all—unless they want to!

Belief and Religious Experience
I understand that you might have preferred to call your book of essays The Will to Believe *by another phrase: "the right to believe." Is that true, and if so, why?*
There was an energy running at that time. The "right to believe" implies that one is controlled by mandates of society. The "will to believe" is human intentionality. So it was battling the trend at that time of manipulation by others, which is why I called it "the will to believe."

You said that scientists can afford to await the outcome of their investigations before coming to a belief. But in the formation of religious belief we are forced to come up with some belief even if all the relevant evidence is not in. Is this still your view?
That is my view as far as the process that occurs on the planet. Religious beliefs dictate to an individual how he is to think and operate within his lifetime. In order to be within a belief system, the human being must comport to the system's directions and mandates, whether or not he believes or feels that what he is being instructed to do is the correct thing for him. The scientist is without restriction, without a planned agenda telling him what to do from the outside. So therefore, he has the pleasure of rewriting what may be accepted as science, from his observations, and he

has the leisure (as he is under no mandate to find x, y, or z) to sit back until the entire situation has played out.

You said, "I have the right to believe because such a belief may help bring about the fact believed in, and a fact cannot come at all unless a preliminary faith exists in its coming." You related this concept to religious belief, particularly to the possibility that salvation depends on believing in God in advance of any proof that God exists. Isn't that putting the cart before the horse?

No, and it's not because—as I now know—beings create their own reality, and unless they possess a truth which they feel their reality should be, they cannot create it. Sometimes they have not delineated a specific truth before they materilize or manifest it. But it is still from within themselves that they evolve where they are going, and what they seek to achieve.

In the case of the existence of God, you indicated that such a belief may be justified by the outcome to which having such a belief leads. You justified the systems of "trust" on which societal beliefs and actions are based, but quoted a statement by your contemporary Fitz James Stephen that "In all important transactions of life we have to take a leap in the dark." Doesn't this concept of the ends justifying the means validate the very worst of religious fundamentalism and political totalitarianism?

Yes, to a large degree, but these statements meant much more than that (as I now know, as I now feel, and of which I now have the wisdom). God is not, as religions would have you believe, a separate, independent being, but we—each soul, each creation, each part of creation—have the force within us to create and to manifest. I now know that the trust we must have is in ourselves and in our abilities.

In The Will to Believe *you suggest that there is no common essence to morality, but a guiding principle for ethics: that we "satisfy at all times as many demands as we can" by seeking "the good which seems most organizable, most fit to enter into complex combinations, most apt to be a member of a more inclusive whole."*

You say that we arrive at laws and moral formulations by a kind of experiment, but there is nothing final about the results: "as our present laws and customs have fought and conquered other past ones, so they will in their turn be overthrown by any newly discovered order which will hush up the complaints that they still give rise to, without producing others louder still." Do you still hold this view, or is there some kind of ethical standard for us on Earth to seek, find, and adopt?

First a comment: what an egotistical person I was to think that I could have the answers to everything! I now know that wanting to compartmentalize, catagorize, and justify everything was a conscious manipulative power that I thought I possessed.

Ethics are an invention of those in human form. Ethics do not exist with us at Home because we are in unconditional love. We do not have to dictate or live by a set of standards that will make us be what we would like all people to be. Ethics are a construct to have all of the actions within a group of people be *fair* to each other. Each individual soul is in a body to experience certain lessons. Some of those lessons would be considered ethical by all who are around them, because they do not impact them in a negative way. Other lessons would be considered unethical because the person is wishing to learn the lesson of stretching the boundaries of what is then recognized by society. I now know neither is right nor wrong, and we cannot dictate to a soul to be "ethical" as we understand it if they have a lesson to learn that is "unethical."

Commenting on the relationship of the individual with the divine in The Varieties of Religious Experience, *you contrast "The Religion of Healthy-Mindedness" and "The Religion of The Sick Soul." The healthy-minded religious person has a deep sense of the goodness of life. This can be just natural to someone, but often comes as an act of will. You praise liberal Christianity as the triumph of a resolute devotion to healthy-mindedness over a morbid "old hell-fire theology." Is that still your view?*

That is my view as to the patterns within those religions, but now I see them almost as if they are soccer teams that have different ways of winning their games, with different playbooks for accomplishing that goal. The end result is that they all play the game and accomplish what they put into it. They are regimented by patterns that have been established for them within the religions to which they choose to adhere. The premise is that people are working on themselves in their lifetimes. Where they choose to go fits into what they choose to learn, and fits best into certain patterns of certain groups, so these groups are those toward which they will gravitate. Nothing is wrong and nothing is right. It is whatever the individual needs to further the personal maturation process.

You said that in "The Religion of The Sick Soul," evil cannot be eliminated. From the sick soul's perspective, "radical evil gets its innings." The sick soul finds that "from the bottom of every fountain of pleasure, something bitter rises up: a touch of nausea, a falling dead of the delight, a whiff of melancholy." These states are not just nasty sensations; they bring "a feeling of coming from a deeper region and often have an appalling convincingness." Have you ruled out a deliberate denial by souls that there are lessons to be learned, and their deliberate turning away from bliss? Is the deeper region satanic in any sense?

What I know now is that those who are on a track of experiencing what we consider on Earth to be negativity, wallow in that negativity as a pig in a sty wallows in the mud. They bring forth with them, from other lifetimes, deeper layers of mud. This is their world. Unless they complete the lessons, they cannot wash the mud off and go to the Light. It is not that they choose not to be in the Light, that they choose not to be in the blessings; it is that they are in a pattern—in a trough that they have dug for themselves and cannot see out over the sides. "They know not of what they cannot see."

You said that some sick souls never get well, while others recover or even triumph: these are "twice-born."

My perspective was only of the length of a soul's experience within one physical life. That is true for a single physical life, that

86

some souls do not triumph through one lifetime, because they are so deep in their lessons (which they have not completed) that they must go on to yet another life in order to get out of the depths that they have placed themselves in. Other souls are extremely old and mature, and they easily go through the lessons and get out in one lifetime. We could also be seeing them at the end of a series of lifetimes, where they have dealt with little pieces of their lesson throughout the previous lifetimes and therefore are now ready to complete the lesson and go on to (what we consider pleasurable) living in the Light.

When they are in darkness, in negativity, is it satanic? Is there an evil force which is contrary to the nature of God?
Sometimes a soul combines with the energy of the negative side for a deeper experience, a deeper darkness, a deeper sensation of the lack of unconditional love and the lack of God the Creator. So yes, but not all souls deal with possession by or combination with the evil satanic forces.

So there is such a thing as Satan—a personal opponent to the Godhead?
On the Earth's dimension, the plane of human existence, there is energy that is of such form.

Which God permits to exist?
It was with the blessing of the Creator that Satan came into existence, so that souls would be able to experience the depths of deprivation and degredation as opposed to the goodness of the Creator.

So there was a fallen angel called Satan, who said (in Milton's words), "Evil be thou my good"?
Yes.

So the myth is not a myth at all!
Definitely not.

And the legions of devils?

Breaking off parts of the evil were souls who chose to pick up pieces to experience, whether or not they remained within it. A lot of them experienced it and then moved back to the Light, leaving the evil to be picked up by someone else who saw it as a tool for their lessons.

This happens only in Earth's dimension, not in the dimension of Light?

Where I exist now there is nothing but unconditional love. There is no hate, there is no fear, there is nothing that you would consider negative.

Are there other worlds in which the negative atmosphere also exists?

Not as it does on Earth, which is unique in that everything has a polarity. There are other planets where there is just (what you would consider) negativity, for people to go there and have an immersion course, and planets where there is just lust, or just pride, or vanity, for people to go and experience.

You discussed St. Augustine, Bunyan, Tolstoy, and popular evangelists, focusing on what you called "the state of assurance" they achieved. Central to this state is "the loss of all the worry, the sense that all is ultimately well with one, the peace, the harmony, the 'willingness to be,' even though the outer conditions should remain the same." Is this state of inner harmony more important than the beliefs of the person achieving it?

The word "belief" is not broad enough to readily explain the human soul who has the ability to feel, and who can only truly learn through feeling, which transcends language. The "state of assurance" is a reconnection with the tranquility of the soul or inner essence while still in your human form.

So you still would hold to a state of assurance?

Yes, by "assurance" meaning: feeling, being, believing, becoming.

Is the state of inner harmony more important than the belief of the person achieving it?

A person can believe in something, but if they don't experience it, and become it, it means nothing. If they cannot feel one in peace, any belief is unserving. They must progress through the earth phases of accepting, having faith in, believing in, knowing, and then becoming the concept.

If that belief were in something negative, could they have a state of assurance?

They could have an intellectual convincing of themselves, but it would not resonate with their inner self. The state of harmony comes from the soul's recognizing its connection to the universal consciousness.

You stated that religious experiences connect us with a greater reality, not accessible in our normal cognitive relations with the world: "The further limits of our being plunged into an altogether other dimension of existence from the sensible and merely 'understandable' world." Were the mystics in mind?

It's true of any searcher of the soul, searcher of the inner balance between living in a human reality while being part of a universal consciousness. It is tapping back into Source. It is recognition of what and who they are. Mystics dedicate their lives to this pursuit to the exclusion of all others. The common man can also achieve this realm.

It's the grunt we give when we know we're right.

Yes, so long as the rightness comes from a true feeling, a resonance with the truth, not an intellectual agreement with what has been programmed into it.

In Pragmatism and Religion *you attacked "transcendental absolutism" for its unverifiable account of God, and defense of a "pluralistic and moralistic religion" based on human experience: "On pragmatistic principles, if the hypothesis of God works satisfactorily in the widest sense of the word, it is true." How does this apply to our situation today?*

It applies to our situation today if we wrap our heads around words and theories and belief systems. I now know that the unproven, the unverifiable, truly is verifiable if we go inside and connect from the inside by feeling, by becoming. It was not verifiable on paper and therefore of little interest to me because I could not tear it apart in an intellectual way. Now I feel—I am. That is what I could not do in human form, because I did not allow myself. Hence, I had to believe that my intellect was supreme, and that the intellect would always lead me to the answer. I was of the belief and impression that if it could not go through my mind, if it could not be seen by my eyes, if it could not be felt by my hand, then it was not real.

Now I know that I cut myself off from the richest of the sensations that can be experienced by the human body, which is tapping into a piece of the soul's love and companionship, and the energy of and communion with the souls who come from the Source. I look upon it as an expansion of awareness, yet I did not allow myself to sample it while in human form.

That's a very modest comment. I wonder whether you are being a little harsh on yorself. In A Pluralistic Universe *you say that religious experiences "point with reasonable probability to the continuity of our consciousness with a wider spiritual environment from which the ordinary prudential man is shut off." Weren't you recognizing what you just said?*

I was recognizing the possibility because of observing, talking to, and dealing with others who were at the point of being able to reach that contact. While in human form I never achieved it. I longed for it as I met those who were already there, but I was not willing to give up the machinations of my mind in order to go into my heart. It is not being hard upon myself; it is just stating the reality of the life I lived with the emblem you call William James.

Thank you for your assessment. We value the contribution you made on Earth very much. Do you find in your present life that there's intellectual stimulus as well as spiritual stimulus?

It's fun, it's interactive, it's dynamic. We're able to debate much as we did on Earth, but our debating is not of the truth of things but how it will be construed, how it will be taught and used, what we have experienced to enrich the experience of other souls to change and complete lessons they are currently working on, and sometimes, to wonder how we came to the conclusions we did.

Thank you, William James, for your help.

Commentary

Toni: William James seemed to be having fun with the dialogue. He relished being able to debunk his earthly egotism, and was compelling in his thoroughly humble attitude. When he spoke of the contrast between what he thought while on Earth and what he knows now that he is at Home, there was an awe that I sensed in his feeling that "No one in physical form can come anywhere near to understanding the 'completeness of being' on the Other Side" or the unconditional love of the Creator.

Peter: The conversation about "karma" involved my suggesting the term "consequence" as an alternative. William James discussed the differences, constructively outlining the semantic restrictions both words might have in use. His main problem was that the established term "karma" largely belongs to the historic teaching by some religions that suggests the possiblity that individuals' karma could result in their appearing in the next incarnation in a non-human species (such as a cockroach). He considered this supposition rather ridiculous. He also denounced any retributive element in karma. We do not suffer consequences as a result of our misdeeds.

Despite James's gentle display of modesty concerning views he has now abandoned in his present life ("what an egotistical person I was"), he has maintained many of his former positions;

for example, "religious beliefs dictate to an individual how he is to think" but "the scientist is without restriction." One important statement he made is that God is not a separate, independent soul, and each soul has the God-force within itself enabling them to create and to manifest.

Speaking of ethics he made some challenging statements. We cannot simply measure people ethically, because they may have a lesson to learn which itself is unethical. People are working on themselves in their lifetimes. Nothing is inherently right or wrong but is related to each individual's need to further the process of personal maturation. Sometimes a soul combines with the energy of the negative side of life for a deeper experience: its sensation of the lack of unconditional love and the lack of the Creator's presence.

The negative in life has a purpose, James declared. Satan is not mythical but real. It was with the blessing of the Creator that the Devil and its assistants came into existence in order that souls would be able to experience the depths of deprivation and degredation—in contrast with the Creator's goodness. But negativity exists only in Earth's dimension. "Where I exist now there is nothing but unconditional love. There is no hate, there is no fear, there is nothing that you would consider negative." In this respect Earth is quite special. There are negative elements in other worlds to which spirits may go, but Earth is unique in that here everything has polarity.

In this universe seemingly turned upside down, James still asserts that the call of religion for people to believe in the divine is correct. But theirs must be more than mere mental belief. People must go inside and find that assurance which is an amalgam of feeling, being, believing, and becoming. "A person can believe something, but if they don't experience it, and become it, it means nothing."

William James still has ideas to challenge us—ideas that are debated at Home, in the realm of unconditional love, where "it's fun, it's interactive, it's dynamic," and where people have a real concern to make things plain for those of us who are still locked in human lives.

"It is no small thing that a western medical office is called a 'practice,' because the practitioners are constantly practicing their thoughts and ideas upon a needy, bleeding, physical being."

Florence Nightingale
1820-1910

Biographical Note

Florence Nightingale was born in 1820 in Florence, Italy, and named after the city of her birth. Her wealthy British father, William Nightingale, a Cambridge graduate, believed in giving his two girls a sound classical education at home. She was taught mathematics by her father and by a skilled tutor, but her mother was impatient with her neglect of domestic responsibilities.

At seventeen, she received the first intimation of a spiritual call to serve the medical needs of the poor. Nursing at that time was largely left to working-class women and prostitutes, and was almost wholly unorganized. She became actively involved in the reform of the Poor Laws and in campaigning for improved medical care in the nation's infirmaries. This led her in 1845 to tell her family about her vocation, much to the distress of her mother who wanted her to marry.

Richard Milnes, an aristocratic English politician, sought her hand in marriage, but she eventually rejected him to remain true to her life's work. A pioneering hospital in Kaiserwerth, Germany, that she visited impressed her by its methods, and she returned later for a deaconess training course. While there, Nightingale received a strong spiritual confirmation of her desire to go into nursing.

She had met Sidney Herbert, a leading politician and reformer, socially. They were mutually attracted and remained life-long close friends. Herbert greatly aided Nightingale's pioneering nursing work in the Crimea, and Nightingale advised Herbert in his political career.

In 1853, for one year, she took the post of superintendent at the Establishment for Gentlewomen in London. Her sympathetic father arranged for her to be supported by a large annuity that allowed her freely to pursue her career.

Then Herbert, now the British Secretary of War, recruited Nightingale as the Lady-in-Chief of 38 nurses to serve the army in Turkey in its field hospital at Scutari, during the Crimean War. Her detailed reports about the horrific conditions for the wounded began to concern the British public. She combatted the poor quality of care given to wounded soldiers by overworked medical staff, who were grappling with the results of official indifference. There was a lack of medicine and good food, and a neglect of hygiene, so infections were common, many of them fatal. Nightingale and her compatriots began work by thoroughly cleaning the hospital and equipment, and reorganizing patient care. Although she met resistance from the doctors and officers, the changes she instigated improved conditions in the wards and mortality rates fell dramatically. She sent Herbert detailed statistical reports pinpointing the needless deaths in the army's Crimean hospitals. To the public she now became famous as "The Lady with the Lamp," and her compassionate care and organizational skills led rapidly to the establishment of an elite nursing profession.

Taken ill in the Crimea, she returned home a sick woman and remained largely confined to her room for the rest of her life, but, responding to Queen Victoria's invitation, she took a leading role in writing the strongly statistical report of the Royal Commission on the Health of the Army, which resulted in the creation of an army medical school. In 1860, a public fund created to recognize her services was used to establish the Florence Nightingale School of Nursing and Midwifery at St. Thomas' Hospital, London. Her *Notes on Nursing* helped to set standards and to popularize the profession throughout the British Empire. Abroad, she also inspired a thorough reform of the U.S. Sanitary Commission's methods during the American Civil War.

As a gifted mathematician, Nightingale continued working on statistical analysis of health care issues. She developed a Model Hospital Statistical Form for hospital administrators, inventing what is now called the *pie-chart*, and was an innovator in the collection, tabulation, interpretation, and graphical display of descriptive statistics. Queen Victoria gave her the Order of Merit, Britain's highest civilian honor. Thereafter, the frail Florence Nightingale "retired to her bed" in 1896, and died in 1910 at 90 years of age.

The Dialogue

Early Experiences

Your father encouraged your education but your mother appears less supportive. I imagine she was upset when you turned down your suitor Richard Milnes. Were you closer to your Father than to your mother?

Very definitely—our ideology was that people could do whatever they set their mind to. If they had the abilities to aid others (even aiding others as far as business went), it was their duty to use those talents that they possessed rather than to remain within the confines of the societal dictates of what people might and might not do. Father was a free thinker in believing that there were no restrictions coming down from on high, separating the roles of males and females. People should follow their pathway rather than being put away onto a siding—which a marriage would have been in my case.

So he talked you out of the idea of marriage?

Not that he talked me out of it—he left it up to me to make the decision. There was no pressure placed upon me by him. Instead, he created an excitement within me to move forward with my dreams.

Why did you turn Richard Milnes down?

I saw marriage as being like a freight train placed upon a siding and left to decay. I saw it as missing the opportunity to find out what I could do with what I was. I found the prospects to be boring and also frightening in their lack of continued stimulation and learning. The position of *Haus Frau* did not appeal to me.

Your classical education and mathematics meant more to you?

Much more—it was exciting. It was a way to connect with the universe and not be in a house taking care of mending and cooking and children.

You give me the feeling that your father was goading you on a little.

I don't know if it was goading; it was encouragement, but the inner direction came from myself. He did not dangle a carrot out in front of me and have me follow it, but he gave me the reins and let me gallop along.

Is there any particular classical author who influenced you?

The whole trend of the free thinkers brought to me the fact that you don't have to follow a set pattern. Your world is your own creation.

Would you have married Sidney Herbert if he had been free?

I would have considered it. I don't know if I would have done it, considering where it came in my life—I was not finished with developing myself and the role for a woman at that time.

But you were, in fact, very close to Sidney. Were you ever physically close?

That's not a nice thing to ask a lady!

Let me rephrase the question. Did you feel that you were able to support each other emotionally through thick and thin?

Oh! Yes, assuredly.

Feminism and Spirituality

Your feminism was very practical: You fought to study mathematics, to be a nurse, for every woman's right "to bring the best that she has, whatever that is, to the work of God's world" and "to do the thing that is good, whether it is 'suitable for a woman' or not." How do you now view the opposition you had to face for your viewpoint?

It was born out of pure ignorance. It was based upon patterns which had been set out by a society that was male-oriented. I hate to use the word stupid, but it was actually stupid that an incredible source of power was allowed to languish just because it was born into the female body. I didn't hate, despise, ridicule any of them for their ideas or for their beliefs, because I recognized they were doing what they truly thought was correct. In society they had the idea that women were incapable of any higher educational studies, and that women were emotionally incapable of dealing with stress, yet no man at that time, save medical men, ever attended a childbirth. They depicted women as weak, overly sensitive beings who had to be cared for and protected from society, from violence, and from anything that was not fashionably genteel. At the same time, outside the privileged classes, when you got down to the poor people, those women worked hand in hand with men in the fields, and had the same strength, saw the same problems, butchered the animals, did everything that a man did, and their sensitivities were not impacted.

Do you feel that our generation protects women adequately from exploitation?

Women put themselves into positions to be exploited, and each individual will experience what needs to be experienced, so there is no need to protect someone from something because, if they choose an experience, they will go round the protection to experience it.

Surely, poverty drives women into a position of being exploited.

There is a distinction between exploiting and allowing yourself to be used to accomplish something. We choose our life's lessons and therefore our station in life.

From your sense of God's call when you were seventeen, to your book Suggestions for Thought, *to your later studies of Hinduism, and to your friendship with Mary Clare Moore, you possessed a strong spirituality. Can you describe your spiritual journey?*

It was unique to me: I was searching. From a very early age I felt something inside of me that was alive, that was connected with the universe. I discovered parts of discussions on that connection with the divine in the different studies that I undertook. For me, spirituality was the discovery of my soul and my soul's purpose, and I firmly felt that my soul's purpose was decided by my Creator when I came down here, that I was being led and directed. I now know it was with my assistance and agreement that all these things were happening to me. I cannot say that I was fully in agreement with any pattern or religious system at the time I was doing my searching; I was open to whatever was there.

Was it Socratic in any sense—asking lots of questions?

Asking questions, but mainly feeling the rightness of what was going on. I did not accept anything as truth unless it felt correct to me, unless it vibrated with my being, and then, regardless of how it was condemned by others, if it felt right to me it was the right thing for me.

Were there "peak moments" in your spiritual journey?

There were so many in my life! My peak moments were when I discovered the truth of what I had been feeling; when I went into places where the whole of society said I should not have been; when I was able to help other souls on their journeys; when I was able to bring comfort and give kind words and physical assistance to those in need. It was when I was able to be a presence of gentleness and femininity and niceness to them while they were in a situation of total chaos and knew nothing but anger; I could then bring in the gentleness which was a part of me.

Was the field hospital at Scutari a spiritual experience for you?

I could feel a connection, soul to soul, with many of those whom I was able to assist, and I felt the strength of my identity rising inside.

Mathematics

Was your belief that social phenomena could be objectively measured and subjected to mathematical analysis in any sense a religious belief?

No, I looked upon it as a practical way of explaining why belief systems that society has could be proved to be wrong. [Laughs] It was a way of indirectly saying that the sexist views that were out there could be mathematically proved incorrect.

What part does mathematics play in your life now?

Very little, because I am in touch with everything and everything is in touch with me. I know that were I to sit down I could explain things mathematically, as one can with geometry, and as one can with vibration. You can explain everything here with sensitivities. Mathematics was the means of communication in the incarnate world. We have other means of communication here, so it still has import but it is not controlling.

The Crimean War

You said in respect of the Crimean War, "I stand at the altar of the murdered men, and, while I live, I fight their cause." Do you believe war can ever be just?

I have to tell you the souls' feeling on justice. We do not believe in justice, because justice is an invention and a necessity for humankind. It is a necessity in the world where there are dualities and opposing polarities about things. Here we do not have polarities; we evaluate what is going on and make a decision whether the observed action is something we choose to do ourselves. We make no determination of "rightness" or wrongness."

You said, "I can stand out the war with any man," but in fact you fell sick in the Crimea, and when you returned home you were substantially confined to your room for the rest of your life. What was the nature of your illness?

It was a combination of things. There were physical ailments which I allowed to come into my being because of the grief I felt for what I saw. I was not able to separate myself from the inhumanities that I saw heaped upon innocent young boys. I internalized the magnitude of war and it eroded my constitution, physically, mentally, and emotionally. I could not and did not at that time go into my soul. I had lost the ability to contact my soul that I had had prior to that period. I became immersed in the physicality—I was not able to dig myself out. It was as if a record was repeating itself over and over and over and over. I tried to stop it, but there was so much of me involved in what that record portrayed that it was like living in nightmares day, evening, and night.

Some people have diagnosed you as bipolar; do you have any thoughts on that?

The diagnosis of bipolar would probably fit with the current profile of symptoms supporting that diagnosis, where a person is totally consumed at one time by thoughts which are abhorrent to them, which generally create their depressions, and then can just begin to touch their highest points again. In re-living everything I had gone through, I hit those points, the highest and the lowest. It would be accepted by many today as being bipolar.

How, in your experience, would the bipolar sufferer like yourself be able to escape from that problem?

If they spent time with a good teacher, feeling their soul and their spirit, and were able to understand that they create their own reality, then instead of being a player within that reality who has no control over what is going on, they would thereby be able to create a reality that would stabilize where they are seeking to go.

Hospitals and Nursing Issues

How should we treat returning soldiers, both the sick and wounded, and those who are apparently unharmed?

They have a term for it now; they call it Post Traumatic Stress Disorder. It is because there are stresses upon not only the visible body but the invisible body as well, things that people are forced to do disagree with their true essence as a soul. It creates a vibration that is destructive. What is needed for returning personnel is to recognize that each has experienced hell upon Earth, and they must be brought to realize that now they can create heaven on Earth. It is more a spiritual discipline than one for medical or psychiatric work. It is getting them in tune with their essence, their core, and stabilizing what they have.

You said, "It may seem a strange principle to enunciate as the very first requirement in a hospital that it should do the sick no harm." How do you view modern western hospital care?

Barbaric! It is no small thing that a western medical office is called a "practice," because the practitioners are constantly practicing their thoughts and ideas upon a needy, bleeding, physical being. It is a necessity because of the situations bodies place themselves into, and the things they do, such as cutting the lawn and getting a foot into the lawnmower, or putting tiles on the roof and falling off.

Something must be done to try to get them back into one piece, but the modern medical doctor looks upon the person in front of them as a pattern from a book that must be mended the way the book shows them. They don't go in and ask why this happened in the first place, so that when they mend what has to be mended, there does not have to be a recurrence. They see the body as a slab of meat, not someone embedded with a soul. They must become more conscious that what happens to a person is part of their life's lessons, their life's experiences, and treat not only the physical ailment, the physical infirmity, but also treat the part of the lesson which came with that devastation. Most doctors are totally incapable of doing this, so therefore, the patient must align themselves with a person or a group that will be able to deal with the reason for which they came to see the doctor in the first place.

Do you have a preference for any type of current medical system of care?

Any spiritual healing technique which marries with the physical manipulations, whether a need to suture, to set bones, or to do surgery. I don't mean to say that these procedures are never needed, but the energy that is within the body is that which has to be dealt with, to prevent a recurrence and to go through the healing process. Any that you might call "the eastern philosophies"—Chinese medicine, Ayurveda, and Energy Healers—can re-start the energy flow within the body to heal it, a gentler attunement to the soul's energy within the body. Healing must be a marriage of the physical, or body adjustment, and the spiritual, which is energy adjustment.

You said, "No man, not even a doctor, ever gives any other definition of what a nurse should be than this: 'devoted and obedient.' This definition would do just as well for a porter. It might even do for a horse. It would not do for a policeman!" How do you view the comparative status of nurses and doctors in hospitals today?

There have been some changes in some hospitals, and the changes have come from necessity when there have been insufficient physicians to meet all of the medical and care requirements. Doctors have also begun to realize that they need assistance in caring for people if they don't choose to sit at the bedside and to look after their patients' minute-by-minute needs. Some have also begun to realize that dictatorship (the obeying part) is counter-productive. Letting an intuitive nurse begin a treatment instinctively while the doctors are en route will save many, many people. It is becoming recognized that women do have the abilities that were not recognized in my day, and, but for the path they are on, they could all be doctors, and many are becoming doctors at this time. There is also beginning to be a blending of nurses and doctors in the physician assistance program. There is a total change going on now, but in some parts of the world the old definition of nurse still rules.

Florence Nightingale, thank you for your wonderful help.
It has been a pleasure to have been here, and I am very happy to see that women are getting their day.

Commentary

Toni: Florence Nightingale, while forceful in some of her statements, felt quite demure in her presentation, and gave a sense of understating some of her remarks. She would rather talk about her work and what she had accomplished while Florence Nightingale, than speak about her personal life. When discussing her ailments, there was a wistful edge to her remarks, that if she had only been able to recognize the problem at that time, she would have been able to do much more before going Home. Clearly, she is monitoring earthly developments in patient care, and I sensed that she gently pushes from Home for changes to help those in need.

Peter: There is a real problem with the popular sentimental view of Miss Nightingale as the lone figure of "The Lady with the Lamp," bringing succor by night to the wounded soldiers lying in the field hospital at Scutari during the Crimean war. As she helpfully explained, her life meant very much more than that public stereotype. She stood for four things above all: faith in God, feminism, good health care, and effective social organization.

The two men closest to her during her life, her father and Sidney Herbert, gave her reason and room to excel, but she did the hard work. Enthusiastically she embraced an education of a quality few girls in her day ever received. Her leap into nursing was a truly startling choice for such a high-born young lady to make. As she made very clear, "From a very early age I felt something inside of me that was alive, that was connected with the universe." In her day that feeling was termed "the call of God," but already she was looking beyond the traditional formulations of faith, not least because the established religion of her day, like marriage, supported a societal status quo which placed upper-class women firmly in an inferior position to men.

The call of God, her feminist conviction, and her fruitful friendship with Sidney Herbert, combined, gave her both the opportunity and the inner strength to serve in the Crimea. There her nursing zeal and her groundbreaking statistical reports proved to the skeptics in power that women-run field hospitals were much better at saving lives than those organized by men, thus striking a great blow for women. We did not discuss her statistical work greatly, but the historical record speaks for itself. At least her skill and contributions were correctly recognized by fellow statisticians for their ground-breaking quality. She was elected by both the British and American statistical societies as their first woman member.

Now that she is back Home again, Florence evidently possesses an up-to-date world view. She gave a fascinating account of her Crimean PTSD and agreed with historians' best-guess diagnosis that she suffered from a bipolar disorder, and she helpfully detailed what this experience was like for her. She sees the inadequacy of care given to returning soldiers today, and was scathing in her attack on medical "practice," which treats the body like "a slab of meat" and cares little or nothing for the soul's energetic role in causing and curing ill health. For this reason she did not come out in favor of the surgical approach, which has its place, but spoke more enthusiastically of energetic models of medical care. Nevertheless, there were some modern trends of which she really does approve, especially in the relationship between doctors and nurses in many hospitals today, although she credited such change to sheer necessity rather than enlightened social policy.

Florence Nightingale's soul lives now in the dimension of unconditional love and universal knowledge. It is a society without need of the concept of justice, because there are no polarities, and one in which even her mathematical skills are largely unused, as issues are analyzed and explained by "sensitivities." It is also a vantage point from which Florence is able to keep pace with the continuing rise in the status of women on the planet, and the developments in nursing care and medical practice that she did so much to enhance during her life in human form. She is truly an example to us of that spiritual realm to which our souls aspire.

"A soul, before it comes down into the body of a child,
knows what it's getting itself into, and chooses
to experience what it does."

Margaret Sanger
1879-1966

Biographical Note

Margaret Sanger was born Margaret Louise Higgins in 1879 in Corning, New York, the sixth of eleven children in an Irish stonemason's family. (Later, she would point to her mother's 18 pregnancies as the basic cause of that lady's early death at the age of fifty.) She escaped the family's poverty by undertaking training as a nurse. In 1902, shortly before completing her nurse's training, she married William Sanger, an architectural draftsman. The couple had three children and moved to Greenwich Village in New York City where William became an artist and she returned to nursing. They joined a group of radicals and, now a socialist, Margaret Sanger took part in supporting labor strikes.

In her work with poor women on New York's Lower East Side, she became very sensitive to the effects of unplanned and unwelcome pregnancies. She wrote a newspaper column on sex education, "What Every Girl Should Know," and battled the censors who stopped her from writing about venereal disease on the grounds of obscenity. She promoted the idea of family limitation as the way working-class women could free themselves from poverty. Because women had difficulty obtaining effective birth control advice and devices, and often resorted to dangerous abortions, she challenged the 1873 United States federal law that made it illegal to mail any "obscene, lewd, or lascivious" books and prohibited the dissemination of contraceptive information.

In 1914 she published *The Woman Rebel*, a monthly paper advocating feminism, including the right to practice birth control. Issues of *The Woman Rebel* were banned and Sanger was indicted. She jumped bail and fled to England, leaving behind 100,000 copies for U.S. distribution of a pamphlet, *Family Limitation*, containing details on a variety of contraceptive methods. While in England, she enlarged her justification for birth control by suggesting that women needed to enjoy sexual relations, free from the fear of pregnancy.

Seeking greater publicity for her cause, Sanger returned to America in 1915 to face charges. Her five-year-old daughter, Peggy, suddenly died, and in a wave of public sympathy, the charges were dropped. She began a nationwide tour to promote birth control and was arrested several times. In 1916 she opened a birth control clinic in Brooklyn, New York, which was rapidly shut down by authorities, and Sanger was incarcerated for thirty days. She appealed the closure of the clinic and was given a high-court ruling permitting doctors to be allowed to give contraceptive information to women for medical reasons. This decision opened the way for physician-run birth control clinics and research to be established.

Divorcing William but keeping the name of Sanger, in 1922 Margaret married oil magnate James Slee, who became the chief financial backer of the birth control movement. The campaign's membership grew and gained helpful support from the medical community. But, attracted by the idea of using birth control to reduce genetically transmitted mental or physical defects, Sanger became associated with the eugenics movement and was accused of advocating the limitation of population growth on the basis of class, ethnicity, or race.

In 1929 she formed a birth control legislative lobby but faced such strong opposition from the Roman Catholic Church and from many doctors that the campaign folded. Although birth control won some advantage in court cases, Sanger's powerful radicalism proved too onerous for the movement she had started. She was forced by younger women to take a back seat in the organization which, from 1939, was called the Planned Parenthood Federation of America. Thus sidelined, she remained busy on the international scene. In 1927 she had helped to organize the first World Population Conference in Geneva; then, in 1952, she was instrumental in the creation of the International Planned Parenthood Federation. She also helped in establishing research funding for the birth control pill.

In the 1966 landmark privacy case of *Griswold v. Connecticut*, the U.S. Supreme Court's decision declared birth control legal for married couples. Shortly afterward, Margaret Sanger died in Tucson, Arizona, at 86 years of age.

The Dialogue

Motherhood

You said once, "No woman can call herself free until she can choose consciously whether she will or will not be a mother." Were you thinking of your mother?

I thought of my own mother, but I also thought of the pressure brought upon myself and other women, that we had no choice in the matter. We were told by society, and by the husbands to whom we were given, as it were, that we must do what they wished, rather than follow our own inclinations.

You managed to have a relatively small family, I suspect because you took the law into your own hands.

A little bit, yes.

Do you blame your father for your mother's large number of pregnancies and early death?

Yes—but it was more than just my father—it was the whole of society: the pressure brought to bear by her family and by her father upon her, and the way she was raised to believe wholeheartedly that she had no choice in the matter. She was, as it were, breeding stock to provide a family for her husband.

Do you see this going on today in parts of society?

Not so much in the majority of societies at this time because of the reduced need to have able-minded bodies...

Able-minded bodies?

...which could be used, as farmers and as herders did, for breeding, and for bringing in the necessities of life. Nowadays there is much more import put on people's needing to have the wherewithal to feed the family. That was not considered in the past; it was assumed that more-hands-would-provide-more-food-would-provide-more-money.

There are still parts of the world where women bear large numbers of children.

When their husbands can find a need for them, yes.

You said, "No woman can call herself free who does not own and control her own body." Was your radicalism, and your well-publicized exercise of free love, a help or a hindrance to the movement for birth control?

I don't know that my mind was on intervention-from-the-outside birth control so much. It was a matter of a woman not having to submit herself to her husband at his will, but when *she* chose to participate. Birth control was a secondary thing. I thought of it as interdiction in a completed act, where the woman did not choose, or was unhealthy enough not to choose to go through childbirth at that time. It was by way of improving her health rather than the prevention of a pregnancy. My personal preferences didn't hinder me, for I wasn't too concerned with what others thought of me.

Did people listen to you as much as you would have liked when it was obvious you were exercising freedom of choice in your male partners?

There were very few people who really listened to me! There were some who would have liked to say they listened to me and sympathized with me, but because of the positions they were in, being under the domination of a husband, or being controlled by the dictates of society, it was more advantageous for them to scoff at what I was saying, and even to condemn what I was saying, than to identify with it. It was a very dangerous time for a lot of women, when they sought to gain somewhat less important advances in controlling their own lives, than just in the situation of childbirth.

You said, "Woman must have her freedom, the fundamental freedom of choosing whether or not she will be a mother and how many children she will have. Regardless of what man's attitude may be, that problem is hers—and before it can be his, it is hers alone. As it is the right neither of man nor the state to coerce her into this ordeal, so it is her right to decide whether she will endure it." Given the need for women to have "every child a wanted child," how do you now see the relationship of husbands and wives concerning family planning?

In the modern age I would have thrived, where women and men jointly make a decision to bring a child into the world with the understanding that the man will participate in the upbringing of the child, even from the early stage of night feeding and diaper changes.

In my age, the man simply provided the sperm and then was not concerned with the offspring until it could be interacted with at, say, the age of five or six, or older. The woman bore the entire work, the entire consequences of that sperm uniting with her egg. Women were even ostracized, to a degree, in the later stages of pregnancy, when they weren't exactly what the husband would like to show to the public. Although some men did find their pregnant women beautiful, most men found them to be less than pleasant.

So the woman bore the entire brunt of going through the pregnancy, the physical discomfort, and—Oh, Yes!—the pain of delivery, whereas the man found it advantageous to be at the local tavern during the gnashing and the screaming, so he did not have any memories of what he had begot. Then the woman in her weakened condition, because deliveries were not what they are now (unless she had relatives or friends who could assist with the care), had to feed the child, nurture the child, be there at all times, with absolutely no assistance from her husband. It wasn't until the child was of an age to be able to interact and not be that demanding upon the male that he then stepped back in and took pride at what he had done. And still, the only thing he had done was contribute the sperm.

Day Care

You said, "Dire poverty drives this mother back again to the factory. It is the fear of the loss of a job, debts, and another mouth to feed that compels her to leave this newborn infant in the care of anyone who has the room to keep it. Any friend or neighbor who works at home can take care of this little waif." Is your ideal that every mother should be at home to care for her children?

Not as a overall mandate. It depends upon the richness of the contact between the mother and child, and if there has been an opportunity to bond with that child. A child at an early age spends a lot of time sleeping and is unaware of the mother's absence if she has to go back to work.

At the same time, the father, whether he is absent, or present but not producing enough for the family, may demand that the wife provide funds now to take care of this child which is hers (and it is always in the beginning designated as *hers*); then the woman is forced into a situation of going back to work. It becomes a mindset with some women, who have continued in the breeding phase, that they cannot have a quiet moment to themselves to identify with the child, if they do not want that child. Then it is immaterial to them what happens to that child, as they fulfill the other requirements that their husband or society places upon them. So it makes no difference to them what happens to the child.

We have seen a considerable increase in day care and care for very young children. What is your attitude toward that?

It is mixed. There is a sadness that is a necessity for some who would choose to spend time with a child who is wanted, but financially it is impossible for them to spend that time because the mother must earn funds to keep the family together. There is also a happiness that day care allows some to have children and to interact with them totally in the period of time that they have with them, by giving them the funds to provide both the day care (if they are careful in choosing it), and the necessities for that child. If the idea is just to have a storage facility for the child, it saddens me. If it is to be able to enrich the life of the family, and the mother takes full advantage of the time with the child to nourish the relationship, it is providing a necessary evil...

Evil?
...meaning that she is not with the child, but it's necessary because it is the only way in which she can provide and have enough time to spend with the child.

Do you have a vision now of the spiritual development of children? How do you see their spiritual needs being met in the day care situation?
A soul, before it comes down into the body of a child, knows what it's getting itself into, and chooses to experience what it does. Some choose a broad experience, where in a day care center there's interaction with a lot of people, and they become socialized much earlier than if they were just at home with a parent (or individual). Then there are other souls who want to experience the feeling of abandonment and being unloved; they are just warehoused until they come of an age where they can interact. So it is something that they have chosen before they come here, knowing the path that their biological parents are upon.

Limiting Reproduction
You said, "War, famine, poverty, and oppression of the workers will continue while woman makes life cheap. They will cease only when she limits her reproductivity and human life is no longer a thing to be wasted." Is limitation of reproductivity still a weapon for women to gain their fair place in society?

No—particularly not since women now adequately participate in many arenas in the warring process. My thoughts at the time were that providing males to offer up as the ultimate soldier was the thrust of some warring nations. I now know that that idea has shifted, and that the number of available sacrificial bodies does not have anything to do with war. Warring can be done now by the smallest nation by recruiting others, by training others in their ideologies, by employing stealth, by having more powerful weapons. It isn't a matter of reproduction with them—it's a matter of ideology, so I would have to back off from my statement of that time.

In The Case for Birth Control *you declared that children should not be born when either parent has an inheritable or sexually transmitted disease, or serious illness such as heart disease. You also included cases where children already born were not normal and so parents should not have another child. You suggested women should be at least twenty-three years old and men twenty-five, and that their previous baby should be at least three years old before their next baby arrives. What is your view of these issues now?*

It sounds a bit like creating a kingdom for the gods! I laugh at a lot of my brashness at that time. I was creating the utopian world where I would be dictator. I was totally unaware of the fact that souls choose the pathways that they are on, that they choose to come into them as children, and that they choose to experience them in adulthood. This would be a world which, even if all of my desires were met, would still be in total chaos. Based upon the lessons a person wants to learn, the second child (even if the woman is 27 by that time) could be too much for her—whether born immediately after the first or after a three-year period—because what she needs to experience is overwhelm. So it was very presumptuous of me to say that this arrangement would create the perfect world, because the Earth's dimension is for experiencing, and if everything is perfect we will experience nothing.

What's your view of the "morning-after" pill?

[laughs] Generally, it is a good thing for those who are not ready to experience parenthood when they make the decision to couple, and haven't taken any precautions, and who are in a situation where, because of age, infirmity, and situations such as rape, the woman is not ready to bring another being into the world.

The next possible stage in the process of ridding oneself of an unwanted child is abortion. What is your attitude toward abortion?

At the time of my humanity I considered that if this was something you had thought out and wanted, it should go forward, regardless of how situations change. But, at the same time, if it were something forced upon you, such as another pregnancy when you already had two or three in diapers, it would be a release. Since now I know that the soul does not enter the body in such circumstances, any of the religious implications of killing a soul—because you cannot kill a soul—are taken out of the mix, and, as with the morning-after pill, I believe that abortion is something which does have its place.

If I were to argue more sensitively, what about late-term abortions? Isn't there a point where abortion becomes too horrendous to endure?

You have to discuss this situation from the spiritual and also the physical viewpoint. The implication upon the body—physically, emotionally, and mentally—is where the person could convince themselves, or society could convince them, that they have killed another human being. That can be devastating. From a spiritual point, again, I know now that you cannot kill the soul, so there would not have been a soul within that agglomeration of cells, regardless of its size, when its growth is terminated.

Dealing now with women's feelings, some women have had many abortions. Doesn't this harm them spiritually and emotionally?

It's their pathway. It gives them spiritual trials, it gives them emotional trials, it gives them mental trials to let them experience

115

and to make choices. This may be the major lesson that they came into this incarnation to learn.

So all we can do here on Earth is to shrug our shoulders and say, "This is her pathway," as she has her fourteenth abortion! That seems extraordinary!

We must know that we have no way to affect another individual. What we say, what we think—unless we couch it in such terms as to be totally in control of that person, we can have no effect upon what they do, and it should not affect us as we do not own that woman. We are not, as husbands have always been, the masters who dictate what shall or shall not occur. To assert that we should have a say in this, or a reaction to that, is to take us back to where we used to be, where a woman's body was not her own and was the property of her husband and of society.

Your concern was also that "children should not be born to parents whose economic circumstances do not guarantee enough to provide them with the necessities of life. A woman should not bear children when exhausted from labor. Not for two years after marriage should a couple undertake the great responsibility of becoming parents." Are you now no longer legislating for anyone?

I know that I can no longer legislate for anyone other than myself, my soul. Again, I was trying to change society's image of things. I was trying to do exactly what husbands were doing and what society was doing, which was to dictate what other people should be allowed to experience. I now know that it is not my place to dictate the experiences of others, to change their pathways.

World Population Control

Your critics state that you were in favor of eugenics—controlling the reproduction of various races, such as black African Americans. Will you comment, please?

The interest I had in eugenics was part of my desire to create a utopia, a world that I thought was the best for everyone, and with that desire I had a little bit of an elitist sensibility concerning white Anglo-Saxon Protestants! When I returned Home I realized that I had already been in the body of a number of different nationalities, some of whom I had railed against while in human form as Margaret Sanger. It struck me as quite ironic that some of my most worthwhile experiences in past lives had been as one of the people whom I had thought less than myself, and who should be eliminated. The feelings I had at the time were strong. So far as I was concerned I had the answers to the utopian "mix" for our planet—particularly for myself and for my friends. I can no longer espouse that view, knowing what I know, and recalling now what I should have remembered but which was beyond my reach.

Let me ask a question relating to our world's huge population. Where is the world going in terms of population control?

It's going to be taken care of by the Earth with earthquakes, hurricanes, natural disasters. It is a response to over-population but also to the devastation that too many people have on too small an area of land.

So there's a relationship between humanity and the Earth?

The Earth is a living, breathing organism. It is well aware of the burden that it's carrying in particular areas. By burden I mean over-population and the total depletion of natural resources because of over-population. Those who are unaware that the Earth is alive pay the consequences when they "write her off" as non-interactive. She wins in the end.

Is global warming a reality? If so, where is it going to lead us?

Yes. It's corresponding with a lot of other things that are happening. As of now, exactly where this is going to go is determined by the mass consciousness of the souls who are on the planet. In the short term it is going to contribute to the total warming of the oceans, primarily the large bodies which are the cooling mass for the planet, the Atlantic and the Pacific. This is going to climatically change what most people consider as normal weather. It is going to continue the 2005 experience and have a great impact on hurricanes and typhoons. There are areas being hit by hurricanes that have never had hurricanes before.

Is it going to go on getting worse?
There are a lot of things coming up that will affect the Earth's natural resources and the various climates around the globe. The position of the planets lining up across the galaxy will have an impact on the planet Earth and what goes on in both the minds of the beings on the planet and the natural forces on the surface of the planet. As the time approaches for all of the planets to line up, there will be an energetic shift upon the entire planet Earth. Depending on where the group mentality of the planet is at that time, it will determine how the energetic shift will impact the surface of the planet.

Earthquakes: Where are they going to be?
There are going to be more earthquakes in the area of India, Pakistan, Indonesia, along the ridge of volcanoes of the Caribbean, on the west coast of the United States, around the plates of the north and south poles. There's a total shifting in the mantle of the Earth.

You are well qualified in birth control; what qualifies you as a Doomsday seer?
[laughs] Well, as you would say, I sit around the tavern fireplace and talk with the guys! It is a fact that when you are in an energetic form you are tapped into the energy that is both living and non-living—that is everything. All is energetic and energy is everything. When you are tapped in, the knowledge of one is the knowledge of all.

Does this include the knowledge of what we can do to help ourselves with these disasters?
The main need is to tap into your own energy, the part of your soul that is inside you, the part of creation that is inside of you, and—joining with other energies—to shift what is going on, to shift the behavior patterns and even to shift the energy patterns

upon the planet. If enough force is applied to the patterns, they can be halted.

Margaret Sanger, thank you very much.

I did not come to this conversation to be present as a geologist, but I thank you for listening.

Commentary

Toni: I had a vivid impression of a huge tavern with an enormous fireplace along one wall, and groups of people sitting and talking together there. Margaret Sanger was the most earthy of those we have thus far interviewed. She was almost *physically palpable*, as if we were sitting together discussing the issues of the day. She readily laughed at her former brashness and at the futility of her time spent proselytizing. Now she knows how each soul has its own pathway and choice of which path to follow in physical life. So she came across as a vital yet humble spiritual being.

Peter: Margaret did not apologize for once having embraced eugenics, but simply stated how irrelevant that episode was, now that she remembered her many racially diverse incarnations. She had moved on in other ways, and applauded societal change where some men are now fully involved in the planning of and care for their children. There was a wistful response to the day care issue: how good it would be to have the mother stay at home, if she could afford to do so. But *warehousing*—just parking a baby at a day care facility—saddened her. She would not prescribe now when and how couples should have children.

Discussing the "morning-after" birth control pill and abortion, including late-term abortion, she took the view that it was the woman alone who could choose the pathway she is on. Abortion did not represent a killing, as the infant's eternal spirit was never involved in a termination of pregnancy by either means, and the eternal spirit could not be killed anyway, so there was no wrong done.

Then our discussion of world population control took an unexpected turn. The Earth, she asserted, is a living being and is taking population control and depletion of resources into its own hands. Hurricanes, earthquakes, natural disasters, and the effects of global warming are now all going to seriously challenge humankind. Not only that, but the lining up of the planets of the solar system in the near future will bring major physical changes to the Earth. She said that in order for us to meet this challenge we must, both as individuals and collectively, tap into our own soul energy. She offered no details on how this should be done, and our discussion time was up.

"One of my big lessons within that lifetime was to feel abandonment. It was what put me into self-reflection, first in the imaginary world, and then grasping what was reality."

Eleanor Roosevelt
1884-1962

Biographical Note

Anna Eleanor Roosevelt was born in New York City in 1884. Her father was U.S. President Theodore Roosevelt's younger brother, and her mother came from a wealthy New York family. Her parents both died when she was only a child and she was raised by her grandmother. A shy, awkward girl, she was educated by tutors until she turned fifteen, when she was sent for three years to a high-class English school for girls. Back in Manhattan, she became involved in social service work at the Rivington Street Settlement House, growing into a young woman who, despite insecurity concerning her physical appearance and her sense that she lacked social graces, had already developed a great and lasting sensitivity to underprivileged people of all kinds.

In 1905, she married Franklin Delano Roosevelt (F.D.R.), a distant cousin and an aspiring politician, Over the next eleven years they became the parents of six children. Later she wrote, "I was fitting pretty well into the pattern of a fairly conventional, quiet, young society matron," but at the start of World War I she broke the pattern, volunteering for work in navy hospitals and with the American Red Cross.

When women's suffrage was established in 1920, Roosevelt evolved politically and supported the League of Women Voters and the Women's Trade Union League: "I became a much more ardent citizen and feminist than anyone about me in the intermediate years would have dreamed possible. I had learned that if you wanted to institute any kind of reform you could get far more attention if you had a vote than if you lacked one."

Then in 1921 her husband, F.D.R., was struck down with polio. She put aside her shyness and became deeply involved in the politics of the New York State Democrats. From 1928 to the day of his death, despite his devastating affair with her own social secretary, she dedicated her life to supporting F.D.R.'s political career. She also taught at a private girls' school in New York City and was involved with a nonprofit furniture factory.

After F.D.R. became President of the United States, Roosevelt—briefed to be his eyes and ears—began to travel around the nation. She inspected Depression relief projects; became an advocate for the poor, minorities, and the disadvantaged; promoted women's issues within the Democratic party; supported anti-lynching campaigns; promoted minority housing projects; investigated working conditions; and supported labor's right to organize. She even broke with precedent as First Lady and held press conferences in the White House. During World War II she sought to encourage international good will by visiting U.S. military bases abroad to raise the morale of US servicemen on active duty.

After F.D.R. died in 1945, Roosevelt carried on with her work. She was chosen by President Truman to serve on the U.S. Delegation to the United Nations General Assembly. At the U.N. she helped to guide the drafting of the Universal Declaration of Human Rights, which was adopted in 1948. She was a member of the National Advisory Committee of the Peace Corps, and Chairwoman of the President's Commission on the Status of Women.

Eleanor Roosevelt came to symbolize independent, politically active, twentieth-century women. She was the first woman to speak to a national political convention, to write syndicated media columns, to earn fees as a lecturer, to appear regularly on radio and television, and to hold regular press conferences. She died in New York City in 1962, at 78 years of age.

The Dialogue

Abandonment

When your mother died of diphtheria, you looked forward to living with your father, who had been separated from her, but he died two years later of acute alcoholism. What effect did that double loss have on you?

It made me become very introspective. I always was a thinker, but I began to plot and plan. For a while I lived in an imaginary fairyland world where everything was just exactly as I wanted it to be, regardless of what was going on around me. I had quite an imagination (which I revived, after all my political experiences, when I began writing the books), but it made life very tolerable for me. Unfortunately, I had created imaginings of what it would be like to live with my father, totally disregarding his infirmities and his addictions. So life was never as I would have actually wanted it to be. It put me into a position, in mid-life, of realizing that I had to accept what was and be aware of what was going on around me, and to deal and work with that instead of creating an imaginary world.

Did you feel abandoned?

One of my big lessons within that lifetime was to feel abandonment. It was what put me into self-reflection, first in the imaginary world, and then grasping what was reality. This grew into my drive to change what the world actually was into something much more palatable to me: a place where there was more a sense of equality and where those less fortunate were afforded respect.

Prohibition

Later you wrote in 1939 about Prohibition, "It dawned upon me that the law was not making people drink any less, but it was making hypocrites and law breakers of a great number of people. It seemed to me best to go back to the old situation in which, if a man or woman drank to excess, they were injuring themselves and their immediate family and friends, and the act was a violation against their own sense of morality, and no violation against the law of the land." Do you see it in those terms now?

Yes and no. I believe those words as concepts just as I wrote them, when I see an addicted person who is down there in physical form. Now, my overall perspective is that we have certain lessons that we wish to experience when we are down there (such as that we are going to be an alcoholic), and we need to experience them. Whether it is legal or illegal to have the substance, we must have it—because it is the addiction itself that we have to work through. The same with illegal drugs. They are all illegal, but if people need the experience of being heroin addicts, they must be able to obtain heroin in whatever way is necessary. It would not make much sense to legalize heroin because we would be offering the person an opportunity to euthanize themselves.

Marijuana?

Marijuana is not as addictive. It does have some medicinal purposes for which it can be used. I feel it does not lead to much more abuse than alcohol.

But it has problems that are not recognized, such as causing sterility.

They have never begun to examine all the problems with alcohol, as well; simply said, it kills! And as for marijuana causing sterility, that might be considered a good thing if people have already fried a good section of their brain.

The other side of the equation is society as a whole. I haven't yet understood the relationship between an individual's life lessons and societal needs. If you liberate people to take any drug they want, won't you cause chaos?

If a person's soul is incarnated at a time of chaos, it is because they need to experience that chaos. We cannot say that any time is right for one thing more than for another. I can only have feelings about my experiences while in human form, and the knowledge that people must be enabled to do their life lessons. As a whole, here in spirit form we do not plan for trends within society. We do not plan, for instance, that we will only have people incarnate who are not going to be in need of self-medication, so that there won't be any social chaos. We can only say that there are people who need to experience addiction, so they go through all of the associated problems, learn their lessons, then renew their strength, so that they can move on.

If addicts all choose to incarnate at the same time, then we do have a problem with society, but it is no different from a time when those who choose to be dictators and power-hungry people are on the planet all at the same time, and you have wars. We do not plan during our between-lives what effect we are going to have on other people (unless it is a person with whom we have entered into a contract). We are only concerned, when we are on the planet, with what an experience will mean to us as an individual.

Are you saying that the reincarnated spirits make these choices which are not in any way controlled by anyone on your side of the divide?

Quite true—the choices are between an individual soul and their council, the advisors who help them decide which lessons they want to learn. There isn't a game plan set out for all of North America, or all of Canada, or all of Britain.

You strove very hard for the best in society during your lifetime. How does such striving by people like you fit in with the overall pattern of people who are drunks, drug addicts, and dictators?

When I was in body form, I felt it was my purpose to make life as comfortable and as fulfilling as possible for individuals, whether or not they were moneyed, or politicians, or in a position where they could give some direction to society. It was part of my dreaming, my utopia, my imaginings, that I was immersed in so often during my life. I thought I could project this ideal out for society, that I could take a drunk and make him a productive member of society. It just doesn't happen like that.

Social Activism

You had support. Your uncle Teddy Roosevelt taught that you "owed something back to those less fortunate." Why were you, a member of the upper class, so interested in social work? Was it Teddy or your own utopia that drove you in that direction?

It was the total picture, as I was seeing it. I had a dream that I could put myself into, which made me feel great. Then I had this beautiful person, Teddy, who thought he could solve the world's problems, from riding on his horse into battle, all of the way through to running the country, and that he would be able to provide for those less fortunate. The entire Roosevelt clan thought they could share what they possessed to level the playing field. Every one who feels for other people wants to provide for them, whatever their basic need may be.

Did you contribute to the discussion in the White House?

The cabinet and staff knew that a lot of the ideas were mine, and they solicited my help. There were those I had worked with in different organizations who knew how tirelessly I worked to help people, and they gave me a stage to accomplish what I sought to do, even after I was widowed.

Did you feel then that your abandonment by your husband for your social secretary Lucy was one you accepted because of your sense of the inferiority of women?

No. I considered it to be—this will seem awfully unlike me!—the sexual drive of men who just have to be pampered and played to. I considered it an unfortunate need on my husband's part, when I provided him with what he needed. But he needed variety. The abandonment I felt was just one more lesson in my abandonment by my parents. I was even able to accept it a little bit better because of the strengthening I experienced through losing my parents.

How in touch are today's policymakers with those less fortunate than themselves, compared with those days?

Because of all the machinations going on with governments, which are so much bigger, and because it is so much more dynamic, involving other countries, politicians don't have time to go out and meet people. They have to spend all of their time just learning about this or that little country they might want to help. We had the time because we were building a country. We were not trying to control the world. We were trying to build stability into what we had. We made the time to meet the people.

So, how do you view America these days?

[laughs] The Empire of America nowadays is like a puppeteer's stage, where the government stands behind the little puppets and pulls the strings, totally oblivious of the effect on the audience, just wanting to move the puppets. They only wish to have a return for themselves, whether it be additional power or additional money, though mostly power.

Feminism

You wrote, "I took it for granted that men were superior creatures and knew more about politics than women did, and while I realized that if my husband was a suffragist I probably must be, too, I cannot claim to have been a feminist in those early days." What caused you to turn into the great women's leader of your later career?

Recognition that a woman can be a self-thinking, self-directing person without the need of a man. In reflection I began to appreciate the contributions I made, albeit from behind the curtains when Franklin became incapacitated. In public, I dared not let on about my power, so I played the dutiful wife, wiping the brow of my husband—the "Power."

Was there a particular moment when your realization occurred?

I had always been very concerned with what was going on in government, once we got into politics. I was just a confidant at first. I did not appear to have a part in what was going on, but we would have pillow talk. F.D.R. and I would sit down and discuss the implications of current events. I thought he was just talking out loud, thinking out loud to himself. It was many, many years before I realized that some of the things that I said in reaction to his wonderings were things he accepted and implemented.

The New Deal?
Yes, among other things.

How did that come about?
He was very aware of my imaginary world and my way of creating things. We went back to it. We sat around one cold weekend and were planning the perfect environment, not only for ourselves but for those around us, and for the common man as well. We came up with all the different options that could be developed, where everyone would have an input into the way their lives were lived, and which things would have a positive impact on them.

Earlier in our discussion you said, "This will seem awfully unlike me." To what extent, as you change by being in the different dimension at Home, do you feel that you are still your self as Eleanor Roosevelt, and how much do you find yourself lifting out of that sensibility?
At Home you have all the knowledge, not only of the life you have just lived, but also of the lives of everybody you have been. In human form I was very conscious and aware of everything I said in public, and the import that would have upon the thoughts of others toward me, toward my husband, and toward the administration. So I was very careful never to talk about personal things—never, in particular, to comment on sexual drive and things of that nature. Now, being at Home, my perspective is of freedom, where I don't have to care or be concerned with what people are going to think. I can say what I feel.

Justice and Peace

Perhaps you will say what you feel about race and peace in America. In 1943 you wrote, "We cannot settle strikes by refusing to understand their causes. We cannot prepare for a peaceful world unless we give proof of self-restraint, of open- mindedness, of courage to do right at home, even if it means changing our traditional thinking and, for some of us, a sacrifice of our material interests." Looking at the peace issue first, what is your assessment?

My words then are substantially an explanation of what is still going on in your world. At this time the United States claims it has entered into various conflicts supposedly for the benefit of the country that they are impacting. In point of fact, it is because they think they are going to be able to take over, benefit from, or control something within that country. They don't at all concern themselves with the feelings of those people, with their beliefs, with their particular customs.

It is the same as it was with the race riots and the problems of my time. During the race riots, those who could have had an impact felt it in their pocket-book—that they would have to pay correct wages. They chose for their own political futures not to infringe upon the rights of others by forcing industry to pay a decent wage. Also they would have to contribute a little more in taxes to make living wages. They would have to acknowledge the fact that they were using people. They weren't willing to do that if it took money out of their pockets, and if they had to give up some of their cherished beliefs about their superiority over others.

One of the cherished beliefs of superiority among some in America is linked to possession of atomic weapons. You said in 1954, "The conscience of America is a very real thing and if we use this terrific weapon first, there are few of us in this country who could live with our own conscience." Since that day, the stockpile of such weapons has increased considerably. What would it take for the world to get rid of weapons of mass destruction like atomic weapons?.

First, sanity, and second, trust and faith in others, which will only come when the people in physical form begin to truly feel what the others on the planet feel, when they come to know for certain that destroying another person benefits no one, that if you love another from your soul you cannot harm them. If you believe in all of the tenets that have been preached for centuries within the religions, the primary basis is love. You do not need to protect yourself.

Some say that the proliferation of atomic weapons makes a much more dangerous world, with rogue states, dictators, and terrorists who would be willing to do anything.

That is what the United States and countries throughout the world are going through at the present time. You will be held hostage by small groups of people who are choosing to employ various means of terrorism against you. Again, if these terrorists could feel not their fanaticism, but instead the love of another soul, they could not do what they have done, what they do constantly. They could not blow others up by themselves. If they felt their religious beliefs, they would know that the only way to their heaven is to love.

How do you feel about the United Nations' actions since the signing of the Declaration of Human Rights?

I give them about "C Minus." They are so consumed with their own importance and their own plans, instead of just going in and taking care of the mess.

What did you mean when you said, "One of the first things we must get rid of is the idea that democracy is tantamount to capitalism"?

What I meant was although the common little man has the vote, it doesn't give him any more money in his pocket.

Quotes from My Day: "When will our consciences grow so tender that we will act to prevent human misery rather than avenge it?" and "I know that we will be the sufferers if we let great wrongs occur without exerting ourselves to correct them." Which great wrongs are we most ignoring in America and the world today?

To begin, my feelings have changed with the new insight that I have now. If I were to write that today I would say, "We can only lead by direction; we cannot change anyone. It is their choice whether or not they will amend their lives." The great wrongs we have to get rid of are thinking that we can change people, thinking that we can control others, thinking that we don't have to feel, that we don't have to be anything but black and white, that we don't have to foresee the repercussions of what we do. Black-and-white thinking is, "It's right; it's wrong." Feeling and loving is knowing that energy goes out to others, and they can be healed by the energy that we give out to them.

Until people feel and love, the world will not change. Governments respond only with thinking; they don't try to feel the reasons terrorists react in the way they do. They don't try to feel the terrorists who may believe that their country has been improperly invaded, that their rights have been taken away from them and given to others. If this great country could only feel the anguish of having their government, on which they so pride themselves, obliterated by someone else, or of having part of the country, say, east of the Mississippi, given to others to control— until they can feel things like that, they cannot improve the world.

Eleanor Roosevelt, thank you so much for coming and talking with us.

I fear that I sound as if I were on a soap box. I hope that what I say is recognized as my feelings from Home, colored by my feelings from life.

Commentary

Toni: Eleanor Roosevelt seemed shy and reticent but had the quiet forcefulness of a good teacher. It was almost as if she were bridging the various stages of her earthly life from being an insecure introvert to becoming an author, ambassador, and expert. She talked very rapidly, which challenged my channeling ability. She seemed to want to be heard before we could even move on to our next question. All the while there was a steely confidence in what she said. Meeting her was truly inspiring.

Peter: Eleanor had plenty to say about the shy girl's imaginary utopias that endured well into her adulthood. She acknowledged a naïveté lasting for many years during her marriage, until she awoke to the really solid impact she had been having on the thinking and policy making of her President husband. Startling in its simplicity was her quiet acknowledgement that she had played a genuine part in the shaping of the New Deal, and that her contribution to policy making was well-known by the Cabinet and White House staff. We learned how F.D.R. sat down before a warm fire with his shy, introverted wife, brainstorming dreams for the future, and U.S. national policy was changed for generations to come by some of the things that she suggested. Teddy Roosevelt, riding into battle on his horse, must surely have been in her fertile imagination on those days. This mental closeness with FDR makes her numb, muted response to his affair with Lucy all the more difficult to understand, until the realization comes that Eleanor's fanciful world always provided her with a way of dealing with abandonment, shyness, and the rough behavior of the real, very male, world.

The spirit who incarnated as Eleanor Roosevelt is now at Home in a different dimension from Earth. She now understands intimately the lives of those with whom she once lived, and has a broader spiritual perspective. Interestingly, she can feel both worlds at once, as her aside concerning FDR's sexual drive illustrated. There we could actually "feel" her spiritual self overcoming the reluctance of her former incarnated self.

This duality poses a broad question about all these dialogues with leading individuals. How far do the leaders don their former mantle and answer us in their human voice, and how far does their spiritual self predominate? What we conclude is that their former personality is always present, and we are left to judge the degree of spiritual balance that has been achieved by each individual.

For many, the real eye-opener might have been that little glimpse we were given of the method by which the spirit world helps souls to incarnate. Piecing the bits together, we see a spirit organization involved in counseling those individual souls who are ready to return to Earth. They are helped to decide on the life lessons that they want to receive or endure. The souls may also choose to draw up binding agreements with some of the members of their peer group, as relational issues they will explore together on Earth.

But when the time comes for the souls to depart, there appears to be no overall plan for the life of the planet which must weather the storms they may bring along with them. If there are lots of souls choosing to experience power issues, Eleanor asserts, power struggles will be the chaotic profile of the planet. This randomness in each soul's freely choosing what issues to experience can be quite alarming from the human perspective.

Talking with Leaders of the Past

"When I first began amassing my fortune, because I chose not to be poor any longer, I was ruthless. I felt it was not important who I stepped on to get where I wanted to go."

Andrew Carnegie
1835-1919

Biographical Note

Andrew Carnegie was born in 1835 in Dunfermline, Scotland, the elder son of a hand weaver. After steam-powered weaving came to Scotland, the financially challenged family emigrated to Allegheny, Pennsylvania, USA. At the age of thirteen, Carnegie began manual work in a textile mill, where his literacy skills brought him rapid promotion to clerk. Within a year he had advanced to become a Western Union telegraph operator. In 1853 he became the personal assistant to Thomas Scott, who was in charge of the western division of the Pennsylvania Railroad. He made improvements to the running of the company and, from knowledge he had gleaned, informed his boss of a forthcoming strike, which resulted in its being put down.

Now enjoying an increased salary, Carnegie used bank credit for his first investment. This was in a sleeping car company which was successful, and rapidly his stake more than tripled his income. Further gains came in 1859 when he took over Scott's managerial position. His second investment, in an oil company, also brought him a substantial profit. By 1863 his annual salary of $2,400 was dwarfed by an investment income of about $40,000. Aged 30, he resigned from the railroad and, with financial help from Scott, created the Keystone Bridge Company to replace the region's existing wooden bridges. He also created a telegraph company that proved highly profitable. His Freedom Iron Company, formed in 1861, began using the new Bessemer steel-making process.

Carnegie opened his first specialist steel plant in 1875 in Braddock, Pennsylvania. Henry Clay Frick's Coke Company had been a supplier to Carnegie's company. During a fiscal crisis in the coke company, Carnegie purchased half the stock of the corporation. In 1886 he published pro-union views, and later, when Frick organized an industrial coalition to resist striking labor, Carnegie had a large enough stake in the coke company to force a settlement with the workers. He developed a radical anti-monarchical view in his publication *Triumphant Democracy* (1886), which sold well in America, and he controlled 18 British newspapers in which he promoted his radical views.

After a courtship lasting 17 years, Carnegie married Louise Whitfield in 1887. He was then 51 and she 38. The couple had one daughter, Margaret. With his annual personal income now exceeding $24 million, Carnegie published his viewpoint in *The Gospel of Wealth* (1889), in which he argued that morality required the wealthy to be socially responsible and to give away their fortunes. His offer to help the Philippines buy their independence from the USA failed, and that same year, while he was away in Europe on a family vacation, his positive image with organized labor was utterly destroyed when Frick, who had been given the authority to handle a strike at Carnegie's Homestead works, broke the strike brutally in a murderous shoot-out in which the state militia were used to protect strikebreakers.

From 1898 to 1901, Carnegie consolidated his businesses as he moved opportunistically into finished steel products. This placed him in direct competition with the steel magnate J. P. Morgan. Then he accepted a defensive offer from Morgan, who bought out his personal investment in Carnegie Steel for $480 million. At the age of 65, he was called "the richest man in the world," although that designation properly belonged to John D. Rockefeller.

This huge increase in his liquid assets enabled him to change course. From 1901 he became a full-time philanthropist. He had already funded the building of over 2,500 libraries throughout the English-speaking world. Now came the Carnegie Institute of Technology, an American universities' research institution, a Teachers' Pension Fund, and the Carnegie Endow-ment for International Peace. In 1911, he set up the Carnegie Corporation to make grants to colleges and universities, and for scientific research. Now he had only one-tenth his fortune remaining, having given away over $350 million.

Finally, Andrew Carnegie bought the Shadowbrook estate in Lenox, Massachusetts, where he died in 1919 at 83 years of age.

The Dialogue

"Car-NEE-gie"

Andrew, I had the horror of listening to a radio broadcast where they pronounced your name in two different ways within one minute. Which of the syllables should we stress: "CAR-negie" or "Car-NAY-gie"?

[Laughs] "Car-NEE-gie." I was never overly concerned how people pronounced my name. The only thing that really concerned me was whether they listened to me.

So we still don't have an official guideline?

Various members of the family stressed different syllables, depending upon how convenient it was for their associates and workers to pronounce the name, which depended primarily upon their lineage.

A Scot would say "Car-NEE-gie?"

Yes.

Early Years

You grew up in poverty, the son of an egalitarian idealist. What were the main lessons your parents taught you that made you so successful?

"Stick-to-it-ness," to be able to focus on whatever you needed to accomplish, and to put your entire effort into it. It was the only way that you could get out of a situation other people put you in, and to have some direction and control over your own life.

But when you came to woo Louise Whitfield, you took a huge amount of time in your courtship. Your mother was unhappy with your choice. Was it her opposition or the pressures of work that made you take years to stick-to-it and get married?

At the time it wasn't my focus. It was a very pleasurable side, but it took me off course. I respected my mother and loved her dearly, but I did not let her influence my personal feelings about things. There was definite thunder between her and my dear beloved, and I tried to put earplugs in and not hear the thunder. It came at a time of my life when making something of myself was all-important to me. I did not feel that I could give to a wife the time necessary to develop the relationship. I waited until I was in a position of stability and financial security, so that our children would not have that same sense of loss and want that early on I had experienced so frequently.

When you said, "making something of myself," did you feel that was something you had not achieved?

During that time identity was very important to me. The policeman and the fireman had an identity; they were recognized by all, their worth was known by all. I felt no direction had been given to me within the family. It was as if a beacon was drawing me forward to become known, to create an identity, to be able to know who I was.

Was there a particular moment in your life when things all came together?

It was when I saw other people continuing down the same paths as their fathers, not making anything up themselves, continuing to flounder, continuing even to go to the soup kitchens at times.

This was in Scotland?

Yes, but I declared at that time it was not going to be me. I was going to move upward and onward beyond the limitations of my birth.

The Gospel of Wealth

In The Gospel of Wealth *you suggested ways to dispose of surplus wealth. It could be left to the families of the rich, or bequeathed for public purposes, or philanthropically administered by the rich during their lifetimes. Did you ever ask whether society should actively control the extent to which people become wealthy?*

I never asked myself that question because I knew that within a human lifetime people can do anything they set their mind to do. If there are regulations that you may not sell apples on the street corner, the enterprising person is going to rent an apartment quite near the street corner and convert their front window into a pass-through to sell apples. There is always a way to do what you need to do, whether or not the society has put through rules and regulations that seem to mitigate against what you wish to accomplish.

You may have missed my point. You were described as the "Richest Man in the World." Should you have been allowed to become so "stinking rich?"

Yes. I believe that in the way I disposed of my wealth, I showed what could be done with money. The foundations, the scholarships, and the other gifts all showed that I could manage money and could use my money to help others. What better use was there for that money but to go to someone who knew how to use it?

That's exactly what you said when you saw the man of wealth "becoming the sole agent and trustee for his poorer brethren, bringing to their service his superior wisdom, experience, and ability to administer—doing for them better than they would or could do for themselves." Weren't you equating wealth with wisdom, surely a common error made by the rich?

There are some who think they are wise and intelligent just because they have money, but if a person has obtained the money through his own planning and ingenuity, he does have intelligence, knowledge, and wisdom. The reverse is the person who has not been able to obtain money through his wits. I hold a distinction that a person who is of Old Money does not necessarily have wisdom, but a person who has New Money most assuredly has wisdom—or they would not have the New Money.

Would you say that the plutocrats who are in charge of America in this generation have the wisdom to know what to do with their money?

Certainly not!

Most of them have New Money.

Not as I define New Money. New Money by my definition is created when people have gone out to get it by the sweat of their brow. These current plutocrats are people who, because of friends and relatives, have been put in a position to make money. Numbers of them have several generations of Old Money behind them. The only New Money people are your moguls, such as Microsoft's Bill Gates. He has the knowledge, he has the wisdom. He is using his money to help others. He has put out more money to help children and to help eradicate disease than parts of the Unites States government have done, because he knows and appreciates what money is for.

You said the duty of the man of wealth was "to set an example of modest, unostentatious living, shunning display or extrava-gance; to provide moderately for the legitimate wants of those dependent upon him." How can you justify your owning a big Scottish castle, and your gift of large family legacies?

What I was trying to say was that a person who has a degree of wealth should not spend all of his money on himself and not use it to help others. If a man is as rich as, again, Bill Gates, he has built a multi-million house for his wife and children. To some it would be ostentatious, but to him it is proportionate with his wealth, to provide for the needs of his family. So it depends on the degree of wealth that you have, and what you do with the rest of your money, and what proportion of your total wealth is used for your wants and needs.

In 1889 you wrote, "It is more difficult to give money away intelligently than it is to earn it in the first place." What can we do to halt the current steep increase in financial inequality in America?

Inequality is based upon so many things. You can educate everyone to the same extent, so that they have the same opportunities. Yet, if they do not possess the same initiative, they will not be able to reach the same level of financial return. So there is nothing we can do to ensure that all are put on steady footing, unless we give each a pension, a monthly stipend, so they are all paid the same.

Would it not be better to give schools throughout the country the same amount of money per child?

That is part of educating all people. Everyone should be given an equal opportunity.

So you would give the children of the poor the same opportunity as the children of the rich?

Yes. It is not realistic in society for that to occur, but we can endeavor to do that. If we live in a utopia where we provide the same amount of money to educate each student, that amount of money must be within the education system. If the rich, who have additional money, wish to provide a leg-up for their children, they will take some of their own money to hire tutors to make sure that their children get better opportunities. We can never equalize everything—that is an impossibility. Our government can only strive to provide the same for each and every citizen. We cannot ask a person with education and initiative not to use what they have worked hard to obtain, even if it gives their children an advantage over others.

Making and Giving Money

Your biographer Joseph Wall wrote of you, "Maybe with the giving away of his money he would justify what he had done to get that money." Your daughter Margaret Carnegie Miller spoke well of you but said, "Tell his life like it was; I'm sick of the Santa Claus stuff." Did the lives of your underpaid steelworkers ever weigh on your conscience?

Not until toward the very end. When I first began amassing my fortune, because I chose not to be poor any longer, I was ruthless. I felt it was not important who I had to step on to get where I wanted to go. It wasn't until I amassed my fortune that I stopped and looked around at what else was going on. Within the family I could be extremely miserly with money if I thought I could use that money to make more money somewhere else, instead of giving them what they wanted or thought they deserved. That was true of my employees, both in the factories and in the household.

When I had time for reflection later in life, when constant driven action did not account for every moment of my day, I began to see the effect my various practices were having on the people around me. Having seen that, I then realized that I had made a god out of money—and also that I had actually become a god to all of those people, and that I had to take care of them. It was then that I reversed the way in which I handled my funds, and my thinking that money would do everything for me and me alone.

So this isn't just your thinking at Home now, but an awareness that began during your physical lifetime?

Yes, but unfortunately, not until near the very end.

What triggered that new thinking in you?

It was having time to stop and see something besides myself. To open my eyes/awareness to what was going on around me.

You said that there were only two incidents in your career that you regretted. One was the strikebreaking disaster at Homestead by

Frick, the other was turning your back on your mentor Thomas Scott. How do you view those situations now—and do you have any other regrets?

Well, from Home we have no regrets. What we did was what we had to do to learn what we had to learn, so there are no regrets. If I were to return again to physical form with the knowledge that I have now (although that doesn't happen because we come down with amnesia), I would wish to be a benevolent person throughout all of my lifetime, if I had the means to do so. If that is a regret, I can only say that we get an opportunity (after learning a lesson), to go back and, hopefully, do something for an outcome we would like to see accomplished, so there is a feeling of completion. I do regret that I turned my back on my mentor because I would have come into awareness much sooner than I did.

An awareness of what?

An awareness of the evils that money can bring to you, if you let it control your life.

You saw yourself as a friend of the working man. According to labor historian Harold Livesay, "By the standards of ethics and conduct to which we would like to hold businessmen today, he operated extremely ruthlessly." (You've admitted that.) What do you think of our global business practices today?

I see throughout the planet stepping stones for the myriad of ways workers can be handled: from the child sweatshops, where they are locked in rooms for twelve hours a day; to the countries which provide four to eight weeks' vacation a year for their employees; to the companies that are employee owned, where they vote their own salaries. You can find anything out there. I began ruthlessly, but as I became aware of the conditions some people were forced to live in, I somewhat mitigated my stance toward things. I had what you could call a bad case of tunnel vision when looking at a lot of things, and I only saw whatever I would allow myself to see.

The various conditions in the world today are only seen by those who choose to see them. Those who perpetrate bad conditions and injustices upon the people do not choose to see them, as I did not choose to see them either. The rest of the world, which feels a degree of fairness and justice, sees the problems and inequities. What people choose to do about such problems depends upon how much involvement each wishes to have in the situation.

Peace and War

You were concerned about world peace. How do you view terrorism today?

I viewed world peace and war only as to how each impacted business. Did it take away workers who were needed? Did it provide business to manufacture the products of war? What did it do? It was a pattern, not an abrupt disruption of something. It began slowly and had cycles to it. Terrorism today creates an abrupt disruption for businesses, such as the World Trade Center. That stopped dead so many operations: insurance businesses, accounting firms, those that had headquarters in those buildings. The threat of terrorism impacts transportation, not only of people but of products from place to place, with the worry that goods might be contaminated, might be used to hide bombs. Terrorism is an insidious plague on the world. As a businessman I never had experience of overcoming terrorism of that kind.

You're not a businessman now.

As a resident on the Other Side I can see a cycle that people are going through, as the entire planet is going into a period of chaos. I watch with interest the machinations of industry and finance.

Wealth and Poverty

You wrote, "Man does not live by bread alone. It is the mind that makes the body rich. There is no class so pitiably wretched as that which possesses money and nothing else." How do you view the cultural standards of our consumer society?

It seems that you have raised a generation of moneyed people, where the parents and grandparents went out and worked as hard as they could to provide money so that their children and grandchildren would not have to work as hard as they had. We now have the result you are seeing, which is a generation of children and grandchildren who do not know the value of money, do not realize the work that is necessary in order to get the money. So their idea is, if they have it—they spend it. They don't need to save it because it will always be replenished, won't it? Doesn't money grow on trees?

People have lost the work ethic. People have lost the sense that they are responsible for themselves. They don't appreciate that if they don't put money aside for the time when they are not able to work, they won't have money. There has been an entire shift in the realization of what it takes to have money, produce money, save money, build money, build an empire. Very few have any idea what that takes. Those who do have some idea of how to develop an empire—such as when Bill Gates did it almost by accident—usually have had the good fortune of being in the right place at the right time and having it almost easy in that what they produce is needed by all.

Like the first of your investments?
Yes.

Like most of your investments?
Sometimes I almost had to work hard to be in the right place at the right time—kept my ear to the road to see if the trends were real. I had a lot of help in that regard.

In the answer you gave (on the consumer society) you seemed to ignore two-thirds of the nation. Many are working fit to bust. Both husbands and wives are working. The children are "minded." But they can't make enough money because they are so badly paid. They don't have health benefits. Life's a struggle and they can't pull themselves up by their bootstraps.

There is a segment which is like that, but within a lot of those homes you will still find television sets, microwaves, TV dinners, a plethora of bags from fast food places, because they have been brainwashed by what is deemed "necessary" by American society. They will maintain an automobile before they look into health benefits, when public transportation would fit their needs. It is the way that society has been trained by the media and by the previous generations.

My final questions are for your interpretation of a scriptural text. How difficult is it "for the rich to enter the Kingdom of Heaven"?

[Laughs] Everyone has equal access. Regardless of what is done while in human form, all souls return Home. Whether the person has been a pauper, the richest man on the planet, an ascetic, a scholar, an illiterate, wracked with disease, blessed with health— all have equal access to the eternal.

So Jesus was wrong?

Like most of his parables, it was not to be taken as literal truth, but as an example of how to lead a better life (all basic religions exist to give you a pattern for life, and not to give you any definitive answer about life). He was speaking to the crowd who would think that if they did not have money they were nothing. They could add richness to their lives because there were those who helped each other. They knew how to have a community, contrary to the rich who did nothing for anyone. So he spoke to the values of their life, and also to the fact that as souls they had come down to learn lessons. They would learn those lessons and become richer in heaven than the rich man who did nothing but sit back and not fulfill any of his life's lessons.

Thank you, Andrew Carnegie, for your help.

Thank you for inviting me.

Commentary

Toni: Andrew Carnegie had a solid professional feel, more physical than ethereal—so much so that I almost looked for his physical countenance. He was forceful and dominant in his delivery and unequivocal in his pronouncements, unlike mellowed "older" souls. There was almost no reference to souls needing to learn lessons and no recounting of the Freedom of Choice refrain repeated by others.

Peter: It took me somewhat by surprise when one of the world's richest men of yesterday chose to talk about Bill Gates, the world's richest man of today. Carnegie was somewhat ambivalent about whether Mr. Gates had needed to work as hard at gathering wealth as he once had done, but he was forced by our questions to admit the relative ease with which he also made a mammoth fortune for himself.

For a while we were feeling somewhat unsure whether the soul who had once incarnated as Andrew Carnegie really had left his previous personality behind—there was a bagpipe-sounding Scots bravado coming through at first. But then came his great admission: "When I first began a massing my fortune, because I chose not to be poor any longer, I was ruthless." Clearly it was only after he had been bought out of his business empire by J. P. Morgan that he took the time to plan his philanthropic retirement and began to examine his former ruthless methods of self-enrichment.

That said, Carnegie never fully let down his guard. When confronted by us on his upper-class interpretation of the consumer society, his response was to criticize the working poor for having a television set in the home and a car outside in the street. (Was there a little spiritual time-warp here?) His understanding of social norms appeared at that point to have remained locked into that of the self-made man. Yet, in fairness, he did not let the *nouveau riche* off the hook, either. To have wisdom about money you must first have worked hard for it, he asserted confidently. Inheriting wealth from Daddy doesn't qualify a rich person for the pantheon of the rich-and-wise. There was an over-simplification in his remarks here that bordered on superficiality.

I felt a little edgy in asking the classic question from the Christian gospels concerning the rich not being able to enter the kingdom of heaven. Here Andrew's answer describing the original setting of Jesus' teaching was unexpectedly useful. He explained elegantly how Jesus' teaching was aimed at helping his unsophisticated audience to better understand their own life lessons, and he directly affirmed that all souls return Home from their incarnations, whoever they were and whatever they may have done while on Earth.

We were reminded of the strong personal drive to succeed severally displayed by Dwight Moody, Florence Nightingale, and Margaret Sanger. Andrew's precept of "stick-to-it-ness" applies to all of them, and made them into the successes they once were.

Here, then, was someone who amassed a fortune but still preaches that you can prove your wisdom in knowing what money is for by giving it all away (give or take a million or two left over for yourself). We wonder how Francis of Assisi and Karl Marx would comment on all that! Perhaps we will ask them one day.

"I have seen so much of the heartfelt work I tried to accomplish written off as my being the right person at the right time and the right place, instead of people feeling the intensity I had for what I chose to do and what I chose to accomplish."

Winston S. Churchill
1874-1965

Biographical Note

Winston Leonard Spencer Churchill was born in 1874 at Blenheim Palace, England, son of an austere aristocrat, Lord Randolph Churchill. His mother, Jennie, the daughter of a wealthy New York financier, largely left his early upbringing to a nanny, Mrs. Elizabeth Everest. Though he sought closeness with his parents, they largely ignored him, and his lonely childhood dogged him throughout his life. He was educated at boarding schools, including Harrow. At this leading boys' school he showed unwillingness to study, despite his genuine ability. Strong in fencing, he became a cadet at the Royal Military College in 1893.

Churchill entered the army as a junior cavalry officer and served in India where, in addition to excelling at polo, he began serious self-education. On leave in Cuba he wrote his first newspaper articles about an insurrection there. Returning to India he assisted his regiment in suppressing a revolt on India's North West Frontier. He wrote about it for the London press and in his first book, *The Story of the Malakand Field Force*, published in 1897.

Again on leave from India, Churchill embedded himself with Lord Kitchener's army in the Sudan, where he took part in the battle at Omdurman and wrote about the campaign as a war correspondent. He left the army and published both a lengthy account of the war, and his only novel (*Savrola, a Tale of the Revolution in Laurania*, written in 1900 in the heroic Ruritanian style), but failed in his first attempt to be elected to the British Parliament. So he went to South Africa as a war correspondent. On his way there the train was ambushed. He fought, was captured, and subsequently escaped. While remaining a war correspondent, he rejoined the British army and took part in notable battles against the Boer separatists. On returning home he published two accounts of the war, and, now a popular hero, he was also elected as the Conservative MP for Oldham.

In Parliament Churchill soon showed his political interests, opposing his own party's overblown military budget and its policy of increasing trade tarrifs. He deserted the Tories in 1904, crossing the floor of the House of Commons to join the Liberal opposition. He continued with his successful writing, publishing a large biography of his father and an account of his recent experiences in Africa.

In 1905 the Liberals were swept into power in a general election, and Churchill became Under-Secretary of State for the Colonies, his first government appointment. He was later appointed President of the Board of Trade, where he championed free trade and supported social reforms. After a whirlwind six-month romance, Winston Churchill married the beautiful Clementine Hozier in 1908. The couple had five children.

In 1910 he was promoted to the senior government post of Home Secretary. There he ran into severe criticism for his personal handling of gang violence in the fracas of the Sidney Street Siege. He was more successful when, demoted to be in charge of the British navy, he initiated modernization. This included the unpopular but far-sighted development of the battle tank. During World War I, his management of the disastrous Dardanelles Campaign led to further demotion in a government reshuffle. He rejoined the army, though still a member of Parliament, and fought on the Western Front.

On his return he was given war-related ministries, then in 1921 was put in charge of the Colonial Office. The Liberals were in disarray, and Churchill sought help from local Conservatives when he stood for election in 1924 as an independent "Constitutionalist." He now became the Chancellor of the Exchequer but was badly advised and made "the worst decision" of his life by returning Britain to the Gold Standard. This led to serious deflation and resulted in the 1926 General Strike, during which he adopted a strike-breaking stance that strongly echoed Mussolini's anti-communist activities.

The Labour Party was on the rise to power, and Churchill, who was unpopular with the Left, was not given a ministry in the coalition government. He devoted himself to writing, publishing *My Early Life*, a biography on his ancestor Marlborough, and other books, and commencing work on his *History of the English Speaking Peoples* (which was published in the mid-fifties). He was notable for opposing Indian independence, and virtually alone in Parliament when he warned the MPs that the military were quite unprepared to stand against Hitler's Germany. His support of Edward VIII in the young monarch's matrimonial crisis resulted in his being shunned for a time by his political contemporaries.

Vindicated for his tenacious and unequivocal opposition to Hitler, Churchill returned to serve in the government at the outbreak of World War II, and was appointed by King Geroge VI as the Prime Minister in a coalition government, which lasted from 1940 to 1945. His powerful oratory, both in Parliament and in America, rallied people to the defense of Britain. Despite some notable blind spots, overall he proved an able military strategist, and forged a crucial strong bond with the American President, Franklin D. Roosevelt.

When the war was over, the Labour Party won an election on its strong socialist program, for which he had shown disdain. He was Leader of the Opposition until 1951 when he returned as Prime Minister until 1955, during which time he published The Second World War and was awarded the Nobel Prize for Literature in 1953. In the same year he backed a coup in Iran to safeguard British oil interests. He ordered the British army to quell the Mau Mau uprising in Kenya, but in Malaysia and

Singapore Britain's weakened military and economic power forced him to make arrangements for their independence.

Following his retirement as Prime Minister, he remained as a member of Parliament until 1964, but spent much time painting with oils at Chartwell, his home in England, and in the south of France. Winston S. Churchill died in 1965, at 90 years of age.

The Dialogue

Introductions

Winston, I once wrote a letter on behalf of a student group, congratulating you on your eightieth birthday. I never got round to sending one on your ninetieth.

There were so many who wished me well I could not respond to all of them. The fascination so many people had with me amazed me a little bit. All I was, was the consummate politician and not necessarily the *Everyman* for everyman.

Toni drew a picture of you in her first adventure in artwork. Apparently it came out quite well. You were an artist—your preferred medium was oil, wasn't it?

Yes, definitely oils. That was the only thing that was accepted as collectible, worthwhile art, outside of charcoal, which was rather messy and more used for preliminary sketches than completed artwork.

Come on—there are English water-colors!

But there was a permanence with the oils; you could build up the layers and make a statement with it. I found watercolor was a bit on the wimpy side—a rather damp day could blend your finished product into something other than you chose.

You sound as if you are building one of your famous walls again!

You can build walls with many things.

Adventures

You were close to two wonderful women in your life: your nanny, Mrs. Everest, and your wife, Clementine. What did they mean to you?

My nanny was security, warmth, a caring, sharing person who let me know that it was all right to explore, to be myself, to be bombastic at times, if I chose, so long as I was truthful in what I did. She was a terrific teacher, a confidante as much as anything else. At times I almost felt as though she were growing up with me, so much was our closeness and the way she was selfless when it came to me.

Then my dearest, my sweetest, my rock, my support, my wife, was everything to me. She kept me on the straight and narrow when I wished to waver.

What did you wish to waver in?

There was a time when, with the pressures and all of the nay-sayers in Parliament, it got to a point when I wondered if it was worth it all, if I shouldn't just chuck it and let them have a go. She let me know, in her own quiet way, the impact I was having, and the firmness, the stability, I was providing for the nation.

This was in the thirties—your "Wilderness Years"?

Yes. It was the years when I could have just walked off and not looked back.

In fact you filled them writing one or two quite good books, didn't you?

[laughs] Yes, that was my escape. It was so easy to lose myself in the pages, and to write off all the little humans running around on two legs who wanted attention, and wanted to sway me this way and that way.

Clementine kept you on the straight and narrow.

She kept me on the straight and narrow; she kept me true to myself and true to my ideals. She was my pep squad preparing me for the battles ahead—she had such faith in me.

You are said to have been an "able but lazy" pupil at Harrow. Is that true?

I guess in those people's opinion that would be true. At that time, I didn't want to work if I didn't have to. It was easy to sit and watch the world go by. It was easy to play mind games and take enjoyment in literature and various other aspects of life, and not have to exert much energy.

Except for your fencing.

One must have an outlet for one's aggression. At the time it was unseemly to be over-aggressive verbally—it was very easy to nip that little bugger with the end of a lance.

As a young man you were all for glory. You fenced at Harrow, played polo in India, rode in the last great British cavalry charge at Omdurman. Then you wrote and wrote about it. Was this vanity, your need for attention, or did you want to cultivate an heroic attitude in others?

More than anything else I wanted to understand myself and what it meant to me. I went into all those things because I felt a need to do them. It was an expression of who I was, yet I wasn't sure why I was doing them. In writing about them, I got the feeling there was more to it than just the act of doing. I found the driving force within me was victory—of whatever kind—of being able to come out on top, being able to save the day for people. There was something in the pit of my stomach which drove me to win. Competitiveness was the gentleman's way of diffusing aggression.

The current literature for boys was full of such ideas, wasn't it?

It was to try to give them a manual of behavior, a sense of propriety in growing up and dealing with their feelings, emotions, and energies in a gentleman's acceptable way.

Do you feel we don't have as much adventure now as you did?

There are not the opportunities that I had—there are no Calgaries. Those days we went on fox hunts. They even forbid that now! Where's the adventure? Where's the sound of the trumpet and the hammer of hooves across the moors? That's all gone. It's as though gentrification has occurred and we no longer wish to link the wildness of the out-of-doors with the dealings inside the mansions, the castles, and the Parliament.

Oratory and Language

In 1908 you asked a Scottish audience, "What is the use of living, if it be not to strive for noble causes and to make this muddled world a better place for those who will live in it after we are gone?" When did you first realize that you were gifted as an orator?

Almost from the beginning. [chuckles] I was able to turn a phrase that would get people to do whatever I wished.

You practiced on Mrs. Everest?

Yes, of course, and other adults who unwarily came into my lair. I enjoyed being able to get those so much older than I to pay attention to me, and to pay deference to me. It became a game and a passion of mine to mold other people with oratory. I practiced on the chaps at school. I practiced on anyone who would listen.

So you didn't need to be taught?

I did not need to be taught manipulation by oratory. That was something which came naturally to me.

You believed in using simple language.

Simple language was needed for the masses. Basically, I spoke simple language unless it was necessary to appeal to those who felt themselves superior to others. I have been known to be able to talk down to them from above, with their own language, and make them feel it. But most of the time I spoke to the gentlefolk and did not wish in any way to belittle them, or to make them sense it was not heartfelt, that it was not coming from one of their own, one of their peers. The simple language had the additional flavor of making them feel I was one of them.

You didn't have much Latin and Greek. Did you have foreign languages?

Languages other than English did not interest me. English alone can take a lifetime to master with all of its nuances.

You were very proud of your own language.

Very proud. I did not see a reason to learn to speak a language in a country I had no allegiance to and where I would not live.

How do you view the debate in America on whether English should be a compulsory language?

These are strange times now, where the definition of a country is created more by its people than by its boundaries. It's defined by the fact that an empire (as we had) may encompass a multitude of languages, and yet the people are all of the empire. In the United States they have parts of their dominion where Spanish is the language, such as Puerto Rico. To say that those who are citizens of that great country cannot, when they come to the continental United States, speak their native tongue, would be to disenfranchise their ancestry.

The bigger issue is the influx of people from Mexico.

That is the bigger issue, but is it not doing disservice to those who are American citizens who speak another language to suggest they may not speak it? The whole history of the United States has been one of the "melting pot." All the Italians, Germans, Swedes, and many, many Spanish nations have come into the United States, the Polish, the Russians—within their own neighborhoods some have never learned English. Would the United States now go and tell the grandmother and the grandfather who remain in the home that they must speak English?

That's not really the intention. It is rather whether the official literature of the individual states is put out in two languages, for people doing business with that state.

I think they have to keep their own counsel on that, being cognizant of their history. I would say that the language of the country must be one understood by all.

Self-Sacrifice

You said in 1936 that we have a great inheritance representing centuries of achievement. "There is not one of our simple uncounted rights today for which better men than we are have not died on the scaffold or the battlefield." Was your view of the martyr forged by the Churchill heritage, or by your history reading, or by the personal sacrifice you had to make to endure the indifference your parents showed toward you as a child?

It was a blending of all of the above. I wanted people to feel the depth of our foundations, that sacrifice was necessary in order to accomplish anything. That if people were not willing to stand up for what they thought was right (which in prior times had led to massacres, and martyrdom, and purges), their country would not move forward. It was analogous to my pulling myself out of the familial pit I was in, of loneliness and detachment, because I wished to go forward. I wished to follow the energy that was deep within me to go somewhere, to be someone, to mean something to my country and to her people. I knew what I could achieve for other people was what I had achieved for myself, which was to move forward and to create that which was of my own making and not the direction in which others would have had me go.

You are now back Home. We've noticed in conversation with other people a difference of feeling about certain issues from the perspective of Home. From where you are now, do you see sacrifice and martyrdom, whether on the scaffold or the battle field, as necessary for the soul's achievement?

Here at Home we look upon achievement as learning lessons. If a soul has never been in a situation which takes personal sacrifice in order to develop, evolve, or work through its innermost desires, then the battlefield, the martyrdom, the persecution are still needed for it to experience those things. It is not a requirement for humanity that there be wars at this time; it is just that individual souls wish to experience those things. We cannot learn lessons for other people. The sacrifices we made should be a guideline for others so as not to repeat what we went through (but it does not seem that people read their history as well as I did).

Empires

Following the collapse of France in 1940, you told the House of Commons, "Let us therefore brace ourselves to our duties, and so bear ourselves that if the British Empire and Commonwealth last for a thousand years, men will still say, 'This was their finest hour'." With your current perspective, how do you view the British Empire?

In some respects the British Empire is much as it was during my lifetime. It has certain trends, such as its fascination with the royal family, that have not changed, and probably will never change. It is almost as if the royal family are pets of the people—very well kept, well groomed, well-paid-for pets, but nonetheless treated as such. Every little trick that they learn, stunt they perform, is accepted and applauded—or condemned.

However, the Commonwealth is changing in its attitude toward other countries. Since the Empire has shrunk, we have become more reclusive and less concerned with helping in other arenas, but then we are no longer in the position of protector of a piece of our own.

But the Empire was a militaristic-based organization; it wasn't just a question of royalty.

The militarism has changed, for sure. We have almost become a country of—I would have to say, as in my time—pacifists. The country, while it attempts to hold up its end in aggression throughout the world (such as by its membership in the NATO forces), does not have the support of the people.

Iraq?

A good example of that is what happened to the Prime Minister [referring to Tony Blair] when he supported the inclusion of British troops in the invasion of Iraq. A good portion of the people would have ridden him out of the limelight.

How do you see that reaction as wrong from your perspective?

I don't see things as right or wrong. I see it as a shifting of the consciousness of the people as a whole, from centuries and centuries of being the dictator, the military boss, the head of an empire which stretched over several continents, where the majority of the lineage of aristocratic families got their titles from their service on foreign land for the honor of the Empire. It was a militaristic period which those who were there needed to experience.

The current pre-occupation of the people is dealing with those who come to their shores but who are different from them. Some, for whom they used to be guardians and dictators, are now entering and wish to take up the rights and the mantle of the country they believed was their protector and, therefore, which they would like to help protect. But those at home are now fighting what they see as a literal invasion of their country. This is turning into an internal battlefield, even within Coventry, Bradford—and throughout the entire land.

How would you compare the British empire of your day with the American empire of today?

[laughs] We had a sense of who was in charge, we had a sense of propriety, we had a sense of loyalty. While we had a few talks in back rooms over brandy and cigars, we did not go out and hang dirty laundry from the street corners. My view of America is that it's a free-for-all. There is no sense of family. There is no sense of history. There is no sense that you have set positions in life where you have responsibility to others and to yourself. If the man on the corner, who has no education, wins one of your lotteries he can decide to put all his money toward becoming President of the United States! Supposing he put together enough of a media blitz, it's possible he could be President—yet have no sense of what he was getting himself into, except that (in his own mind) he would have supreme power.

Society and Sobriety

You were noted for repartee. Once when the Astors were staying at Blenheim with your cousin the Duke of Marlborough, Lady Astor said, "Winston, if I were your wife I'd put poison in your coffee." You replied, "Nancy, if I were your husband I'd drink it." How do you view that relationship with Nancy Astor?

We laugh about our nudgings and pushings and asides. We played a lot to those around us, rather than having any intent behind what we said. It was word games. It was good press and a little bit of envy of each other concerning our respective stations. She chafed somewhat under the role of "female," even privileged as she was.

You respected her?

Yes, I did.

Your drinks were not usually coffee, but alcoholic. In 1936 you won a bet with Lord Rothermere that you could abstain from spirits [hard liquor] for a year. Were you an alcoholic or a heavy drinker who was alcohol-dependent?

I don't really define myself as either. I enjoyed the taste and the effects of spirits. I found that it took the edge off the proddings of other people. [laughs] It allowed me to relax and sometimes not be held responsible for what I chose to say. In that way it was a help to me. There was no time when I felt totally dependent upon spirits, and I did win that bet because, during my entire human life, I had the willpower to win whatever bet I made. That, again, was part of my need to succeed, to be on top.

World War II

Going on to the Second World War, critics assert that, on the night of November the fourteenth, 1940, you knew about the raid on Coventry many hours in advance. They say you "let the city burn" rather than reveal that the Allies had broken the secret German intelligence codes. How do you respond?

True, too true, alas! We all had sacrifices to make. It was a decision based upon what we saw would bring us to ultimate success. The potential in having the German code could save thousands if not millions of lives. A lot of the townspeople had been evacuated, but it was necessary that some pay the price for our being able to save the others, and potentially change the tide of the war, which it did.

You seem frequently to have excited criticism, as you did in South Africa, and when you were Home Secretary. Critics have even alleged that you ordered the firebombing of Dresden as payback for the bombing of Coventry. What did you most regret in your life?

I could say, "Regrets I've had but few." If I were still in human form, of all the experiences of that Winston Churchill, I would have regretted not doing what I could for others. Yet I know in my current position that everybody chooses the lessons to learn, the things to experience. For some, what appear to be egregious outcomes were what they had agreed to endure, and I was but the facilitator of their lessons. From this viewpoint, I did a bonnie job of what I had to do.

Why did you firebomb Dresden?

It was not just for Coventry; it was for England herself. It was for all the bombs, for London, and the sense of security that was ripped from our fabric.

You said some harsh things about the Islamic world. One of your milder comments was, "Individual Moslems may show splendid qualities, but the influence of the religion paralyzes the social development of those who follow it." How do you view both that statement and the present hostile international relationships in the Middle East?

We have a tendency in human form to criticize that which is almost diametrically opposed to what we believe, and take a stance against things that are different from whatever we wish to see exist. When we were dealing with Moslems in many countries, they did not respect our way of life, but we thought they should as we were providing help or direction for them. We did not respect them.

161

What is occurring now is that religion is again being used as an excuse for certain people to direct campaigns against those whom they do not like. As I railed against Moslems, they now are railing against all non-Moslems. It is a harvest for which we laid some of the seed in times past; it is now beginning to grow and has given a foundation to the hatred that they now exhibit. As ye have sown, so shall ye reap.

My comments also acknowledged that religious belief systems may take all freedom away from the individual. They do not exercise their freedom of choice because they are not aware that they have any choices—they blindly follow the clerics. They never think about going into their heart and soul to see what resonates within themselves. They are mere lemmings.

Are those Moslems correct who say this is another Crusade?

It depends on who is defining Crusade. If the definition is a religious war, based upon the interpretation of a few of the religious tenets by their hierarchy, who have convinced the congregation of their righteous beliefs, then it is a Crusade. If you refer instead to a search for the truth, then it is not a crusade.

Do you see that in terms of the religious right in America?

I don't see any of the religious right in America advocating that you must go out and kill others to keep your religion from being suppressed. The religious right in America is simply verbal, creating some discontent among some parties, but they do not advocate bombings and self-destruction as a means of getting their point across. Their strongest thrust is one of prejudice and intolerance—not very Christian of them.

New Foundations

"I feel that Christian men should not close the door upon any hope of finding a new foundation for the life of the self-tormented human race." You wrote those words in 1950. Today, humankind seems no less tormented. Can you tell us from your present perspective, what is that new foundation for human life of which you spoke, and how we should seek it?

162

The new foundation is what your Spiritualists or your New Age people—whatever you want to call them—call "discovering your souls," discovering the love that is within them, discovering their connection to the Creator. It is something that is going to be virtually impossible for a large majority of the population, because they are not mature enough as souls to be at the point where they can have that self-realization. People on the planet at this time are at all stages of development. The energy of the planet is reaching a crescendo and everything is being magnified to bring it to a completion. There will be a lot of forces rising up in the next few years, as saviors and prophets. It will be a very interesting time for you all.

Winston Churchill, thank you so much for being with us.

I hope I have been able to answer some of the questions that have plagued my human history.

Are there others you wish to answer now, something which nags you?

I cannot say "nags" because that isn't a concept we know here. It is just that I have seen so much of the heartfelt work I tried to accomplish written off as my being the right person at the right time and the right place, instead of people feeling the intensity I had for what I chose to do and what I chose to accomplish. I am not by any means saying that to blow my own trumpet, but I mean it as an example for other people, that they, too, may get out of the dreamland in their head of what they want to accomplish, and can fulfill their dreams, their plans, if they will only go forward with them.

Commentary

Toni: Ever the orator, Winston was proud to share his views with all. At times he sounded bombastic in stating his beliefs like a no-nonsense, make-no-excuses politician, whom I could see waving the Union Jack so that none could mistake his loyalty. I felt his regret that time had moved on, and that many young people will not experience the sense of self-confidence that the warrior's own life evoked.

While he did not display pride, I felt his satisfaction with the contribution he had made to other people's learning, as he went with us through the lessons he had set up for himself. I sensed that he had enjoyed his human experience as Winston Churchill immensely, and that he still advocated people should live and play heartily. At other times there was some diffidence in his manner, suggesting he wanted his words to help us draw our conclusions about him. And in parting from him, being somewhat clairsentient, I sensed a faint but quite unmistakable waft of cigar smoke in the room!

Peter: It is really interesting to witness the dichotomy that spirits can experience on returning Home from planet Earth. On the one hand they are in an unconditionally loving, non-judgmental atmosphere, where, once their life-review is over, they no longer have self-blame or regrets; on the other hand they are still able to dive emotionally right back into the character of their former human personality. This was true of Churchill, not so much in what he actually said as in the tone of his recollections. He was caught up within his human character a lot of the time, but was still able to prove that he has a good grasp of what is going on today. This knowledge was rather tested over the issue of English language use in America (I blame my off-the-cuff questions), but he was so aware of the current British and American political scene that he made sharp comments about both. He found humor in American politics and his hyperbole, in the parable of the lotto winner standing for the U.S. presidency, was outstanding for its multiple barbs.

If we rather lingered on his youth it was because the insights into his character ran so deep. Nanny Elizabeth Everest clearly had a profound effect on his childhood. Books, no less than his formal education, sharpened his verbal rapier and his love of history. But above all, his was the determination never to give in, matched by an overarching desire to win. He was able to acknowledge that this drive got him into trouble, but still, his human self had few regrets. Even where he clearly wanted to put the historical record straight, his allowing the German Luftwaffe's bombing of Coventry was deemed necessary action. The Dresden fire-bombing was viewed quite coldly, almost brutally, as if it was "easy to nip that little bugger with the end of a lance," as he did in days when he was fencing champion at Harrow. But he did it all for King and Empire, and clearly would do it all over again, given the chance.

Winston Churchill is remembered most for his wartime leadership, spirit of adventure, and tenacity, but there was another side, which we glimpsed in his love of history and literature. This was the Churchill of stirring speech and poetic illustrations. In consequence his "New Age" answer to my question on the desire he had expressed for a new foundation for human life was not wholly unexpected, corresponding with other souls' comments from Home. We thought his phrase "New Age people—whatever you want to call them" showed that he wanted to distance himself from any specific spiritualist movement. Nevertheless his answer was in line with what may best be termed the "spiritist" thought of the Masters and Leaders. Looking toward the fulfillment of human destiny he made four points:

First: The way forward is in discovering our connection with love and with the Creator.

Second: Most people will not be mature enough to make this connection.

Third: There is an energetic crisis on planet Earth that is soon to reach its dénouement.

Fourth: The role of the prophet will become important in the coming years.

He did not predict the end result but said evenly that it would be "very interesting."

"I was in that lifetime psychotic, although I would not have admitted it in that persona. Yes, I did play the psychotic. Who but a psychotic would be so ruthless, so unthinking, uncaring, uncompassionate, and diabolically cruel."

Adolf Hitler
1889-1945

Biographical Note

Adolf Hitler was born in 1889 in Braunau am Inn, Austria, the fourth of six children of Alois and Klara Hitler (a.k.a., Schicklgruber). His strict father was a customs officer. Adolf studied well at first but stopped working in high school, which he left without qualifications. The sixteen-year-old wanted to be an artist but was twice rejected by the Vienna Academy of Arts. He earned a little money selling paintings to tourists, but became homeless. In 1910 he found lodgings in a house for poor working men where he painted, listened to Wagner's operas, became anti-semitic (blaming the Jews for Germany's financial difficulties), and started to voice anti-democratic views.

During 1913, Hitler crossed the German border to Munich, where he might escape Austrian military service, but he was apprehended, then declared physically unfit and released. World War I started and he enlisted in the Bavarian army as a messenger. He was notable for the total obedience he gave to his superior officers. For gallantry on dangerous missions he was twice awarded the Iron Cross, and was decorated with the Wound Badge for a leg injury. Just before the war ended he was hospitalized with temporary blindness, a reaction to mustard gas, and a military psychiatrist diagnosed him as hysterical and psychotic.

After the Armistice, the Bavarian army assigned Adolf to the suppression of socialist insurrections. He blamed liberal politicians, Jewish financiers, and Communists for the humiliating Guilt Clause in the Treaty of Versailles, and for financial reparations levied on the German people. He refined his views by taking army propaganda courses aimed at ascribing blame for the war and its outcome. In 1919, the army ordered him to infiltrate the small German Workers' Party where Dietrich Eckart, a founding member, befriended him, inflamed his growing hatred of Jews and Marxists, and taught him public speaking.

Leaving the army, Hitler became a party activist and firebrand speaker. He organized swastika-decorated, uniformed supporters to drive large crowds into Munich arenas, where he addressed them on nationalist and anti-semitic topics. In 1920 the party changed its name to The National Socialist German Workers Party (Nazi Party). The party leaders opposed his dictatorial style, but he drew on his grass-roots supporters and won, assuming complete control in 1921 as Führer (Leader). Many businessmen and war veterans, who later rose to power as Nazis, were attracted by Adolf's fiery speeches and joined the movement.

In 1923, the inexperienced Führer and his paramilitary followers attempted a military coup in Munich to take control of the Bavarian state. For his part in the "Beer Hall Putsch," Hitler was arrested and sentenced to prison for five years. However, the widely reported April 1924 trial had greatly enhanced his reputation, as did his book, *Mein Kampf* (My Struggle), which he had time to dictate while incarcerated, and he was released in December of the same year. There followed a more carefully crafted anti-Semitic campaign, and the refinement of the Nazi command structure. Then the Depression gave Hitler his chance, and in the 1930 election, empowered by negative rhetoric and fiscal promises, the Nazis rose to be the second-largest political party in the Reichstag (Parliament).

Hitler boldly campaigned for the German presidency in 1932, despite the shooting death in his apartment of his niece and mistress Geli Raubal, which was declared a suicide. Before her death, he had begun his lifetime relationship with Eva Braun, then nineteen years old.

In a complex series of political events, Hitler steered the Nazis toward control of the Reichstag. The government fell, but he failed to become Chancellor, despite promising his party's co-operation. Political chaos continued into 1933 when the aging German President Hindenburg dismissed the current Chancellor, who had failed to create a coalition government, and appointed Hitler as Chancellor in his stead. Almost immediately afterward the Reichstag was set on fire by arson. Hitler persuaded the President to agree to emergency powers, and banned the Communist Party, which he blamed for the fire. An election gave the Nazis a working majority and they pressed through special powers for Hitler's cabinet, giving it governmental control of Germany. Political and labor opposition was banned, and the power of state governments more than decimated. Nazis now controlled everything. All in unifom pledged allegiance to Hitler personally, but rebellious paramilitary supporters and other opponents were murdered en masse in the "Night of the Long Knives" (1934).

In a public-debt-generated boom, both German military expansion and infrastructure work brought high levels of male employment. The concepts of Ayran superiority and of eugenics to purify the German race on political, racial, homophobic, and other grounds took root. Women were to be seen only as homemakers and childbearers. In 1935, Jews were stripped of German citizenship and suffered increasing public harassment. By 1938 Hitler had sanctioned waves of destruction and confiscation of Jewish property by the thugs of the uniformed SS and Gestapo. He revived conscription, re-occupied the demilitarized Rhineland, and tested his military might in the Spanish Civil War. He formed an alliance with Italy in 1936, which was later expanded to include Japan. Planning to enlarge Germany's borders, he ordered the SS to undertake a systematic, eugenics-based genocide that eventually killed well over 12 million people, 6 million of whom were Jews. Hitler was directly involved in the planning of the gas chambers used in his "Final Solution," in which the total elimination of the Jews was his primary concern.

Hitler forced Austria to unite with Germany in 1938; then his forces occupied Czechslovakia. When he invaded Poland, however, Britain and France declared war, but his army marched on to occupy Denmark, Norway, The Netherlands, and Belgium, followed by France, which surrendered in 1940. He persuaded Mussolini's Italy to join the war, leaving Britain as his main target, which he ordered to be bombed systematically before launching an invasion.

In mid-1941, Hitler ordered his forces to invade Russia, Ukraine, and the Baltic States. After initial success, Soviet opposition and bad weather halted his troops at Moscow. Thereafter the German Reich suffered major defeats: in North Africa at El Alamin in 1942, and at Stalingrad, where the German army in Russia was wiped out. He began to lose control of the military situation and of his mental powers. Italy fell to the Allies; then sustained bombing of Germany was led by the U.S. Air Force. On D-Day in 1944 the Allies landed on the beaches of France and the march toward Germany began from all directions. Hitler survived assassination, responding with the slaughter of thousands. He was surrounded by the allies in Berlin but would not admit military defeat. Finally, in an underground bunker, he married Eva Braun. On the next day, April 30, 1945, the couple committed suicide and their bodies were incinerated by his order. Adolf Hitler was 56 years of age.

About the Dialogue with Hitler

The week before this recorded interview took place, the Masters unexpectedly told us that they would ask the soul-who-was-Adolf-Hitler to appear fully in character for the first part of our discussion, and then speak with us in his true soul-self in the second part. We agreed to go along with the idea, which clearly was of importance to them. We have marked the sections of the discussion accordingly.

In Part I, Toni, who is sensitive to energy changes, remarked that Hitler came in with a flourish and a burst of energy. Afterward she reported, "I did not like the energy that first came in. It was restless, like someone pacing back and forth. I always had the feeling he was very conscious of who might be around. Almost paranoid, he was looking over his shoulder but with an air of 'I'm a force to reckon with. You must do as I say. You must recognize who and what I am.' His energy did not have the dynamic smoothness of the other leaders; it had a rough abrasiveness."

In Part II, the soul, now free from the Hitler persona, appeared to Toni as "very calm, collected, and matter-of-fact, as are the majority of souls with whom we have spoken."

Dialogue with the Dictator

Adolf, the Masters assured us your spirit is very much alive and that we may interview you. I personally survived seven bombs the German Luftwaffe chose to drop close by on two nights in 1942, so our historic relationship got off to a bad start. Other people are probably angry with me for even deigning to talk with you, so perhaps we are making progress. Let me start by asking some fairly straightforward questions to set the scene for our discussion on why Adolf Hitler's spirit is where it is now. Is that all right with you?

Go ahead. It's a pity we didn't get you though, with all the other non-combatants who were all conspiring against us.

Eight-year-old boys were conspiring against you?

Everyone was conspiring against us. Some of our strongest supporters were youths of that age.

Early Days
When you were a youth of that age did you regard your father as a tyrant, and was he?

He was a disciplinarian. He shaped some of the ways I found I could act against others and how to show deference under the guise of respect to put tyrants at ease. I had a grudging respect for him when I looked back upon it.

But you didn't like your father?

It is not always necessary to like a person in order to respect them and what they stand for and to know of their strength. In a lot of respects my father was weak because he could only push those less strong than himself. I was able to master pushing everyone: pushing those who were stronger than I, pushing those who conspired against me, pushing everyone in the nation to do as I wanted. I, alone, reigned supreme.

But you weren't able to push the Vienna Academy of Arts, which twice rejected you as a student.

They were such wimps! Dullards! They did not recognize talent; it was strictly prejudice against someone who was better, more proficient than they.

They probably had left their high school with some sort of certificate, but I don't think you did.

It wasn't necessary. I had all of the information I needed. I had the talent, which came naturally to me. Certificates do not give the measure of the man; accomplishments do.

Making money by selling your paintings with your talents was extremely hard, and you went bankrupt—or, at least, you were homeless. Was that a display of your talents?

No, in fact my talents went to people, not to pigment art. The role of artist let me examine all sorts of people without them realizing.

[A cell phone rang at this point.] What an annoying contraption that was. Is it some kind of eavesdropping device?

It was a telephone. Can you see them from Home?

[His agitation was very apparent.] Home? I don't know what you're talking about. I don't pay attention to things like that.

Home was a working men's lodgings in Vienna, at one time, wasn't it? What was the effect on you of living there?

I knew I wanted to go further. I knew I wanted to prove to people the worth I had. I wanted to gather a corps of people who shared my beliefs and, yes, who could do my bidding. I wanted to prove to everyone that I knew the right way to do things and was their superior.

You had help from people selling your paintings, including a Jew. It wasn't all your own work.

I let him have a pittance of what I could provide; they have a mind for finance. It was all part of my plan to get to know people and to find their strengths and weaknesses, and how to use people with them eager to assist me.

How was your relationship with your mother?

I did not care much for her. She was weak. Little more than a *Hausfrau.*

Your mother died of breast cancer when you were eighteen. Was the cancer caused by your attitude?

[Almost shouting, and glaring from left to right.] I don't know what you're talking about!

I think you do know what I am talking about because you have a vision now of what it is. Was her breast cancer caused by your attitude?

If you truly believe that energy can create disease in the body, then, yes, it was. But it was because she put herself in a position to absorb and transmute those energies. I wanted to be rid of her sniveling accusations of my worthlessness. She did not see who I was.

What attracted you to Germany more than Austria?

The Germans knew, they had drive, they had strength within them, they had conviction. The Austrians were weak and idealistic, not thinking very much of the future. They took the position that if you ignore something it will just go away.

When and how did the point of view you now express all start?

I dabbled with it as a youth, but while I was in the military was when it came full bore onto me. When I saw what was going on around me, I saw the different traits people had, and the different ways they reacted to fear, and to being put into life-threatening situations. I realized fear was a valuable tool to use against people.

I'll ask you more about your war experiences in a moment. Let me stay with Vienna and ask how you became attracted to Wagner's operas, and what they meant to you.

I saw them as being very spiritual, as a way to connect with the mystical. At that time I began to study the inner traits of people, what you might call the occult. The music seemed to me to be the key. It carried energy which could transport you to other times and places.

Did it transport you into the presence of the Evil One?

I don't know what you're speaking about.

Satan?

There is not one energy that is Satan.

Did you ever embrace the idea that you wanted to be evil?

No, I wanted to be powerful. I wanted to create a perfect race of people. I wanted to go back to the true Aryan blood that came at the time of the early Celtic religions.

Aryan blood that you did not have in your own veins.

I had some.

And some Jewish blood, I think.

By mistake, yes, but I did not embrace it; I purged it from me.

Women

Were you ever in love with Geli Raubal and Eva Braun?

It depends what you define as Love.

174

What do you define as Love?

I don't know that I truly ever had a love of another human being. I had a love of power. I had a love of being the one in charge, who dictated, who wrote the manuscript. I had a fondness for ladies who could satisfy me, but it was secondary to the thrill that power gave me—to being able to stand up before a group of people and have them hang on my every word, to have them walk down the street and hail me both in my presence and out of my presence.

So you were not in love, in the romantic sense, with either of those two ladies?

No.

Did Geli commit suicide, or did you shoot her?

I shot her. She had begun to become a clinging liability. She talked too much.

Whom did you pay off?

[laughs] For what? I paid many people for many things.

For the declaration of her suicide?

[laughs] I did not have to pay for that.

Why?

Because I convinced the doctors that it was the right answer.

You had a relationship with Eva Braun, who was 19 at the time, when you shot Geli. Was that why you shot her?

One of the reasons. I was tired of her. She was becoming very demanding, and I suspected she might not have been of the blood she said she was.

Or you were.

[very loud and petulant] We're not talking about me.

Did you see women as inferior to men?

Totally.

That's why you told them to stay at home and mind their babies?
Yes. They had to raise a strong stock of youth to follow me.

Did you shoot Eva Braun on the day of your death?
Yes, I shot her and then myself. The reports of my existing after that time were fanciful at best, from some of the more strident followers, and were also brought out by some people who would like to have had an opportunity for earthly revenge.

Anti-Semitism

What caused you to be so strongly opposed to the Jewish people?
They were deceitful, they were sly, they took advantage of people, they weren't to be trusted, they weren't truthful. They hoarded the money and wouldn't let it outside of their race.

What experience made you feel that way, or was it what others had said? There was a lot of anti-Semitism in Austria at the time when you were a young man.
There was one banker to whom I went for help. He laughed me out of his office because I wasn't the "right type." I didn't have the right background to succeed in anything. I saw them all with their smugness and the way they thought they were so much better than everyone else, how they flaunted the fact that they didn't believe in any of the old religions. They were the only ones who were superior.

Was your attitude formed by the fact that you were failing as an artist and were envious of them?
No! Me envious, never! I was clearly their superior.

Was the anti-Semitism you spoke so eloquently about used by you as a ploy to gain popularity, or was it real?
[smiling] It was sort of both. There were certainly feelings of anti-Semitism in me because of what they stood for, but it was a terrific rallying call. It was later that I formulated my ideal of creating the perfect race, and that definitely did not include the Jews.

You were a dark-haired Austrian with a black moustache. Why did the pure Aryan image of a clean shaven German with his blond hair and blue eyes appeal to you? Did you believe somehow in the Wagnerian myth, or was it sexual?

It was not a myth—I believed in the Wagnerian history of the powerful ones, of the race, of what they could do, of the way with their very presence they could bring fear to people.

Did you fancy these blue-eyed, blond-haired young men?

I found them appealing and at times very satisfying.

Were you bi-sexual?

Yes.

Looking at the Jews in particular, and all the other people you put to death, why were you involved—even to the point of planning the architecture of the gas chambers—in the genocide of so many different types of people? Were you afraid of them?

[At this, Toni said that she could feel his fear.] No! Afraid? I wasn't afraid of them; I wanted to prove that I was better than them. They were not pure and, in order to have a pure race, all must be eliminated. That was why those who were mentally and physically deformed and deficient (even my own people) were sterilized or succumbed to mysterious illnesses.

You were opposed then to anyone with a psychological illness?

Yes, and those physically deformed who hurt the eye.

War Service

In World War I, after you had won two Iron Crosses and a Wound Badge, you collapsed hysterically claiming blindness. Your psychiatrist diagnosed you as a "dangerous psychotic." Were you mentally ill, and when did it start?

I was not mentally ill, I just did not want to go back, to see any more at that time.

You mean the psychiatrist made a mistake and you were not a dangerous psychotic?

I was very clever in manipulating them to change my orders.

But you are not going to manipulate my questions, Sir!

[smirking] I don't see that I am trying to manipulate you, Sir!

The history of what you did suggests you were a dangerous psychotic. I'm asking you to deny that that is true.

Of course I deny it. I was a genius. I was creating a utopia, and but for the underlings who went against me, I would have succeeded. We would be ruling the world at this time, if the betrayals had not existed.

Are utopias created with the blood of millions of people who die at some dictator's hand?

Yes, if those people are not fit to be part of the new society. They are the foundation upon which we can rise up and build. They are the fertilizer for our crops.

Adolf, I see you simply as evil, and I wonder when did you make the decision to be evil: was it in the First World War?

I don't perceive myself as evil. I see myself as a dictator, a director. I see myself as the one who could be followed by the right people to create a magnificent empire. If that is evil, what of the other heads of countries, are they evil?

The "other heads of countries" had not put the whole of Europe to the sword, and thrown away the lives of millions, and had grandiose ideas to rule the world. You were unique in that respect.

I was no more unique than Attila the Hun, Alexander the Great, or other earlier leaders who sequestered large land masses off the backs of the people who were living there, and accomplished that by plundering and pillaging.

From Weimar to the Third Reich

Was Dietrich Eckert of the German Workers Party a major influence in your life?

He was a key who turned me in the direction that put me into the limelight, to let people know who I was, and to feel my dynamism, so that they would follow me.

He taught you how to speak in public.

He helped polish me, yes.

What did your ability as an orator mean to you?

Control. Utter obedience.

You became the Nazi Party Führer; what was your main ambition at the time?

To be god-on-Earth to people.

Including to be the master of Europe?

Yes.

When did you forge that ambition?

As people began following me, as people hung on every word, as I felt power radiating out, as I felt the way people reacted to my presence, I knew that this was my destiny.

Did you personally order the Reichstag fire, the "Night of the Long Knives," and "Kristallnacht"?

Indirectly, yes; directly, no.

Who did the ordering of the Reichstag fire?

It was by a committee. We were discussing various ways to turn the common folk against those whom we did not favor.

What about the "Night of the Long Knives"?

It was more of the same. It was all a plot to strengthen the inner core by winnowing the group.

You needed a committee—you couldn't do it on your own?

I was involved with a lot of different things and could not myself go out into the streets and perform it. It had to be done by people who believed in it. It had to be done by people who were ruthless in their handling of the situation. I, also, did not want to be seen by anyone at that time as the Common Soldier who had to get his hands dirty.

Pope Pius XII has been called "Hitler's Pope." How did you view your relationship with him and with the Roman Catholic Church?

I found him to be a little bit of a clown. He was manipulated by a few words if you dangled little carrots in front of him and told him you were going to be a good boy.

Did you believe in God?

I believed in the power that controlled the occult. I believed that the symbols in existence came from an all-powerful source. I believed in, and even searched for, the Ark of the Covenant, because within it was the answer to eternal life. I believed in the power of rituals performed by masses of people.

Did you believe in heaven and hell?

No. That was strictly a religious concept. I believed in reincarnation, and I believed that I was, in fact, fulfilling the destiny that I had begun in another life.

Well, it didn't end up as you wanted. What were your biggest mistakes: Churchill's Britain, the Eastern Front, declaring war on America, or something else?

Getting America involved. That was probably the biggest mistake because they brought in supplies, determination, and forces that I had not anticipated. I had grossly underestimated what they would bring to the table.

Did you declare war on America because of your pact with Japan?

It just seemed the right thing to do at the time. Japan was definitely for it. They wanted the Hawaiian islands. They wanted to be able to extend into another part of the world of a type similar to their own country.

You don't acknowledge a mistake in going, as Napoleon went before you, to the gates of Moscow?
No.

But it resulted in your German army being wiped out in Russia at Stalingrad?
A lot of that had to do with the fact that the leaders in the field did not fulfill their obligations to the Reich.

You are taking the position that you made no mistakes, but other people did?
Yes. They were incapable of fulfilling their obligation; they could not follow the simple directions that I gave to them.

But you did make a mistake in bringing America into the war?
It turned out to be one. It wasn't a mistake at the time. It was a miscalculation.

Dialogue with Hitler's Soul

[Toni remarked, "There is a shift, a definite change in the energy. The energy I am feeling now is of a regular spirit. It is not the force we've just been talking to."]

"The Great Experiment"
The Holocaust survivor Elie Wiesel wrote about you as follows: "I take on this essay with fear and trembling because, although defeated, although dead, this man is frightening." He saw you as "the incarnation of absolute evil." Now that you are back Home, do you see yourself as the incarnation of absolute evil?
I saw the person whose part I was playing at that time as being what a human would consider as "absolute evil." But I am no different from any other soul who plays a part in order to learn

physical lessons and to help others with their lessons. I was selected and agreed with others to be evil incarnate on the planet during the time I was Adolf Hitler.

You say "selected and agreed with others." Can you be more specific?

First, I would clarify that the energy you are speaking to now is not the energy that you have previously spoken to. That was the force of the energy of the human Adolf, as he existed. That was to give you a taste of the energy which is sustained in a personality, or physical being. You now speak with the sum of the soul energy that at one time played the role, if you will, of the person your history knew as Adolf Hitler. When we are at Home before incarnating, we plan what we, ourselves, wish to learn. We then make contracts with numbers of other souls who wish to experience this or that while co-existing with us. My agreement was to be a despicable despot, and theirs to be my victims.

Can you hop in and out of that energy when you have come Home?

Yes. You can go back and can revisit any of your prior existences, parts, plays (whatever you want to call them).

Tell me about the choice that was made and why it was made.

We are in our soul form at Home—that is who you are speaking to now, the soul form of the person who was at one time on the planet as Adolf Hitler. Before entering into that lifetime, I conveyed the idea that something had to change in the consciousness of the planet. We had to put forth to the people the necessity for compassion throughout the planet, because that concept had not been thoroughly engrained in the people and was not disseminated among the masses. We came up with this idea ("we" being myself and millions of other souls) that a way to do it was to show gross inhumanity as measured by what humans themselves perceived as "inhumanity to man." With this, we would develop a wave of compassion throughout the planet, which would provide a framework for compassion from that point on throughout human history. This was then arranged so that I would be a ruthless, immoral, psychotic...

So you admit you were psychotic?

I was in that lifetime psychotic, although I would not have admitted it in that persona. Yes, I did play the psychotic. Who but a psychotic would be so ruthless, so unthinking, uncaring, uncompassionate, and diabolically cruel.

You said that millions of spirits were involved in this decision?

Yes, all of the victims who went to their death in the death camps, and all of my countrymen who chose to be ruthless mini-psychotics, and the ones who worked in the death camps. A perfect example is Mengele and his experiments, and all who volunteered to be his guinea pigs—so it could be written into the patterns of what is just not done to another human being.

Why does the Creator permit such a decision to be made?

What you are doing is taking and creating a god-form outside of humanity. You are creating, as most of the religions do, a man in a white beard and a white robe. But that which is "God" is the energy within all of us. Each of us is a piece of all creation. When we return Home we are rejoined with that larger creative energy. So it is with the consciousness of creation that we agree. There does not have to be a consent by one Person, one Soul—God. It is the agreement of all of the energy, whom some of you call the "God-Force," that sets up a negative pattern so that we may experience all these things, even if what we choose to experience may be totally unthinkable and abhorrent to the majority of people in human form at the time when it occurs. We see it as a lesson or an experience that we wish to feel in human form.

So was this experiment, conducted with the approval of millions of souls, a success?

It was a success for the majority of those who have been in human form since then, those who have been able to feel what went on, those who were able to feel the abject evil, the abject hopelessness of the victims. That has created a compassion for all who might be placed in a situation where things are so totally beyond their control, and unjustified.

But you weren't able to stop Pol Pot, who came later, in his slaughter of innocent people?

That was coming from a different realm. That was in a country with a conflict between different tribes. That was another example. My example as Hitler was more massive, involving many communities and countries. Pol Pot was philosophical rather than driven by a desire for genetic purity.

What was the reason they were so keen to pick you for this job?

[shrugs] I volunteered.

What was the basis for your volunteering?

It was from previous life experiences. I had spent time as a marauder in a number of different lifetimes. Part of it was that I had come up with the concept of a way to create a wave of compassion throughout the entire planet.

You were a marauder in previous lifetimes: are you now going to come up with something bigger and worse?

[laughs] No. I don't have any plans to come back in your linear distant future.

Satan and Hell

Some people will feel a sense of relief at that thought! Now, tell me about Satan.

To talk about Satan is to talk about the duality of energy. Satan was chosen by the Source, by the God-Force, to be the opposite of what could be felt and perceived as the God-Force, which is unconditional love, goodness, kindness, sweetness. Satan was chosen to be the exact opposite of that: to be absolute evil, injustice, hatred. At the point of origin, Satan and the God Force are the same.

And as Adolf, were you and Satan the same?

I had the same energy-direction, if you like, to be the exact opposite not only of everything that was from the God-Force, but also of everything that at the time was conceived as "humanity."

Was Satan your Führer? Did you take orders from him?

No. Satan does not exist as a person, just as the old man with the white beard and the white robe does not exist. There is not one force that is Satan, with red robes and horns and a pitchfork.

The force of evil is a real force?

The opposite of the God Force—but it only exists in the dimension of humanity. It does not exist when you come back Home.

And hell?

Hell does not exist unless you create it for yourself when on the planet. Hell was the death-camps.

But when the spirits rose up from the death camps they were no longer in hell?

They returned to unconditional love.

Permitting Evil

What does the Creator achieve by permitting evil?

To be able to experience and know the greatness of what we are. We cannot truly comprehend unconditional love unless we know what the absence of unconditional love is like.

Why cannot we know what unconditional love is like without having to go through torment?

Because there's nothing to compare. If you were raised in a cave with no light, you would not know what light was, unless you exited the cave.

We'll be getting on to Plato in a moment.

It is Plato. Plato is an analogy for that simple principle of having to know the opposite in order to understand what you are.

Many will want me to ask if you are sorry for what you did.

No, because I did what I agreed to do to those who chose to be victims. In doing that, there was a waveform created which allowed all souls to experience the ultimate in evil. I did not do evil from a soul's purpose to be evil. I did evil for a perception and for a template of evil, so people would know they did not have to experience that again.

You've really answered this already but people ask why you did not go to hell?

Because I left the planet, and once I leave the physical there is no hell.

But you were in hell when you were on Earth?

In my later years, very definitely, and throughout my lifetime. I was in a hell of my own making.

As you look back, what was the most awful thing you did?

From my perspective now, no one thing was more egregious than any other. It could be the death camps because they ended the existence of so many millions; it could be the allowing of medical experiments because of the abject horror entailed; others would say it was the attempt to exterminate an entire people. From my perspective, everything that I performed as Adolf I did because it was to set the template to allow people to experience and, of course, to allow my soul to have these experiences as well.

Evil Today

Whom do you consider the most evil people in the world today?

There are many who are evil by your definition. It depends on where you are on the planet whether you would consider them evil. In different African nations, tribes are trying to wipe out other tribes, and they don't care whether you are an infant or a grandmother; if you are of the wrong tribe, you have to be exterminated. There are those who terrorize with bombings and threats of germ warfare in many, many places upon the planet. There are the dictators; there are drug lords in the South American countries who terrorize the people. These are in pockets. There is nobody with a global outreach now, such as I had, but there are many out there setting a stage for change and transition.

So we haven't learned all the lessons you came to teach?

There are some who ignored the lessons, and therefore must revisit them. There is even a segment that denies an extermination took place. You also see those who turn away, holding their hands over their ears so that they do not have to acknowledge the insanity.

The experiment was not wholly successful?

It was successful for a vast multitude. We cannot make any soul learn what it chooses not to.

But at a huge price!

That, again, is your perspective. What is the huge price? No soul was killed for this lesson. The soul is eternal. Those who went through a physical transition during the time frame now will have a different perspective themselves when they choose to return.

Soul of Adolf Hitler, thank you for being with us.

I hope there is something of a learning experience generated by this time we have spent together.

Commentary

Toni: This dialogue was truly a weird experience. In part one Hitler's persona was very threatening and very dynamic. The energy in the room was fiery. There was such an intensity of malevolence that a person under hypnosis in the next room at the center where we worked was transported back to a prior life as a prison guard in a death camp. That seemed no coincidence to us! It was as if the energy in our office leaked out into the adjoining spaces to control them as well. During the entire first half of the dialogue, Hitler was hugely restless, with his paranoia seeping out all over. He was constantly challenging, trying to manipulate—yet at the same time there was an underlying fearfulness permeating everything. The voice I heard was sharp, caustic, and accusatory. It was anything but a comfortable encounter.

In part two, the soul energy appeared—a humble, serene, compassionate, older soul, seeking to explain the unexplainable to our disbelieving human sensitivities. It appeared to sense that what it had to say were concepts that the majority of souls in human form would never accept, and that was all right. It quietly conveyed the way things are organized in the universe. This had a soothing effect upon me, and I found myself empathizing with the soul's desire to have humanity reach a modicum of understanding of the universal laws of energy. Coming from the place of unconditional love, where judgment is absent and there is only observation and evaluation, the soul presented a picture of how its life as Adolf Hitler clearly fits the plan of the God-Force, of which all souls, including this one, are an integral part.

Peter: The first whale we had to swallow was the amazing ability of Mister Nasty to transform into Mister Nice at the blink of an eye. Toni had been told by the Masters that this would happen, but the shock was palpable as the fiery pace of the dictator suddenly gave way to the relaxed energy, easy manner, and Platonism of the soul.

We reviewed controversial historical points about Adolf Hitler: He knew that he had Jewish blood. He shot both Geli and Eva. He was bi-sexual. He did not survive his reported suicide.

While my verbal confrontation with the Dictator makes for interesting reading, what stands out is the account by Hitler's soul (which I anticipate many readers will consider bizarre) that millions of souls at Home had agreed together to sanction and support what I will call "The Great Experiment." This involved sending a powerful soul to Earth with the intention and means to become a bloody tyrant who would order millions of innocent people to die, often in intensely cruel ways, and seduce millions to give him their utter obedience and their lives in following his satanic schemes.

This unthinkable cruelty is explained as providing a stimulus to the task of increasing compassion among the peoples of the world. So, as a result, the experience of this *spirit-designed*, unmitigated blood-letting would be written into the history books with the intent that the attitude of people worldwide would be changed for the better. Having faced the horror of evil incarnate, humanity would more fully and deeply understand the nature of peace, goodness, and love.

I am reminded of Wilfred Owen, a World War I poet. Thinking about his native Britain in one of his poems, Owen makes a sharp rejoinder to the Latin essayist Horace who wrote, "*It is sweet and right to die for one's country.*" Owen called the thought an "*old lie.*" Unnumbered human horrors tumbled into my mind at the soul's shocking statement. I challenged the soul with Pol Pot's subsequent slaughter of Cambodian millions, but I could just as easily have chosen Hitler's contemporary, the Soviet butcher Stalin, or Saddam Hussein of Iraq, or the Contras in Nicaragua, or the juntas in Argentina, Chile, Burma, North Korea, Sudan, Rwanda, and on and on. Were *all* these atrocities spirit-designed attempts to "increase compassion" among the people of planet Earth? Surely not! Then to ensure the job was well done, would there even be worse—total annihilation—to follow?

In our dialogue, the soul said it had personally conceived this Grand Experiment, volunteering for service as the tyrant, possessing the qualifying experience of having been a "marauder" in several past lives. I asked myself, from my purely human perspective, whether millions of spirits might even have been *duped* into dying in agony, so that a duplicitous spirit might taste real blood? I dared to wonder whether it had been even possible that at Home—the fair realm of unconditional love—a little under-cover evil might go a very long way.

We are all bound to ask also whether the Grand Experiment might be said to have sadly failed to produce a more compassionate world. Such a judgment might be an obvious perspective of people alive today—cannot our friends at Home see the potential danger? Are they incapable of asking whether a cosmic mistake might have been made? Or, with our world appearing to be heading towards total melt-down these days, is the God-Force trying desperate measures to capture the attention of a dulled and apathetic, chaos-weary humanity?

As this point in our reading, should we find ourselves holding this negative viewpoint, there appears to be no easy answer. One thing is quite clear, however, that a careful reading of other dialogues in this book reveals that this soul was telling us no lie. Rather, it seems that we have stumbled in this discourse with Hitler on the stark and grisly fullness of the spirit-world's self-training method.

We may just be able to understand that facing up to violence by an angry father or abandonment by a lustful spouse can be lessons which souls have willingly agreed to in advance. but that is only the tip of a huge iceberg. As the passengers aboard *The Titanic* found to their cost, most of an iceberg lies under water. The Grand Experiment with Hitler may be a gigantic challenge to our humanity, but we are forced to admit that it does truly seem to be broadly in line with the universal policy of incarnation that we all come to Earth to learn *tough* lessons.

Difficulty in trying to understand the spirit world raises the question, "whose perspective is it?" We may feel souls at Home are living in a kind of ivory tower, but we really do not know the detail of all they are trying to accomplish. Other souls interviewed for this book have spoken somberly of a coming time of total crisis on planet Earth, from which only a select group of human beings may emerge unscathed. Always they speak of the eternal soul's indestructibility, and hence give an escape clause for any and every bloodthirsty episode—Hitler, Stalin, Pol Pot, or whoever is being used by the spirit community. While our limited human perspective portrays bad things happening to good people as inexplicable, unmitigated disasters, our guides back at Home see disasters as important and necessary spiritual experiences, to which all of the eternal souls involved have both always and willingly agreed in advance, drawing as their guide on the wisdom of the omniscient and loving God-Force, of which we are a part.

Maybe the Grand Experiment of Hitler the Great Dictator did not totally achieve its goal—maybe it did. Maybe what we see as a failure to produce world-wide compassion was not a total failure after all, but a necessary progressive spiritual lesson in negativity. And there are so many other negativities: HIV/AIDS, malnutrition and starvation, and alcohol and drug addiction, for example, all of which cause great misery and lead to squalid, painful deaths. The spirits assure us that, when viewed with eternal eyes, facing such horrors is the right way to grow in understanding, at the deepest level, of the eternal opposite—unconditional love, the very essence of the Source. We have to learn to put aside forever the old human concept of a capricious, judgmental divinity. The spirits tell us pain and suffering is *essential* to our spiritual growth and maturity, and that (always with freedom of choice) we have accepted *in advance* all such dire tests that life will bring us.

Fortunately, whatever nightmares may follow, it will not be for Adolf Hitler's soul to accomplish again. He is not coming back—we have his word for it! We are left with the thought, however, that if someone worse than Hitler is to come, or if some trigger-happy or merely stupid leader—an American, Russian, Iranian, or North Korean were to start a nuclear conflagration, the folks back Home will soothingly reassure us, as we make our tearful, blood-stained return through the veil of death, that our eternal souls (all of which will have survived intact) had already made the choice to be afflicted. So perhaps—because, while we were enjoying the lush fields of Elysium, we agreed to all these horrible things in advance—we only have ourselves to blame.

At least, if we are going to blame ourselves for agreeing to suffer we won't be able to blame an old man with a white beard, sitting on a cloud in heaven dispensing divine judgment. Nor can we accuse a nasty man with horns and a tail, carrying a pitchfork. Neither exists, the spirits tell us, even though their story likes to linger here on Earth. The crumb of consolation is that there is no heaven or hell back Home, but only in mental states here on our planet. And there is always the eternal Home in the realm of unconditional love, where the soul of Adolf Hitler quietly reflects on everything that was done in that life. Enough said!

"In the beginning Hinduism was a practice of compassion,
but a person cannot be compassionate towards another
unless they believe in equality ... that all people are the same."

Mohandas K. Gandhi

1869-1948

Biographical Note

Mohandas Karamchand Gandhi was born in 1869 in Porbandar, Gujarat, India, the son of Karamchand Gandhi, Chief Minister of Porbandar, and Putlibai, his fourth wife. In an arranged marriage, when both parties were aged 13, he was married to Kasturba Makharji. Both families were of the Vasihya, business caste, well-educated, affluent, and devout Hindus. Kasturba bore him four sons during their life-long marriage.

Gandhi enrolled in the law school of University College, London, to train for the bar in order to be well qualified for high office in Gujarat. He sought in dress and manners to become like a perfect English gentleman, with the exception of adhering to his family's tradition of vegetarianism. While in London he was elected to the Board of the Vegetarian Society, members of which encouraged him to read the Hindu scriptures and those of other religions, which he had formerly ignored.

Returning home as a barrister, Gandhi had little success in getting work locally, and in 1893 took a short-term job at an Indian law firm in Natal, South Africa. Here the shy young lawyer encountered fierce racial discrimination. He was ejected from a train, despite having a valid ticket, and suffered other hardships because of his Indian heritage, but he remained steadfast, even refusing to obey an order from a judge to remove his turban in

193

court. His sympathy for the long-suffering Indian and Black populations was deepened by such experiences. Implored by friends to help them defeat legislation in Natal to deny Indians the vote, he stayed on in the country, creating the Natal Indian Congress in 1894, and organizing a widespread campaign to air Indian peoples' grievances, mainly against their British rulers. Returning from a trip home to bring his wife and children to South Africa, he was physically attacked by a mob but refused on principle to sue his assailants.

In 1906 an act was passed in the Transvaal parliament enforcing Indian registration. In response, Gandhi encouraged the Indian population to adopt a policy of non-violent "Truth-Force" (*satyagraha*), involving a seven-year struggle in which thousands of Indians, including Gandhi himself, were punished and imprisoned, and some were even killed. As a result, however, the tide of public opinion in Britain and South Africa rose against the brutal tactics of the South African government, and a compromise settlement was achieved.

This non-violent doctrine of *satyagraha* was developed and used by Gandhi for the rest of his life. It was based on the Hindu *Bhagavad Gita*, Jesus' teaching in *The Sermon on the Mount*, books by Tolstoy and Thoreau, and the peace-loving traditions of his own devout Hindu family and the Jain community. At first, he was patriotic to the British cause. Just as in South Africa, on his return to India in 1915 he urged Indians to support Britain in World War I as a sign of their citizenship in its Empire. But his desire to embrace Indian traditions (later symbolized by his simple clothing and spinning wheel), and the influence of his mentor, G. K. Gokale, moved him permanently away from the imperial culture of Britain toward the dawn of the Congress Party's movement for Indian independence.

Gandhi, now famous in India for his leadership in South Africa, became recognized as a spiritual leader who was also involved in such social issues as discrimination against the Untouchables and the role of Indian women. He carefully assessed his dietary needs, embraced silence on one day a week, studied philosophy and world religions, helped to organize ashrams, and wrote about his search for truth and belief in non-violence. Famine in Bihar in 1918 sparked his activity against British rule. There, the poor farmers of Kheda and Champaran had been organized to strike non-violently against their oppressive, mostly British, landlords. For fomenting this trouble, Gandhi was jailed. A huge protest rally outside the prison resulted in the release of all who had been taken prisoner, and a negotiated settlement between the farmers and their British landlords. Now his spirituality, his success at Champaran, and his revitalizing the Indian National Congress caused admirers to call him "Mahatma" (Great Soul) and "Bapu" (Father).

In 1919, the Jallianwala Bagh massacre of over 1,000 men, women, and childen in an unlawful but peaceful protest at Amritsar, caused widespread rioting by Indians. Gandhi, now fully convinced that Indian physical and cultural independence (*swaraj*) must be advanced, persuaded the Congress Party to condemn all violence. The Indian National Congress' outreach was expanded to a refusal to pay taxes, and to a boycott of all British goods and services (the Mahatma's famed spinning wheel's symbolizing the drive to use homespun cloth). The campaign started well, but when violence broke out in 1922, Gandhi called a halt. He was arrested and imprisoned for six years for sedition. He was released two years later following an appendix operation.

During his absence, relations worsened between party leaders and between the party's Hindu and Moslem factions. Gandhi fasted for three weeks to heal the rift, with little success. He retreated to be occupied with the Untouchable issue and many other social problems. In 1928 he persuaded the Indian National Congress to petition the British government to grant Dominion status to India or face another non-violent swaraj campaign.

In 1930, Gandhi launched a new campaign against the British tax on salt. Marching with thousands for 250 miles to the sea to extract salt, his challenge of the British monopoly was met with violence and the imprisonment of 60,000 followers. Then the British gave way and invited Gandhi to a conference in London, but it failed to address the independence issue. He was put in prison again, where in 1932 he began a fast over the British treatment of the Untouchables' vote, which resulted in some improvements. Then he began a three-week fast against British oppression. After negotiations, the Congress party accepted a revised political role, but Gandhi resigned to retain his independence from political factions.

When World War II broke out in 1939 the British involved India in the war without consulting the Indian representatives. They all resigned, and Gandhi, despite Hindu-Moslem quarrelling and pro-British Indians' objections, created the "Quit India" movement of civil disobedience in 1942, to win Indian independence in the shortest possible time. The result in this "Do or Die" campaign was the arrest of hundreds of thousands of protestors, and many thousands were killed or injured. Gandhi was imprisoned for two years, during which time first his son Mahadev and then his wife Kasturba both died unexpectedly. He himself was ill and was released by the British lest he die in prison and provoke a widespread Indian backlash. Although the Quit India movement was finally suppressed, the new Labour Party government in Britain agreed to give India independence with Dominion status.

Although he opposed British proposals to partition India into religious groups, Gandhi ultimately accepted that the alternative would provoke civil war. He turned away from politics and devoted his time to healing the divisions between the main religious factions. In January 1948, in order to stop sectarian violence and the enforced deportation of Moslems to Pakistan, he began a fast to death. At the very last moment, when his death appeared to be imminent, the factions reached a peace agreement and his fast was broken. Twelve days later in Delhi, when walking to a prayer meeting, Mohandas Karamchand (Mahatma) Gandhi was assassinated by a disgruntled Hindu. He was 78 years of age.

The Dialogue

Vegetarianism

Your mother was very concerned that your early passion to act like an English gentleman should not lead you to abandon vegetarianism. Did your joining the Vegetarian Society in London represent the beginning of your return to the family culture?

I never really left the family culture, but I did experience each culture that I visited so that I might more fully understand what people obtained from their cultures. I never completely abandoned vegetarianism but I was a little more inquisitive when I was out of India. I did not particularly like the feel that animal flesh gave to my body. I could sense the violence of the death of the animal, and felt an aggression that was very unlike me.

Your mother made a vow with a Jain priest that you should not stop being a vegetarian.

Mother believed very intensely that animals had souls, which in fact, some do, but not all. It was for this reason that if we were to partake of the flesh of an animal we would be robbing them of part of their energetic being. Potentially this could contaminate our own purity. Mother's vow alone did not influence me; I had to follow my own urgings.

Does the spirit community at Home, where you are now, have any special perspective on vegetarianism, especially about the issue of animal souls?

From time to time some souls have chosen to spend a life as an animal in order to feel and experience the particular peculiarities of animals, like becoming a leopard to know what strength and solitariness are like, and to experience being an animal of prey. But just as no soul remains in the human body after death, so no soul remains in the animal after death, if there is a soul in that animal. Very few animals have human-interchange souls.

In respect of the human body, there are some human beings who have an actual need to consume animal protein in order to maintain their energy to the extent needed. This has a lot to do with the climate they are in, and what amount of physical exertion they undertake. Even if a human were to kill and consume an animal which had a human-interchange soul in it, the soul would depart before the point of consumption and, in a lot of cases, before the death of the animal. There is no karma (as my people of the time would have said) in consuming animals. Karma is only an experience you undertake, not something negative that you carry with you from lifetime to lifetime. The experiences that "carry over," often referred to as Karma, are merely soul lessons that we do not complete in one lifetime and must continue to fruition in the next.

So the death of the animal is not a big issue because the animal's spirit is out of the body, either before death or before consumption, so that the spirit is not harmed.
Or that it has no soul at all—no human-interchange soul.

Does it have a non-human soul about which we should know?
It has a spark of life that comes from the pool of divinity, from whence human souls are detatched, but it is a minor little spark that exists just for the lifetime of the animal. It does not of itself have a consciousness. It is energetic, similar to the energy which creates the world around us. Everything that we see while we are in human form is composed of energy—from tables, to plants, to mountains, to some of the animals.

How do we know that we are the right people to consume animal flesh? Will it be instinctive?
We have an instinct, a craving, reaching the point of fatigue because the proper nutrients are not in the body.

Someone who is a vegetarian probably shouldn't be eating meat; will they know that instinctively?
If they have made a conscious choice about it, or it has been the way they were brought up—the belief systems of their fathers

becoming their belief systems. If their bodies function well without animal protein, then there is no need to consume it.

What about the agricultural argument that raising meat is a very inefficient way of growing food?

In modern times that is a very plausible argument; however, most meat eaters came from the time when animals far outnumbered humans, who had a wild source which supplied them with all the energy they needed. Because of the life of the hunter-gatherers back in the time of plentiful animals, now some people need both the flesh and the fat in order to sustain the degree of physical labor they undertake.

You seem to be talking in a way Mahatma Gandhi would not express himself.

I am talking from the position of having an overall view now of what happens in and with the human machine. When I was in the form of Mahatma Gandhi, the belief systems I accepted were that animal flesh created a vibration within the human body which interfered with a full connection with the the soul's energy. That was because it diverted the vibrations of the connection to spirit and to higher self by dulling them down, so to speak, by the physical need to divert energy to convert the meat into nutrients for the body. My belief system also included the concept that all animals had a soul and that in the process of reincarnation we might be consuming a distant relative. [smiles]

That is not a position you would hold strongly today?

No, I would not.

Arising from what you have said, is there a way in which people may identify a human-interchange soul in a particular animal?

If one is sensitive to the presence of spirits, in the presence of an animal one would know by looking into its eyes.

Celibacy

You wrote as if you were consumed by your sexuality in the early years with Kasturba, yet you chose a vow of celibacy-within-marriage when you and she were only 36. Why?

I was at that time aware that my life might not be as long as the average life because of the enemies I had created with the programs I was implementing, and by my preaching. I did not want Kasturba to raise a large family without my support. I believed at that time that any excess use of energy, for anything other than for one's calling, dulled the intensity one might achieve and project.

So it wasn't your asceticism or religious fervor? This was a very practical decision?

To me it was a very practical decision; it was not based upon any other belief that was introduced to me.

Did Kasturba go along with that or did you push her into it?

She so loved me that she wanted my every wish to be fulfilled.

Were you successful in remaining celibate?

[lengthy pause] To my shame, because of what I purported to be, I did have an urge and a need during times of trouble on two occasions.

Thank you for your honesty—we appreciate that. I have heard that, as a very old man, you had two nieces lie with you in bed. Was this a test of your ability to remain celibate?

I truly enjoyed my nieces and they lay in bed with me not for any sexual purpose but for story-telling. We would lie there and I would tell them of my adventures and my travels, and of the excitement I had for what was happening in my world.

That must have been nice for all of you.

It was very, very pleasant. It was at a time when I enjoyed the energy of youth.

Indian Progress

You championed women's equality with men, especially regarding the cruel practices related to widows. We still learn of malpractices regarding bridal dowries. How do you view women's position in Indian society now?

To the shame of the country it hasn't changed as much as it should have. In the larger cities, in mainstream society, women have obtained many of the rights that I fought for. In the smaller villages they are still under the same yoke as they were centuries ago. They are still treated as property. It saddens me to see the country has not changed more than it has.

How far do you see India progressing in relation to the elimination of the caste system?

Again there have been major steps in larger areas, in particular the cosmopolitan areas. In the outlying areas and in the hill country there has been very little change. The Untouchables still are not able to get work, or allowed in places with others after dark, or able to own property of their own. The very fabric of some sections of the country is based upon a division of peoples and human rights.

You said, "The only people on Earth who do not see Christ and his teachings as nonviolent are Christians." Does the same problem relate to Hindus and the issue of human equality?

Yes.

What is wrong with Hinduism that it produces this result?

I should modify my "yes" a little. It has been the practice within the Hindu religion because of policies and interpretations which have been utilized as *The Word* for centuries. Because a person follows the Hindu religion it does not mean that they are going to accept these elements which go against the equality of each soul—those created in the image and likeness of the Creator. It has become very comfortable for the hierarchy within some Hindu sects to grant themselves additional power by adhering to the old principles.

So the belief system is all right, but the practice of the religion is flawed?

It is the application of what they construe as laws and not merely historical retelling.

What truth should the religious be looking for in Hinduism that they are missing?

In the beginning Hinduism was a practice of compassion, but a person cannot be compassionate towards another unless they believe in equality, unless they believe that all people are the same. That belief would take away great power from some of the hierarchy and they are not willing to release that power. Over the centuries the restraints imposed by inequality have also empowered those in the middle because they are not as good as the hierarchy, yet they do have somebody they can control, just as the hierarchy controls all. What can be done is to imagine yourself in the place of the lowliest of those in human form, and from that position ask, "How would I choose to be treated if this were my station in life?"

Hinduism retains a belief in reincarnation, doesn't it?

It does, but its interpretation by some Hindus is that, if you are not a good person, as they interpret it, you will come back as some plague: as a locust, or as a cockroach.

Not as a Harijan (Untouchable)?

Not as a Harijan, no. Something that they conceive as even lower than a Harijan.

The partition of India in 1948 was a great disappointment for you. How do you view the relationship between Hindus and Moslems in the Indian sub-continent today?

It is a very tentative one, at times very volatile, constantly in transition. They have not resolved basic issues. They each still preach that they are the one and only, and if you have two kings you cannot have an agreement.

Personal Achievements

You taught yourself to spin and to weave and wear khadi [hand-woven cloth]. You maintained silence one day a week. You ate very simply, and walked a lot for exercise. What did you actually achieve by these practices?

I was able to go into very deep meditative states wherein I was able to communicate not only with my higher self but with many of the Ascended Masters I now walk among. These simple practices put me back at the beginning of human experience, with all the connectedness to the Earth and the earth energies, which allowed me to obtain knowledge and feeling for all that has occurred on this planet.

What do you count as your greatest lifetime achievements and disappointments?

My greatest disappointment was that I was not heard by as many as I should have been. Even those who were aware of what I said failed to become sensitive to my feelings. So they ignored what I was trying to teach them, and where I was trying to go. I feel that the greatest achievement was my example, letting people know that a single person—with the simplest and most basic experiences on the planet—can change the mindset at first of a few people, then of a larger group, then of whole sections of a country, and that sincerity and love can be used to overcome antagonism and hatred.

Pacifism and Satyagraha

In World War II you wrote to the British, "I would like you to lay down the arms you have as being useless for saving you or humanity." But you encouraged Indians in both World Wars to support the British cause. This sounds like a mixed message; was it?

I did not feel it was a mixed message. I thought that the way to change anything was by peaceful measures, not through putting lead into another's body. I encouraged the Indian people to see that if they could emulate the strength of a nation, such as Great Britain, they would gain the power and strength to take control of themselves, the ability to rule as a government, the ability to organize and to put into practice the various rules, regulations, and laws needed to control and govern a people. In our contact with the British who were in the country at that time, we found that they saw our discipline, they saw our dedication, they saw our firm belief in the purpose of what was going on. All of this could be used within our own country to take care of our own needs, and to change the policies which were suppressing so many of our plans.

Yet you told the British to lay down their arms?

As I said, I believed that peaceful means could be used to bring about the changes. My thoughts on violence were always the same—that it served no purpose. I did not at any time attempt to say that what they were doing was wrong, just the way they were doing it was wrong—that they should attempt to go into negotiations instead of going in with force, taking whatever was left of the resistance and trying to beat them into submission.

Truth-force, Satyagraha, has been used very effectively by others, such as Dr. Martin Luther King, Jr. Your attempt in 1922 at using non-violence ended in bloodshed. How do you see that this problem can be avoided in future conflicts?

I don't believe that it can be totally avoided when you get into a situation where fear reaches a high level, and when the person who has that fear has their finger on a trigger or their hand around a club. If you go into such a situation and are faced by a group which is outnumbered, and which believes that your force and intent in getting them to come over to your side is to suppress them in any way you can, there is going to be bloodshed. But if we are able to convince the peoples of the world to listen to each other, and not to pre-determine (in most cases erroneously) what we believe the other side is going to do, then we may achieve a small modicum of peace with change.

You wrote, "There are many causes that I am prepared to die for, but no causes that I am prepared to kill for." Can a modern country reasonably expect to abandon its weapons of mass destruction and still remain safe in the present world?

That's a very difficult question to answer for the very simple reason that it depends who has access to the triggers. If calm, sane people are the only ones who have access to the weapons—people who will communicate with each other—then there is the possibility that all will be able to dispense with weapons and there would be no threat. But in this world, with all of the underground terrorist organizations, and some governments who wish to become more powerful and be recognized as a force (the latest one is China, and Pakistan is going in that direction), they are too happy and overjoyed with their new toys to ever give them up. If they perceive that they might be able to step into and take advantage of a weakness elsewhere, then there will be no peace. It would be foolhardy of those who are being conscientious with their trigger fingers to lay the weapons aside while they have a weapon pointed at them.

You sound more like Winston Churchill than Mahatma Gandhi!

I have spent time with him. [laughs] We enjoy some lively debates.

Truth and Religion

You said, "The Truth is far more powerful than any weapon of mass destruction." You also said, "Truth is God." What is your view of Truth now?

Truth is an impartial, dispassionate telling of the deepest feelings of an individual. Truth is laying bare all the aspects surrounding an issue, so that none can take advantage by hiding behind a gauze sheet, a steel barricade, or any other kind of shield or covering. It is a vulnerability that bares your chest to tell another that "I am what I say," and "I am who I say," and "I will not do anything that you cannot observe me capable of at this moment."   That said, it must be recognized that on Earth a person's truth changes as his perception changes. If your truth at this moment is that you wish no harm to another, and then that other kills your dearly beloved, your truth may become "an eye

205

for an eye." Your truth changes from pacifism to revenge. But if you are fully in touch with your soul, you know that your dearly beloved had an agreement to transition as they did, so that they might learn a lesson. Further that they also were allowing you, and those close to them, to experience desired lessons. In this situation, the soul does not judge but remains in unconditional love and thanks both souls for contributing to their spiritual growth.

So you no longer think Truth is to be considered the equivalent of the word "God"?
To be able to undertake any of the things I have just discussed, one must be totally in tune with one's soul. The soul has the fragment, the part of God which connects all of us. So it is an exercise of the energy of God which allows this to occur.

The recent earthquake in Kashmir reminds me of one in Bihar in 1934. You told your friend Rabindranath Tagore that it was a result of people's sin—and he replied that the cause was a natural one, not a moral one. Now that you know the answer, which of you was right?
Actually, we both were. Mother Earth is a living, breathing force. When we abuse her, when we do not take care of her, she takes her revenge. Sin is not the state of evil but rather the state of ignorance. What we do to injure the Earth has repercussions.

If I remember correctly, the event was one where high-caste Hindus were not allowing low castes or Untouchables into a temple. Does that qualify as abuse of Mother Earth?
It's only on the fringes of qualifying, because it is what little people do to the planet, not their squabbles, that Mother Earth responds to. She responds to the placement of buildings upon her plates, that have to shift for comfort from time to time. She responds to the diminution of her resources without regard to the overall land mass.

The Kashmir earthquake?

206

That was Mother Earth's decision how she chose to respond to things going on with the destruction and almost obliteration of some of her plants and foliage. This is very definitely likely to continue because Mother Earth is awakening more and more to the potential damage that can be done to her by the human population.

You said, "I am a Christian, a Muslim, a Buddhist, and a Jew." Clearly you drew wisdom from each source, but criticized the failings of religious organizations. Do you recommend we should seek the best amalgam of faiths, or is it now time to move away from the various historic formulations of belief to something new?

Each religion I studied and immersed myself in had very good wisdom and instruction on how we should live a human life. One must allow those precepts which resonate to become a part of one, and allow that energy to be internalized in one's very being, and make a personal decision what parts to live by. There is a shift going on and people are beginning to feel their souls, who they are and what they are. They are getting in touch with the divinity inside each of them. Organized religions that were established for the purpose of controlling people no longer have the force to affect those who are becoming (in the most general terms) free-thinkers. They are accepting only what feels right for them. So, to answer your question, organized religions are no longer needed for a person to go and give away the power of who they are to an imam, a rabbi, a priest, or a cleric.

Is the search by an individual for meaning irrespective of the tradition in which that person has been raised?

Correct. The search for meaning comes from within, not from without. It comes from meditating and getting in touch with one's higher self, and going into one's soul to know who one is, because in the process of reincarnation, the majority of souls have sampled of all the religions (as I did in my earthly lifetime) to find their truth and what is reality to them. It is all inside of them, if they take time to go deep enough to reconnect with the wisdom which is inside of them. The knowledge we can gain from reading the scriptures and the history of the religions does nothing for us if we cannot feel the wisdom behind that knowledge. We cannot apply the knowledge unless we know how that comes from wisdom, and that wisdom is what we have partaken of and learned through our previous existences.

Is there hope for a rapprochment between Islam and Christianity in the world?
There is always a hope.

How would it be achieved?
By listening, by sharing, by entering into an arena naked but for the energy, the knowledge, and the wisdom. Then having a fair exchange to appreciate the others' feelings, why they accept what they accept, and by having an open mind and an open soul to sample the others' beliefs. It will be found that within these religions, disparate as people would have us believe, more than fifty percent is identical, and the other fifty percent is merely the way they apply the various beliefs, and the way the control systems of the religion were established at the point of origin. This was done in order to help the people who could not read or write the particular religious tenets. Religion relied upon oral passage of knowledge and wisdom. It is like taking two embryos which came from different sources, and placing them in a dish together, and bombarding them with the energy of the two religious traditions, and allowing them to absorb whatever will make them grow and understand themselves better.

Life Purpose
You have spoken of having many lifetimes. Have you learned in the course of those lifetimes what is the purpose of human life?
The purpose of human life is to learn as much as we can about ourselves and (as they say up here) to learn lessons. At Home we're in an ocean, an all-consuming environment of unconditional love. Here we do not feel hate, despair, or any emotions or feelings that would be considered negative. It is only by assuming a human body that we are able to experience these things, yet in

each one of these seemingly negative experiences of our lessons, our appreciation and wisdom concerning the unconditional love from which we come grows, magnifies, and intensifies. So we come to Earth to partake of the lessons we may learn there in order that we may grow in appreciation of what we have at Home and who we are as a soul, a piece of the all-encompassing divinity.

We're told this by several witnesses but, as an example, let me take that massacre in 1919 of over one thousand innocent people in Amritsar; I presume you will say that they agreed in advance to suffer that massacre?
Yes.

Why is it necessary for that type of experience to take place in order to achieve an understanding of absolute love. Could it not be done in some other form?
It can be done in many, many forms, but those particular souls wished to have the experience of knowing what was going to happen to their physical bodies before it happened—to be able to feel that intense fear of what was about to occur.

How do feelings of intense fear help you feel the nature of unconditional love?
Unconditional love has no sensation to it. It is a state of being in which everything is perfect. In order to understand what everything perfect is like, you must know what less-than-perfect is.

Can't you do it by putting souls into a box and bombarding them with all the experiences they need, and then letting them go Home? Why must you have massacre after massacre and carnage after carnage?
The actual incident of the carnage does not only affect the viewers and the victims. That energy goes out, affecting first the earthly relatives of the people involved and their physical friends. It then goes a step further to the next village, the next town, the next metropolis. It has a wave effect, creating an intensification of

feelings, whether of relief, joy, sorrow, or fear, allowing people to experience, within a small compass, a plethora of emotions which they cannot get at Home.

Some estimates indicate that sixty million people died under Stalin. Why is it necessary for so many to be slaughtered? Hasn't each of those sixty million souls been through some kind of experience like this before?
Not all, but the majority of them have.

Why do it time after time? Don't we learn the lesson?
There's an Earth-consciousness that's being built—not a Mother-Earth-consciousness, but the energetic consciousness within the dimensional plane where humans live. It helps to shape and to form people's beliefs—what is in and out of their comfort zone, what makes them compassionate or ruthless. The numbers which occur in any of these carnages give an idea of the power that the energy ripple will have, and over what expanse in time and space it will occur.

Gandhiji, your remarks are most helpful. Thank you for coming.
It has been very pleasurable. I hope I have been able to clear up some thoughts for you. My soul acknowledges your soul.

Commentary

Toni: Gandhi had a tender forcefulness to him. It was like talking with a very pious person who was also a well-briefed attorney wanting to get his point across. The overall feeling was of a pervasive and peaceful loving-kindness. There was an understatement in his words, directing our thinking to dwell on a path of wisdom and then letting us draw our own conclusions. Gandhi's demeanor did not change regardless of whether the questioning was personal, political, or ideological. It was refreshing to observe such matter-of-fact calmness displayed in this way. He conveyed a reverence for the whole human experience a soul chooses to undertake. I felt a sense of wanting to spend more time with this enlightened soul for pointers on my own soul's journey.

Peter: This was a peaceful but challenging encounter. There was little of the energetic feeling that Gandhi gave out which was Earthbound. His observations reflected the dimension of the spirit world, and he said little that evoked his human self. His sorrow at the lack of progress in India over the status of women, the Untouchables, and the India-Pakistan relationship showed he was fully in touch with events. The modest, sensitive recollection of his personal celibacy was breathtakingly honest. He truly and fully demonstrated this attitude in the quiet moment when he explained (less theologically than I expected) his current view of the nature of truth.

The main surprise for us was his altered view of being a meat-eater versus being a vegetarian. Here the strong, religiously doctrinal approach of his earthly life was abandoned, though he did manage to give solace to practicing vegetarians: "If their bodies function well without animal protein, then there is no need to consume it." He did not fully answer the hard question of whether Earth can sustain meat production, but he cleared a lot of guilt out of the way for hesitant meat eaters.

What came next was surprising when he talked about human/animal interchangeable souls. He carefully explained how souls never die because they always get out of their dying body at the right time. To avoid a long-running subsequent argument among readers, I had to strap myself down in the question-master's chair to refrain from asking the question about pets: "Does Muffy, Fido, or Beauty have a soul?" Animal lovers will just have to spend a bit more time gazing into the eyes of their animal companions, wondering if they really can see them wink knowingly!

In raising the issue of the spirit world's deliberate use of severe negative global experiences as lessons for incarnating souls, I mentioned Joseph Stalin (whose cruelty is still generally under-rated in the West), but not Adolf Hitler. There was significance in the fact that, this time, it was the non-violent, freedom-loving Gandhi, and not the soul of a former bloodthirsty dictator who was giving the same explanation. This helped somewhat, though some may still find the chilling message hard to grasp from the human vantage point.

What was most enlightening, and will be heartening for those people who practice meditation in all its forms, was the thought that the chosen simplicity of Gandhi's life in his ashram enabled him to delve so deeply and successfully into the inner reaches of his soul. Observers have commented, about his extensive ashram and the large entourage following him everywhere, that the Mahatma's poverty cost people a great deal of money to maintain. But his point about meditation was compellingly made. Winston Churchill may have once bombastically slandered Gandhi as a "half-naked fakir," but it felt entirely believable that this spiritually advanced being was a mature, humane, though solitary individual, simply clothed in his own homespun cloth and armed only with the naked truth. He was able over many years of trial and suffering to persuade his often sharply divided people successfully to stand up for truth and justice and, by his astonishing equally practical and spiritual leadership, to bring the haughty British Empire to its knees.

"Man was not made from a monkey. Man was made from a series
of cellular matters infused into an early bundle of cells with
the characteristics that created homo sapiens."

Charles Darwin
1809-1882

Biographical Note

Charles Robert Darwin was born in 1809 in Shrewsbury, England,
the fifth of six children of a wealthy doctor. His mother, Susannah,
died when he was eight. After boarding school, he enrolled at
Edinburgh University to study medicine. There, being an
inveterate collector, he became interested in nature, enjoying
beachcombing for sea slugs on the Firth of Forth, reading his
grandfather Erasmus' theories about evolution by acquired
characteristics, and developing a keen interest in geology, in the
classification of plants, and in the life of marine animals.

Finally his disappointed father removed him from his
neglected medical studies at Edinburgh and sent him to
Cambridge University to study theology and to enter the safety of
the Anglican priesthood. Again, Darwin preferred nature (this
time beetles) to his prescribed theological course. He studied
natural history, mathematics, and theology with Professor
Henslow. Professor Sedgwick taught him geology, and also the
theory of "Divine Design" in William Paley's book *Natural
Theology* (1802), wherein Paley contended that design in nature
could be seen to prove the existence of God. In 1831, Henslow
successfully recommended him to the captain of a survey ship,
The Beagle, as a gentleman's companion for the two-year voyage.

As it turned out, charting the South American coastline actually took five years to accomplish.

During this, his only trip abroad, Darwin spent the majority of his time studying the geological features of the area, documenting and collecting fossils and specimens of the local flora and fauna in great quantity. He developed his concepts of interaction between species and furthered his anthropological studies of the region. He noted fossilized remains of very large mammals in South America, but it was in the Galapagos Islands where he witnessed marked differences in birds and mammals on various islands, suggesting that they had an ability to alter their characteristics. Thus the seeds were set for his theory of natural selection, which came in 1838. Some of his work was later detailed in the five-volume publication he edited and partly wrote, *Zoology of the Voyage of H.M.S. Beagle*.

Starting in 1833 during the voyage, and with greater frequency from 1837, Darwin was laid low from a variety of illnesses. These appeared to have been caused by insect bites, though they repeatedly affected him in stressful situations. In 1839 Darwin married his first cousin Emma Wedgwood, despite her continuing concern about both his ill health and his inflammatory scientific views. She bore him ten children. Three died young, and several suffered physical weakness, which he feared might be due to the ill effects of the parents' close sanguinity.

A truly productive phase of Darwin's thinking followed his return home to London (1836-42). He had become aware that what he wanted to say as a transmutationist ran dangerously against the accepted norms of contemporary Christian thinking, and that his findings would be considered criminally heretical to many people in the church. When his ten-year-old daughter, Annie, died from typhoid in 1851, his fears that his own illness might be hereditary were revived. After she died, Darwin seemingly lost all faith in the goodness of God. He explained his natural selection theory to friends, but they were unenthusiastic, and insisted that a divine element was needed in the process of natural selection. Afraid of publishing an incomplete theory, and sensing that his ideas about evolution, which were highly controversial on religious grounds, might even be dismissed as worthless by his scientific peers, he stalled publication. In the event, the appearance of his book *On the Origin of Species by Means of Natural Selection* (1859) was spurred on by a letter from the Malay archipelago, written to him by Alfred Russel Wallace, a naturalist and specimen collector.

His worst fears proved unjustified. Strong acceptance by the scientific community of his voluminous work in several fields followed, leading him to more research and to his most controversial book, *The Descent of Man, and Selection in Relation to Sex* (1871). Following the publication of *The Origin of Species*, other scientists had begun to discuss human evolution openly. Now Darwin, despite failing health, advanced his theory of sexual selection to explain racial and cultural differences. Then came his last major book, on the evolution of human psychology, *The Expression of the Emotions in Man and Animals* (1872).

Though scientists honored his many and wide-ranging achievements, his books generated stormy debates in public, which continue to this day, principally on the role of God in nature, and the reliability of the Judeo-Christian scriptural account of creation.

Although Darwin did not personally defend his theories in public, he eagerly read about the continuing debates, and he spoke about his research to working-men's clubs, to Cambridge students, and to scientific meetings. Repeatedly battling debilitating illness, he struggled on with his work for another decade. His final experiments resulted in books on plants, and the effect earth worms have on soil levels.

Charles Darwin reportedly embraced Christianity again, shortly before his death at home in 1882, aged 73 years of age.

The Dialogue

Early Days

[Toni: "I'm getting the impression of a very dignified person wearing one of those starched collars and a dark business suit."]

Talk about putting on the mantle of Charles Darwin! It doesn't have to grip you by the throat.
 [Darwin laughs]

Thank you for coming, Charles. My first question is: which had the most influence on you, the dedication of your father and grandfather to scientific discipline, or the social and religious radicalism of free-thinkers and Unitarians, including your brother Erasmus and your Wedgwood relatives?
 I was my own person. I took and sampled all of the regimens that were there. There were some people who were so immersed in their own way of thinking and doing that they were unable to visualize or synthesize anything beyond their own wanderings of thought. They never saw the possibilities and opportunities from the interesting and vital aspects of other people's output and divergences. When you put your heart into it, there was an intermingling of science with the spiritual, feeling the spirit and being able to be truthful to yourself. For me, science was not a solid, black-and-white, immovable object. It had influences from outside that helped it to produce the formulations and the foundations which had already been established, and which could be proven, and reproven, and reproven.
 When I was with my father, and we were immersed in mathematics and scientific experiments, it was like being in a fairyland where everything fell into place. You knew exactly what was going to happen, and you could depend upon a result that would be repeatable for you. To me that was a fairyland because there were no outside influences you really had to worry about. When I say "fairyland" I think some will misunderstand, because it's normally thought to be something within the realm of

imagination. To me a fairyland was having everything in its perfect place, and everything in its perfect position.

With my brother's involvement with spirit and soul, and the interaction of the Creator with what would then be considered plain sterile science, I could see a little bit of an interchange. Now I know that there is a lot of interchange between the two. I dabbled on the edges of what is now called quantum physics. The spirit and the intention of Man had to do with how things evolved and interacted, and the final result. My father and grandfather would never have understood. They sometimes thought the trails of consciousness that I entered upon were fantasy, because they were outside of the strict steel structure that they knew as science.

So they pulled you out of Edinburgh and sent you to Cambridge?

Yes. They wanted me to become more directed. They wanted to take the experimentation and the fantasy out of me until I could have the steel rod up the spine. They hoped the process would mature me. It was also done as a little bit of punishment for my wasting my time on what they considered to be idle, non-productive thoughts.

In fact, at Edinburgh, you studied sea creatures and read your grandfather Erasmus Darwin's theories about evolution by acquired characteristics. In Cambridge you immersed yourself in geology and botany. Was his theory or your meticulous observations the more important in your developing thought?

I think that they both had about the same import. Were it not for his pioneering experiments and writings I would not have had the gentle push to be as thorough, to try to find all the elements that were creating changes in an organism. My own work showed me that there could be patterns, but there also could be some spontaneity in what occurred. And from my brother's beliefs, I realized that such spontaneity could be the hand of a Creator. I now know it is, in fact, the hand of the Creator, through the action of the creation itself.

The Beagle

Then came your voyage on The Beagle. *Looking at it now, can you identify the highlights for you of the trip?*

The biggest emotion that I felt was of being free from the constraints of organized academia. I could feel what was going on with life. I wasn't confined to little tanks and containers of specimens but could see them in their natural habitat. I could see and feel the interaction of the planetary influences, of Earth and the planets upon the waters and through the waters upon the organisms within the seas. It was a time for me of turning the dry ink upon the paper of my books into a flowing stream of answers and of consciousness.

One of those papers was about geology. On the voyage you read Charles Lyell's Principles of Geology. *Then you witnessed an earthquake in Chile and found fossils high in the Andes. Those experiences must have been pretty vital to your development.*

Each of them made me feel like a small boy in a toy store or candy shop. I was able to make discoveries, work with samples, and get explanations for myself of the movement of the earth, the history of the vegetation and organisms of the planet—with Lyell's "bible" in my hand leading me into directions of study. Then I was able to expand upon what I was seeing, and to have some direction to follow up to the next step, which was to put all of it together. It was a time of tremendous growth for me, because it made personal that which had been impersonal. It raised so many questions about development of organisms that, to me, had not previously been adequately explained.

Did the concept of design in nature prove the existence of God?

Yes, it did, because I could see that there was no coincidence in the way changes occurred, that there was a pattern behind the changes, and the pattern had an intelligence because each and every change was something that made the organism more adaptive, more able to utilize the platform upon which it was existing.

William Paley's "Divine Design"?

Yes, but much deeper into patterns of adaptation than had been explored and examined.

Anthropology must have been important as well, because you met tribes of people from Tierra del Fuego and elsewhere.

Yes, and I was able to see first hand that Man, as I had always been exposed to him, came in many varieties, depending upon the pathway that the lineage had embarked upon. There were so many similarities but at the same time tremendous differences, all of which gave me a feeling that there was a reason and a pattern for each direction that had been taken. Man definitely changed to fit into his surroundings.

Was it the anthropology of the indigenous people, or were the flora and fauna, fossils, extinct mammals, animals of the Galapagos Islands, finches, mockingbirds, and tortoises, more important?

Well, the people were not as easy to explain, dissect, and go back generations as were the flora and the fauna. With those you could go back through centuries, both by what was preserved in fossil form, and by what was preserved in layering. You were able to see at a glance many, many generations and the changes that occurred between them. With Man it was not as easy. With animals, depending upon their lifespan, it was easy to see what accommodations they had made to better acclimate themselves to their surroundings.

So you had to use a process of deduction in relation to Man?

Yes, more so than anything else. With the exception of the sea creatures that lived for hundreds of years.

One of whom—your tortoise—is still alive at 176 years of age?

Yes. [see note at end of chapter]

Do you happen to know whether the tortoise was yours? The one that's claimed to be yours?

219

It is. I think he would chafe at being called "mine." He pre- and post-existed my frail human form.

I'm sure it will be very relieved to find that out.
[laughs]

During the voyage you began to have repeated bouts of illness which assailed you for the rest of your life. From your current understanding, can you tell if it was insect bites, Meniere's Disease, or stress-related?
It was a combination of things. I was over-using the vessel that I employed, my body. I would get so occupied with doing something that for periods of time I would totally neglect myself and whatever needs I had. When I had the misfortune of, say, meeting a mosquito that carried something, I would ignore what was happening with my body until I was bedridden. I was not conscious of having any control whatsoever over the energy within my body. I just sacrificed it as a platform and remained in my mind because I wished to understand what was going on, what had happened, and what would happen in the future. I was completely divorced from the sense of the energy coming from my soul, which was telling me to take care of myself and to become conscious of what was going on around me.

So you wouldn't want to hear a medical description of you, but rather an energetic description?
Well, there were many people at that time who were diagnosing different things, different symptoms. I now know it was energetic. My consciousness at that time was that it was just something that was afflicting me, preventing me from being able to accomplish everything I chose to do.

The Theory of Evolution
You held off publishing The Origin of Species *for a while for fear of the opposition it would generate, of which your wife, Emma, was especially fearful. You wrote to Alfred Wallace, "I should avoid the whole subject as it is so surrounded with prejudices," but historians*

suggest that news of his intent to publish similar views provided the catalyst you needed. Was Wallace a catalyst?

I felt betrayed by Wallace. I felt he was being very manipulative in trying to eliminate any competition that I might provide for him. For a time I thought he was assisting me as a counselor, as a guide, but then he appeared to be adopting some of the findings of my research as his own, yet not with the same conclusions. There was a lot of fear, especially from my wife and close friends, that my book would be condemned, and that the condemnation of those in power would wreak havoc on our existence. At the time of writing the book, I felt more deeply for family and friends than while I was on my travels gathering the information that would become the grist of the book. I did not want any harm to come to anyone, but once faced with the impression that information would be presented that I could definitely prove to be false, I threw all caution to the winds and stepped into the fray.

The Origin of Species *and your companion book,* The Descent of Man, *had related theories. Let me take some of them in turn and ask if you still hold that view or if you have modified it. The first theory is that evolution happens with change that is very gradual or happens over thousands of years.*

I can no longer hold with that. If it is needed evolution can occur in a single generation. Changes produced by climate, for example, may occur that quickly. At the time, there were some scientific claims that change can be effected virtually instantaneously, but, although I had an inkling that they could be true, I didn't fully accept them. The concept of rapid change would have been so different from what people had thought or expected to hear, that I did not want my book to read like a fairytale. I wanted the idea to be something that they could accept gradually, knowing that others would come after me who would be able to document changes that occurred in a much shorter period of time. In saying that it could take thousands of years, I removed the influence of the soul from the equation. But in fact, the soul does have the ability of manifesting its own reality and it can create changes instantaneous-ly when needed. I now know that with divine power the soul is able to effect change; it does not take thousands of years.

Are we talking about human evolution in that shorter period of time or about natural evolution as a whole?
Well, what applies to natural evolution also applies to human evolution.

So, in either, change can come very rapidly.
It can come very rapidly; it can occur in the seed, it can occur as the shoot is opening, it can occur with the root structure, it can occur in any one of a number of points as the plant comes up, and as it adapts to variances in climatic conditions.

But you were talking about the influence of the soul upon this. Are you suggesting that a seed has a soul?
A seed has a consciousness within the energy framework of the planet. The planet Earth itself is a living, breathing soul and, to a smaller degree, so are the plants. Human beings have an awareness whereby they can consciously effect changes within themselves with their powers of divine manifestation. The plant does not have that much awareness. It has to rely upon the energy of the whole to know what is needed.

The second theory you advanced was that natural selection was the primary mechanism for evolution. Do you still hold the same view?
I know now that that is a piece of the puzzle wherein those who do not want to take the time or the trouble to evolve themselves drop by the wayside. So the natural process of selection is done by each individual, depending upon the amount of initiative and drive it wishes to put into its existence. If individuals do not choose to go forward, if they choose to remain only where they are, then, because they will not fit the conditions that are coming before them, they will drop out. So yes, and no, I agree with what I had said, but for different reasons.

222

The third theory is that millions of the Earth's species today originated in a single original life form changing through the branching process of specialization.

[laughs] I wanted to believe that everything was just one point of energy moving forward. And I had part of it right and part of it wrong. The fact that all energy originates from one point is true because the Creator is the source of all energy. But once a piece is broken off the Creator, say to become a dog, that does not mean that the dog can become a plant. Once it is started on a line, it remains on that line. It does not break off to join something else— so the progeny of the dog cannot join with acorns on a tree to produce a barking bush.

We're doubled up with laughter here. I think the immediate evolution of the channeler into a laughing hyena is at hand!

Well, I thought we were getting a bit too serious. When in human form I was very serious about everything I did. And I now see that it was arrogance to feel that I was the only one who was discovering the pathways of things. But I do know that oak trees and elm trees remain oak trees and elm trees. Dogs and trees don't mix. So, to go along with the idea that things change, a tree can change from being a huge tree into a dwarf tree to accommodate the soil, nutrients, and moisture, and it will still be from the same source. A human can change from the average height that they had centuries ago (in the neighborhood of four and a half feet), to your seven-and-a-half-foot basketball players, based upon the nutrition that is put into them, the exercise that is given to them. And yet if there is no need for height within that same family, another one can still be of average height. So there is a division—a possibility to evolve based on what is needed.

We have an urgent need for politicians to be humble. Is that an evolutionary possibility?

[laughs] Certainly not!

Do you still hold to your fourth theory, which is that the survival of each organism occurs randomly within the species, and depends on that organism's ability to adapt to its environment?

Well, on a purely physical basis that is what happens. If a single organism, a plant, or a combination of organisms, such as Man, does not acclimate to the surroundings, they will not survive. If an individual man goes from a city into the country, he has to learn to fend for himself. He is not going to have everything delivered to his door if he is in the wilderness. He is going to have to find water; he is going to have to find a source of heat if it is getting cold. If he does not, he will starve and freeze. So in that case, he does have to acclimate. If a plant that is used to growing in semi-temperate conditions goes into cold conditions but does not acclimate its cell structure so that it is less affected by the temperature, it will wither and die. A single-celled organism needs nutrients; if it needs only one nutrient and that nutrient is not available, and it does not change to be able to get nourishment from other substances, it will cease to exist. So anything within the realm of development, when forced to be present in conditions it is not used to, must change or perish.

In the spiritual aspect, if a soul does not choose to recognize itself as a soul, it will not have the awareness, the awakening, and the opportunity to make use of the tools it has learned in other lifetimes. Therefore, it will not grow until it returns to the whole body of the spirits at Home. So on every plane we see there must be adaptation in order to flourish. It may appear as if this is random, but it has a lot to do with the intention of the organism.

The last theory is that mankind evolved from earlier animals by sexual selection. Selection is the cause of the development of human mental abilities and of social organization.

No, I do not still hold with that. I hold that, if we take humans, there were some early humans who were very much like primates because, as they were adapting, they needed to change and go through some of the same evolutionary changes as the apes did. But to say that ape became man is to take out all the variables of intention, manifestation, and influence that the soul has within the organism. It would be possible that if an ape-type structure came down with a soul that had been a man at another time, or in another existence, and wished to morph itself into some of the same characteristics and abilities it had as a man, it could do that.

That's a possibility, but is it a reality? Has it ever happened?
In one or two isolated instances, not as a whole species. It depends solely upon the maturation of the individual soul.

If I'm hearing you correctly, to copy a popular phrase, man was not made from a monkey?
Correct! Man was not made from a monkey.

I'm imagining that "Darwin's bulldog," Thomas Huxley, is turning in his grave as you say that. Maybe he knows better?
He knows better now. We frequently have what we call human debates, where we play ourselves at the time we had the beliefs that we expounded. It's quite an entertaining experience.

Creator and Evolution
What was humankind made from?
Man was made from a series of cellular matters infused into an early bundle of cells with the characteristics that created homo sapiens. When it came to create the experiment, which was on planet Earth, there was a discussion of various ways to do it. It was perceived that it had to be done with a biological form, which could contain parts of the whole, capable of experiencing everything that was <u>not</u> of the unconditional love of the Creator.

Was this one specific act of creation?
It was one specific act of creation but not within the blink of an eye. It was over millions of years of the existence of this planet—which is still the blink of an eye to us.

So God formed man out of the dust of the Earth, then made a woman from a man out of his rib?

If you take the strict biblical interpretation and you wish to find something in antiquity that explains it—yes. If you wish to take it from a scientific viewpoint, DNA (which determines what happens), can be transplanted into any living thing and have it change that living thing into a copy of itself. That is the basis now of cloning as it has been experimented with. The way that the soul chose to come into existence was that it wanted to have a shell or a vehicle of certain consistency, and with certain abilities, and therefore it saw that the right DNA was placed into a living organism.

Did your view of evolution imply creation without divine intervention? Was that meant to contradict the story of creation in Genesis? Firstly, how did you feel then?

How I felt then was that I was trying to grasp with my human mind how I sensed things had occurred, without consciously considering any concept that had come before from the scientific or the religious communities. It was something that was personal to me, and was the way I felt about what had occurred. It took into account various aspects of everything that was there: science, religion, metaphysics, and what we now know as quantum physics, and put that into what the religious groups would say "explained" creation. I did not make a conscious decision to include or exclude divine intervention.

How do you feel now?

Now I know that it's not that complex. Now I know that we are all energy. With the energy we can portray ourselves as we desire. If we choose our human form to grow another set of arms, we have that ability—that would be the most evolutionary state. To me it would be the manifestation of the soul's intention. Each soul, which is a piece of the Creator, is imbued with divine powers. These allow that soul to create what it chooses or needs.

When you're talking about the intention of the soul, would you go along with the concept of "intelligent design" by the Creator?

226

Intelligent design is of each individual piece of the Creator, not of the Creator as a whole. The Creator as a whole is the point of origin of all energy. As various pieces of energy broke off, which we came to call souls, each one of them had the same abilities as the whole. They didn't have to go back and get permission to create new or different aspects of themselves.

We're talking in human terms about intelligent design of the human being.

In human terms, yes, each individual soul does have a conscious design for its own physicality.

So in the debate that is raging at the moment about intelligent design versus evolution, where do you stand?

I take the position that both have it right and both have it wrong. One cannot be totally divorced from the other. The way evolutionary design occurs is by making incremental steps (the evolutionary process) to get the finished product or the end result that you are seeking. So, it cannot be either one or the other. It is because of the one that the other is effected. Because of the conscious design, the change in the organism occurs.

And what about the creation story in the Bible?

The creation story in the Bible served numerous purposes—it was not a scientific book. It was written to show the power of the Creator in creating souls, and in that form it ceased to demonstrate scientific fact or how we can document it as a scientific fact. It then became a guideline for the religious organizations to teach the power of the Creator, and to teach about sin, which, of course, does not actually exist outside of Earth's dimension.

Much has been written about your agnosticism (Huxley's word) or atheism, and whether it developed during your voyage or when your daughter Annie died, and whether you made a deathbed return to Christianity. Can you put the historical record straight, please?

I fought throughout my lifetime with the strict principles of a religion, that things had to be exactly the way *they* said and no other. Then, when I had gone out and found proof and examples and evidence of things that flew in the face of Christian belief, I went through a period of time where I was an atheist. That was because I fought against one source being the Creator, a single source being responsible for everything, when I could see that different organisms determined things for themselves or acclimated themselves. Then I became what I called an agnostic because I realized there was a superior intelligence, a superior planning behind what had occurred. My return, as you might say, to Christianity was for a number of reasons. It was as much for those who remained behind as it was to attempt to give some credence to what I had done, if people were to read my work as a guide, the way they read the Bible.

So did you have a "deathbed conversion," or was it more planned than that?

It was more planned than that. Toward the end, I was becoming quite aware that I was spending more and more time out of my body, talking with the angels and my guides about how the work I had done was always going to be a point of contention on the planet. I thought that if I had the appearance of being a "good Christian" at the end, people would look at it as a possibility and not just throw my work away as having no credence.

In actual fact, most people thought that it was just a tale?

That was inevitable because my ideas went against all the tenets of most Christians.

Evolution and Society
You suggested that human character and mental characteristics are inherited the same way as physical traits. Do you share Herbert Spencer's view that society would improve naturally over time by the evolution of the superior race of human beings?

Definitely not. That idea totally disregards the fact that each soul chooses the lessons that it is going to learn. It chooses the parents that will make it easier to facilitate the lessons it seeks to learn. If one seeks to experience mental illness, what better way to experience it than within a "hive," one might say, of mentally ill people. It is still a matter of selection made by each soul before incarnation, choosing what lessons it wishes to learn.

So some may become superior, but others won't?

Superiority is just a lesson. It belongs to one who has experienced a totally judgmental lifetime. What is superior? If you say "superior," you must say "inferior." And if you say "inferior," then whoever chooses to do a job which is not graded by society to be important (and I cannot think of a word more important than "important") will be rejected somehow. A person such as Mother Theresa, who was not important, who was not wealthy, provided so much for the Earth, because her soul's journey was to touch people and by example to show how you can assist other souls. She knew that a lot of those souls were experiencing poverty and devastation so they could learn lessons, so she did not take and drag all of them out of those situations, but gave them energy. She witnessed what they were doing to give credence and importance to the lessons they were learning. That is what is important—not a superior race as graded by other men, or by other minds.

Evolution of the Soul

Do souls evolve at Home? If so, please describe the process?

Once they are back Home, there is a period of debriefing, as the military say, to find out what lessons have been learned. Sometimes it is at this debriefing that a soul who has not understood, while in human form, the lesson that they learned on the planet, gets the "Aha!" moment, when they realize why they experienced what they had experienced. And if it is truly felt, they can then go back and feel it again very quickly, or not even have to do it at all, because they go from just having the knowledge of the experience to having the wisdom that goes with that experience.

You're starting half-way into the development of the soul.

229

Oh, you wanted to go back to the beginning. I thought you wanted to know about their growth back Home after returning from the Earth. A new soul is born by being broken off from the Creator.

How does that happen?

Simply by the intent of the Creator. The energy that a new soul has is all of the knowledge of all of the souls that exist, but it does not have the wisdom that can be gleaned from the knowledge, because it has not had any experience. It is like a person who watches a rugby match, who knows all the rules and regulations, knows all about the scoring, and may even know all the dirty tricks, yet until they engage in the game, they will not feel it and it will not become a part of them. So the new soul at Home has the knowledge, but not the wisdom of what it feels like, what it can accomplish, how the soul can expand within that knowledge.

So the soul learns by coming down to Earth.

The important part of the equation is Earth, because it's the physical experience which turns the knowledge into wisdom. It is like apprentices first using their studies in a practical manner.

Why do we need that physical experience?

All souls at Home live in the energy of unconditional love, where everything, as you would say, is perfect. If you are blind and you never see the light, you do not know how fantastic colors are. If you are deaf and never hear, you do not know the magnificence of an orchestration. You can theoretically understand it, but you have to experience it for it to become a part of you. And when you experience those colors, the vibration of those colors can resonate in your body, and that orchestration can make your entire body tingle. That is the earth experience. Knowledge of all the pieces of music that create an orchestration, or all the patterns of vibration upon a machine that a color creates, does not let you experience them. It does not give you the wisdom of what it does to a soul, how much it fulfills and enriches a soul.

Such things can only be experienced outside of perfection, because in perfection there isn't anything that can be better or less than perfect. On the Earth, we start with nothing, and we layer on all of our experiences, so that we can become knowledgeable and wise—not just knowing about the writings and the vibrations, but having the wisdom of how they feel. That feeling resonates with the energy in our soul and becomes a part of it, enriching it and allowing it to grow and expand with all of the tremendous ability that we call wisdom. It's like a canvas that is painted. The soul is a plain piece of canvas when it begins, and with every piece of color it experiences, a dab is added to the canvas. With every vibration of music it feels, the paint can be moved around into patterns. And just as the canvas becomes enriched, the soul becomes enriched with the human experience.

What happens to the soul when its search for wisdom is complete? Is there a final goal?

The final goal is to exist in unconditional love at all times with the wisdom of all of the experiences that can be had of what is not unconditional love, with all of the wisdom a physical manifestation can allow by way of interaction, rather than just a commingling. While there is humanity still in existence, that allows the mature soul also to act as guide, but to have a front-row seat in the greatest play that has ever been staged.

Do you remain an individual, not re-attaching to the Creator?

We are all creators, whether in unconditional love or as an individual soul within a human body.

To achieve individuality we broke off from the original Source...

In order to have experiences that are different. It is like a team playing a sport, such as in the Soccer World Cup. In order to succeed each individual player learns to play in different positions on the playing field. Their success is as a team, not as individuals. The winners' experience was of the team but also of each of the individual parts that they played as a team member. They never lose the experiences they have had that are individual, but they have no wisdom of that. They have the knowledge, say from a goal keeper's perspective if they are a winger, but they cannot have the total knowledge of everything that is there. So their individuality encompasses all the things they individually experienced that they have the wisdom of, plus all of the things they gained the knowledge of from being part of the whole.

What was the Creator's purpose in creating individuality?

Unconditional love is magnificent—it is that for which all souls strive. But you still don't know how good that magnificence is until you know what it is like to be without it.

Was individuality needed so that the Creator would know the magnificence of unconditional love?

So all would know.

Charles Darwin, thank you for answering our questions.

I hope that it has been helpful, and I know it will be controversial.

Commentary

Toni: Charles Darwin was very relaxed and matter-of-fact about his evolutionary theories. He used humor to defuse our consternation at the way things are in the world. I felt him smiling all the way through the dialogue, which is typical of the enlightened souls back Home. They try to instill in us that the whole human experience is like a game. You can either fight it and learn the hard way, or sit back and enjoy it; then you will easily assimilate the wisdom you have come to obtain. He was very easy to channel, with a lot of energy, and he came through clear and strong. We both had trouble re-establishing decorum after his "barking bush" joke. I channeled his words, there was a pause, then their meaning hit me. I cracked up and laughed for a long time before recovering and being able to clear my mind to resume channeling.

Peter: Darwin's present opinions march in lockstep with the Masters' teaching, but in an unexpected reversal, those who are most likely to cheer his remarks are not evolutionists but evangelical Christians committed to the current, embattled, Bible-centered dogma of intelligent design. We must be careful not to miss that the subtleties of his remarks are aimed at drawing the two viewpoints together, but they certainly do not entirely commit him to present formulations of the opposing human viewpoints.

Intelligent design is an ancient idea going back in essence to Heraclitus, Aristotle, Cicero, and Aquinas, as well as to William Paley, whose "watchmaker analogy" (contained in his book *Natural Theology*) was read by Darwin at Cambridge. In response, Darwin now sees the divine Creator setting the goals and providing the means for nature's own processes of evolution to take place. This he described as a continuous evolution that really does work according to natural laws—though it does not connect *homo sapiens* with the apes as had been thought by some.

Darwin made out that he was something of a dreamer when young, holding fantastical imaginings far outside of his father's and grandfather's strict scientific viewpoint. Such an awareness of the broader picture represented for him the integration of their rational enquiry with his brother's spiritual insights. This was a constant feature of our discussion. In no respect did he reject science and the scientific method, but for science to be truthful he asserted that it must be seen within the wider cosmic context.

We felt Darwin's soul appeared less encumbered by his physical persona than was the case of many Leaders, although he was rather apologetic about having allowed his soul energy to be sapped, giving way to ill health, and he seemed to suggest that his disease had a mosquito-borne origin. He also confirmed the judgment of many historians that the faulty scientific ambitions of his contemporary Wallace was the catalyst for his eventual publication of *The Origin of Species*, and that he had held back from publishing the book before then because of the hostile public attitude of the time.

The theories expressed in his two books *The Origin of Species* and *The Descent of Man* were somewhat modified by him in our dialogue. His straightforward contradiction of the belief, sometimes attributed to him, that Man evolved from monkeys was quite logical. He said it was remotely possible for such an evolution to take place, but it was not an historical fact, save for minor exceptions. Man, he said, had been made from a series of cellular matters infused into an early bundle of cells with the characteristics that created homo sapiens. The divine design behind this creation was to establish on planet Earth a sentient being who could be capable of experiencing everything that was other than the unconditional love of the Creator.

With this modified point of view, Darwin showed us two things clearly: first, the persistent narrowness of human viewpoints on both sides of the debate about evolution and, second, the way in which the view from Home, radically new as it is to our human minds, is both substantive and logical. Everything is measured in energetic terms. The Creator is the totality of universal energy but is also expressed in the creative energy of every individual soul. So the process of evolution is controlled by the energy of a divine Designer, but the actual method by which it works is the progression of energetic changes wrought by the action of individual energies, both in nature and in humankind. Thus there is a macro aspect to evolution which may be described theologically, and a micro aspect which may be described scientifically. The scientific promise in the fairyland of his youthful first adventures is fulfilled by his present ability to suggest a new relationship between the competing dogmas of science and religion. He said that he even attempted to demonstrate that rapprochement personally, which he confirmed as the reason for his rumored final re-entry into the Christian church.

Darwin's view of the role of the soul as being on a wisdom-gathering mission was clearly expressed. We visualized each soul fragment of the Source entering into a unique experiential life cycle involving frequent trips from Home to Earth and back again. We understood that by this process, and by the personal review made back Home of the lessons of each human life, the soul gains increasing wisdom. The final goal for each soul is that as it continues to live in unconditional love it will do so with the wisdom gained from all its human experience of that which was <u>not</u> unconditional love. The soul is not just an individual but also part of the Source itself. So its contribution as an individual is to contribute a deepened understanding of life to the whole. In this way the wisdom and apprehension of unconditional love is fully assured for all souls, as the Creator intended.

Darwin's Tortoise

The tortoise, Harriet, died on June 23, 2006, in the Australia Zoo, near Brisbane, at the reputed age of 176 years. Our conversation with Darwin took place one month before her death. For the first 124 years of her life, the tortoise was thought to be male and was named "Harry" when Darwin purchased it. This may explain his mistaken use of the male pronoun in referring to her.

Talking with Leaders of the Past

"Synchronicity is a term that is much richer than in my use of it.
It talks of the soul's power as being able to bring to itself,
even from a subconscious level, those things
that it needs to experience."

Carl Gustav Jung
1875-1961

Biographical Note

Carl Gustav Jung was born in 1875 in Kesswil, Switzerland, the
son of a highly educated Swiss clergyman. He learned from an
early age to love ancient languages and literature and to study
ancient religions. He was also deeply interested in metaphysics. In
1894 he began a course of medical studies at Basel University,
and finally specialized in psychiatric medicine. At Zurich he
worked in a hospital with schizophrenic patients, starting a
private practice, developing a theory of word associations, and
teaching in the university.

In 1903 he married Emma Rauschenbach, heiress to a Swiss
watch fortune. She bore him five children, despite his many
affairs, and their marriage lasted until her death in 1955.

In 1906 he published *The Psychology of Dementia Praecox*,
which was read by Sigmund Freud and led the two psychiatrists
to forge a professional friendship that lasted for six years.
Eventually they parted company on theoretical grounds,
especially because of their various interpretations of the nature of
the unconscious. Jung saw it positively as a fount of personal and
cultural creativity, while Freud emphasized its negative role as a
storehouse for repressed emotions. When Jung published
Psychology of the Unconscious (1912) he broke from Freud, who

now clearly considered his younger colleague a threat to his own authority as an analyst.

Parting company with Freud brought Jung a sense of freedom, although he was adversely affected by hysteria, brought on by the horror of World War I. Absent from the practice of psychology for six years, Jung developed his own systematic theories as "analytical psychology," in which he classified personalities into introvert and extravert types, according to the individual's attitude to the external world. These theories were published in *Psychological Types* (1921). After the war Jung traveled widely to North Africa, India, and the United States. He studied worldwide wisdom traditions, Western spirituality, esoteric writings, and alchemy. He regarded these elements, rather than experimental science, critical in understanding the nature of the unconscious mind and the human soul.

In developing his unique approach to psychology, Jung advanced the concept of the "archetype." Archetypes have no form of their own, but work together as an organizing principle of the things we see or do, and appear to be present at all times as the substance of a human collective unconscious. This system of archetypes does not develop individually but is inherited. Thus, while remembered childhood events come from individual memory, the remembrance of past lives emanates from the memory bank of the collective unconscious. Lack of harmony between the consciousness of an individual and the greater archetypal world results in psychological neurosis. Jung's therapeutic work, based on this theory, focused on psychological growth and the development of mature responses.

Among his many contributions to analytical psychology were Jung's concepts of "the animus and the anima" (parts of the psyche), "the shadow" (unconscious aspects of the self), and "synchronicity." Synchronicity was the concept that two events might occur which were linked neither causally (working deterministically through cause and effect) nor teleologically (being created freely by people's idea of the future's meaning and purpose), yet were meaningfully related and were much more than mere coincidences. He believed that synchronous events were indications of how we are connected through the collective unconscious.

Throughout his career, in addition to university lectures, including Yale's Terry Lectures *Psychology and Religion* (1938), he wrote numerous popular articles and books which established his world-wide reputation. In his later years he studied differing personality issues among tribal people, and other subjects including UFOs. Delving into the occult, he had his own familiar spirit, Philemon. He invented the term "New Age." Carl Gustav Jung died in 1961 at Kuessnacht on Lake Lucerne, Switzerland, at 86 years of age.

The Dialogue

World War II

Thank you for coming, Carl. Before discussing two of your theories, may we give you an opportunity to review two items in the historical record of your life: First, in the 1930s you are said to have supported the Nazis, favoring a study of Hitler's Mein Kampf, *and presiding over the Nazi-supported International General Medical Society for Psychotherapy. Later, in 1943, during World War II, you supported efforts against Germany made by the U.S. Office of Strategic Services. How do you now evaluate your actions?*

My actions were those of opportunism. I wished to be a pure researcher into the ailments of the mind, so I took a position which allowed me the most fertile ground within which to operate. Allying myself originally with the Nazis gave me *carte blanche* to work. They were very concerned with any possible mental deficiencies that they might be able to diagnose in people as part of their winnowing process to form the perfect race. It was a terrific aquarium within which to observe and experiment, but then I saw the reason for it. Truly I had not known, going in, why they wanted my research and input. I had thought it was to treat people, not to exterminate them. Once I discovered that, I ran as fast as possible, while still protecting myself from annihilation, to a position (in Germany) where I might be able to help combat the horror that I saw going on. I did not want to be a part of it; I did not want my work, my research, to be used as an excuse for any of the horrendous things they were doing.

Then you came to America to put things right?
And to take my work and let it be known throughout the world as a way to help people, not as an excuse to get rid of them.

Do you feel that this experience has hindered your reputation?
[laughs] I have no concern for my reputation.

Somewhat connected with this is my second question: Unsolved issues remain concerning your alleged racial theories of the unconscious. Can you shed light on that accusation?
It was all for nothing. I tried to explain what the society was saying were trends, at the time of my human existence. One of the theories at the time was that the body which you inhabited made you different from other people. It mainly had to do with environment and opportunities, and not with the color of the skin or the DNA makeup of a person. Of course, I now know and remember that we spirits have all been all races; in one incarnation you might be a totally illiterate bushman of Africa with connection to the Earth, and in the next lifetime you might be a genius of European origin who has very weak human genes with a predisposition towards medical problems. It makes no difference to what the soul chooses to experience.

You were not in favor of eugenics—you didn't get that far, did you?
No, I did not get that far. It was out there as an hypothesis and I worked on it. I thought I might get more opportunity to prove or disprove those theories through the Nazi Party, but I found that their only goal was to obtain even a tiny scintilla of evidence that could justify their extermination of someone that they thought to be less than they.

The Collective Unconscious

You said, "The collective unconscious doesn't owe its existence to individual experience, and is not a personal acquisition. The collective unconscious has never been in consciousness but comes to us through heredity." How much do you hold to your ideas of the collective unconscious now? Is this a collective unconscious of the race or is it a database held at Home?

It is the energy all of us have created. It is the wisdom from all of the knowledge gained by all of the various facets of the energy of creation. It comes from experiences wherever and to whomever they occurred. It is accessible to each soul if they have the maturity to know how, at least while they are in their human form. At home all have the ability to "tap in."

That is true for both the collective and the individual consciousness. Everything is held in energetic form.

Each is a piece of the whole.

Let us imagine a client, Fred, whom I ask to go back to a past life where he finds that he was a butcher in 1850. If I understand correctly, you would say that he is accessing part of the total consciousness of the race, held in the spiritual realm, not necessarily an individual consciousness.

Yes and no. In most cases he is accessing that which is his individual piece of the whole experience, but it is from a larger view, with feed-ins from the rest of humanity. If there is something he needs to experience in this lifetime—or use to correct in this lifetime an experience his individual energy has not undertaken—he is able to tap into the knowledge of the whole to get that experience. It is as if each experience is a book upon a common bookshelf and he decides whether to choose the book that was written by himself, or the book that was written by someone else. In your hypothetical example, if Fred, while living the life as a butcher, had unfinished lessons, he would access his own incomplete work to deal with during the regression.

241

In past-life regression can you access somebody else's life just as easily as your own?

Yes. When a soul has the need to experience, at that moment, a situation it has not previously faced in human form, it reverts to an archetype from the collective database.

So if someone were given a past life experience that she was the famous Thomas Jefferson, is this something where she knows for sure that she is accessing her own past life, or is it just "a life" that she has accessed?

It's just "a life" she has accessed.

In fact she doesn't necessarily have any connection with Thomas Jefferson, according to your view.

Correct, except in so far as we all have connections with everything that is there.

So in a past-life regression we take any book off the shelf in the Akashic (celestial) library, because they're not named, and read what we believe to be our own, but which is not necessarily our own, book.

That is correct, but there are some books that have energy that will draw us, because that energy will give us the pathway to correct something that is hindering us in the present lifetime. The whole human experience of a soul is to learn lessons. If there are unfinished lessons in their individual background that are affecting their present lifetime, they go back to their own books.

So when my client picks up a book given to him in the Akashic library, where I have taken him in trance, he opens it and he sees that he was once a musician. Is that musician's life necessarily, inevitably his, one that he can call his own past life? Or are you saying that we should doubt that we have any knowable past lives, if the possibility is that we are pulling lives at random off the shelves?

It is the influence of the energy. If there is something that remained unresolved or unlearned in a past life, it will pull us to that particular experience so it may be resolved. With an older, more mature soul, there are hundreds, possibly thousands, of prior lifetimes. They have encompassed a plethora of conditions, to broaden as much as possible the human experience. They have been both sexes, many races, a myriad of occupations. Inevitably the client has indeed "lived" aspects of whosoever life he eventually accesses to deal with the issues that brought him to your couch.

So if I'm told about the relationship between church and state and I go into a past-life regression, I might access Thomas Jefferson discussing the relationship between church and state.

Yes, particularly because you are searching to broaden your understanding of your own experiences that you have lived, directly and indirectly through Jefferson.

Then I will think it is my own past life by mistake.

Not by mistake because it is the collective. You share the energy of the experience almost as if you were a spectator at the initial event, and then you chose to jump in and play the role in a re-enactment of the circumstance.

To what extent is your answer shared by others at Home? Is it a common belief or essentially your own interpretation?

It is common. It is the knowledge, the wisdom that is shared.

So you hold that if we are looking, and have a spiritual need, for an experience of some kind, we will access that archetype from any person—it doesn't matter if it was our own soul's past life or not.

It isn't as easy as that. It is all an energetic thing and a balance that has to be struck. The things that have the most energetic pull on us are the things that our piece of energy, our soul, has experienced before, and we have had many, many, many experiences, each one of us from hundreds to thousands. We would be drawn to that other life if there is something about it that could be used to jog the temporal plane with a fact that would have more impact than our own experience. Then an archetype comes into play, rather than the individual experience, because the body will have warm feelings, will have more affinity with something it perceives as being more correct, more important than something else.

Is it possible for us to know, if we want to explore our own historic past lives, that we are doing so, or is this just a matter of guesswork?

To spirits at Home it really doesn't matter because all energy is shared. Here there is no egotistical need to distinguish among yours, mine, and ours. In past-life regressions, if you are directed to a current problem that is hindering your growth, what difference does it make how you resolve it?

As a therapist, you were concerned to help people overcome their problems. Is it ethical therapy for us, when we are taking people into past lives, to send them in a direction that can be accomplished by accessing a life—not their own past life but just a life? So for example, I have a client who can't sleep and I say to him, "Go back to a time when you slept really well." He will go back to a life which, you say, is picked as being the most appropriate life and not necessarily anything to do with his soul at all.

If he had a life that had that strong energy, he will go to his own first, and if he does not, then he will go to another consciousness of that experience. Is it not your intention to solve the problem regardless of the means? If they need to find an archetype of restfulness, what matters the source, as long as it can be used to remedy the current problem? It is only important that the person is steeped in the "feel" or activity of being able to sleep.

We sometimes identify people whom we meet in past lives in regression and believe we are meeting them in our current incarnation: is it real?

That is real. A soul recognizes other souls in whatever form or part they are playing.

Even if the past life that we are accessing is not our own?

In that case it would be your own.

244

Synchronicity
[The philosophical term *acausal* means *without a cause*.]

Your notion of synchronicity, or meaningful coincidence, states that there is an acausal principle linking events having a similar meaning by their coincidence in time. Am I correct?

That is correct, as I wrote in my papers. Basically, what I was saying was that if you set the stage the play will go on. Now my feelings are that we are much more the creators of our reality than I had any perception of when I was in the body. I now see that when we need to experience something, we establish the energy or the signposts that say, "Come to me, so that I may experience this." So for example, if we are looking for employment, we will have the right advertisement come to our attention, because we are broadcasting for it, or we will have an associate come to us saying they have heard about a position. These are the synchronicities that bring everything together. Everything we are unconsciously projecting is giving a result for us, even though we may not have consciously thought about it. So we imagine that it is just something that comes out of the blue (which I called "synchronicities").

When you say consciously and unconsciously, are you thinking about the subconscious mind or the higher self (i.e., the soul)?

Both the subconscious of an individual (who may have entertained the idea before but put it out of their conscious mind) and their "higher self" are bringing in the energies to enable that person to go forward and have new experiences.

Does the "higher self" work independently of the subconscious?

In most cases, yes, because the subconscious is somewhat connected—but not to the specific ego of the person's conscious mind. There is a bleed-over with whatever the conscious mind wants to accomplish but has just put in the closet for the time being. The subconscious is frequently a reservoir for belief systems that have been presented to the person, traumas that they do not wish to face, and the origin of the fears that control

245

one's life. The higher self (and it may have various levels) is the soul's consciousness that contains the wisdom gleaned from all its incarnations and is the connection to the collective unconscious.

In your first category of synchronicity you talked about "an external event that corresponds to that state of mind, even though there is no evidence of a causal connection." Now you're saying that a person's state of mind does cause the external event. So, does the mind aspect come first?

Some energetic impulses originate from the individual, whether on the subconscious or higher-self level of self-consciousness. Then it draws to itself the energy of the idea which was put out there.

Does it ever happen the other way around, that there's an acasual event first?

It can be, but it's not something that happens as frequently as something that is pre-programmed into the subconscious to draw in an event, so that an action may be fulfilled.

To what extent are those acasual events which do not come from the mind or higher self generated by the spiritual powers on your side?

The spirits cannot do anything that the person does not ask for in some way, shape, or form. If somebody is lonely, one thing that could help assuage that loneliness would be a pet. The spirits on the other side could direct an animal into the life of the person, but it is not coming without the person thinking first of loneliness and wanting a companion. So it seems to be acasual, but in fact, it is interconnected.

So you have backed off completely from the acausal approach?

I had to. Still, synchronicity is a term that is much richer than in my use of it. It talks of the soul's power as being able to bring to itself, even from a subconscious level, those things it needs to experience or complete, or some task that will enable the soul to go forward.

Must the soul be able to understand the process? For example, your spirit colleagues tell us that healing takes place through our intention. Does there have to be an intentionality for healing to take place?

Just bringing the energies in—it can be more haphazard than that. Healing is affecting the physical in a direct way. Synchronicity brings energy into a person's arena so that they can interact with it. But it is still up to their free will how they will interact, once it's presented to them. With healing, they are seeking to change physical aspects within their body, so they need to have a definite intention to change the specific thing that is out of order. A synchronicity is just giving you the potential to make such changes, based upon your freedom of choice.

You said that synchronicity was the coincidence of a person's mental or psychic awareness, more or less simultaneously with a corresponding happening outside his or her perception, which can only be verified afterwards. Do you still hold that view?

It is much more a picture of the entire process, rather than the way I divided it originally. It was difficult to accept all that could happen within the energy field. It was much easier to come up with my one, two steps. It had made it easier for me to accept and for others to comprehend.

How do you view the controversy that followed your words, and is still rumbling on among the skeptics?

The skeptics aren't going to believe it's raining even if they are outside getting wet, if they choose not to! I will not try to influence them because they deny anything other than their ego, and when their ego is supreme it will not see an elephant standing on their foot!

There might be a Jumbo synchronicity about such a situation!

Yes, there would.

To sum up your former doctrine of synchronicity: how do you hold it today?

Beautiful things on Earth get drawn to us to experience. Generally, they are brought to us when we are in such a position that we need to take notice of them. You have had a yearning to do something but haven't known what the means were, and that brings the energy to you to help you accomplish what you are seeking to do—generally in a way you would never have considered. We would call that synchronicity. An example would be if a person needs more income and he has a hobby of rummaging through and collecting old books. He sees an advertisement to sell first editions, and when he searches his collection he finds a first edition. He has, therefore, synchronistically brought together his needs and his hobby. All has been resolved simply because what he had only thought nice became a means of providing for his physical needs. It is summed up in the Spiritualist phrase: "When the student is ready, the teacher shall appear." [Jung's phrase is a Chinese proverb current in Spiritualist circles.]

You imply that synchronous events that happen to us are mostly programmed by us rather than by any other source.

Yes, definitely.

Life Lessons

What about non-synchronous events—for instance, something falling into the road causes our death? I suppose that example isn't really about a synchronous event.

Not as I envisioned it. The only synchronicity for us may be that the time has come for us to transition [die]. We happen to go down that particular road at the right time for the mountain to fall on us so that we can transition, but we haven't determined beforehand the exact means of the transition.

In that situation, it would be the soul itself that would be wanting to transition?

Yes.

Are there no accidents?

No. There are no accidents.

So nothing happens to a soul without that soul's previously having a view about it?

It is generally something that the soul has previously wanted to experience. If a woman is in an accident where she is maimed, it is because on the soul level, before coming into the body, she wished to experience what it was like to go through life with a handicap. Yet she was born whole so that she could know what it was like to be whole, then the event happens that makes her handicapped, so she gets the feeling of both sides.

At this time on Earth we have starving babies in many parts of the world. Did the souls of these babies all want to starve? And what of the genocide in Rwanda?

Not that they wanted to starve, but that they wanted to have a place in society where they would influence people throughout the world. Whenever a large number of souls comes together in some manner which seems to be sacrificial or devastating to the human mind, it is because they have agreed to be a spark, a catalyst for psychological, emotional, and physical change on the planet. They don't always accomplish what they seek, but it creates an energy that affects all those in physical form. Those people in Rwanda who survived have found a strength unheard of in that nation prior to the time of the genocide.

This seems abominable cruelty on the part of the spirit world. That so many people should die and suffer torment is hellish!

From a strictly physical, Earth plane standpoint—where everything is judged good or bad, right or wrong—that would be true. From an energetic, soul-level perspective, where the soul wishes to experience different lessons, it is perfectly normal. We do not expect the mortal who is not in contact with his soul to feel and appreciate the beauty of what takes place. Each soul determines its own pathway and the means of its journey. The "abominable cruelty" is a human judgment. Judgment does not exist at Home. Hell exists only upon the Earth.

The "beauty" of dying of starvation in Niger!
The human experience in learning the lessons which allow each soul to experience its desired situations.

There's a lesson in dying of starvation?
A number of lessons, depending on what the soul has experienced previously. It could be feeling the physical suffering, but it could be the feeling that they give to the aid workers which enables them to give of themselves and have fulfillment. Then there are the ways that individual souls see all their relatives depart from them, yanking away all of the support system they have known and leaving them with a sense of helplessness. These are all human emotions which a soul at one time or another comes down in some way to experience. These particular situations represent a crash course in experiencing a lot of things at once, so that the soul may mature at a faster rate.

Why do we have to learn these horrible lessons?
The souls choose them because we gain wisdom. We learn, as you now may see, by the suffering of others, and we get an emotional connection, even though we have not actually experienced it. The soul comes down and wants to have the wisdom of what a person feels it is like to suffer total deprivation, so that when they go back Home, the unconditional love here is so much sweeter, so much more immense.

Personal Freedom

Human beings are conditioned by genes, race, class, education, social environment, consequences from past lives, pre-agreed lessons arranged for them, and by synchronicities—how does the principle of freedom operate in this regard? Is human personal freedom a myth?
Human personal freedom, yes; human soul freedom, no. It is the soul who has the freedom of choice. Frequently the incarnate

does not have a choice if it wishes to remain living in its shell. If, in Rwanda, for example, a person on the side of the insurgents wishes to remain in the body, he must do exactly what he is told, or he will lose his life. He has the freedom of choice to do what he is told, or go to another existence, be killed, and move on.

Souls choose the biological parents they will have, so they know that particular physical traits are already in the body they are going to inhabit. They may choose for it to be easier for them, say, to be alcoholic, by choosing alcoholic parents. That frailty would then be within their genes and would shift the body more easily in that direction. Their freedom of choice comes in because, even though it's there, they may choose different ways to get out of that cycle. But in all of this, the human has no freedom of choice unless he in fact knows of the existence of choices. If a person knows only alcoholics, he thinks that is what life is about.

Let me pick you up on alcoholism: is it good or bad?
It depends on whether you're drunk or not!

I asked for that! I should have asked about somebody who is an alcoholic and gives up being one. It is a free choice which she has exercised "for her highest good." Is the situation good or bad?
The bad is if she has not learned the lesson that went along with it—what it is to be physically dependent on something, and what it means to be able to break that cycle. The good is that she may learn the strength lying within her, that she was dragged into alcoholism because of a lack of self-worth or self-control, or a feeling that it was what she was supposed to do. Now she has gained the wisdom and knows that she doesn't have to be what other people want her to be. She has the ability to choose and to use the strength it takes to tear away from her previous path in life and get on to a new path. That is the lesson learned there.

So good and bad is really a measure of whether lessons are learned well or badly?
Whether they have been learned, or they have to be repeated. Good and bad are earthly concepts because they again involve

251

making judgments, which is the province of the ego of the human existence.

So I could be a soldier in Rwanda, killing and raping people, and if I had chosen to be a soldier that would be my "good."

Yes, if you wanted to be in a position where you were ruthless, in total control, amoral as society would consider you, then you would be experiencing those lessons.

If I then wanted to give up being a soldier, would that be another kind of good?

It is as the Earth society sees good. It means you have moved on to different kinds of lessons—on to a lesson of clarity in which you are now honoring the souls whom you had been abusing up to that time; now you are interacting with them and taking guidance from their energy, acknowledging that they have a right to live and to go on, as you do.

Jesus said, "Love your enemies." The implication is that this is the right thing to do in all circumstances, but you seem to imply that in a confrontation the right thing to do might sometimes be to hate your enemies.

I'm not making that much of a distinction. When Jesus spoke of loving your enemy, he spoke of loving the essence of your enemy, not the actions that he does—that's where the distinction is. You can love the soul who is behind that brutal person and not love the acts that he commits. You still love him at the soul level. You may despise his actions but love the soul behind the mask, because it is as all of us are.

Carl Jung, thank you for your answers and insights.

I hope this has brought some degree of clarity for those who will take the time to read.

Commentary

Toni: Carl Jung was the first Leader we interviewed, and I felt as if I were at the feet of an old professor gently introducing a neophyte to a broad range of fresh thoughts and feelings. There was a tenderness displayed, as if our hands were being held while we confronted a spiritual universal knowingness. Carl repeated concepts with different scenarios, as if to provide alternative ways for our minds to grapple with his ideas. In my relationship with the Masters this is their typical method of dealing with the curious and inquisitive. Jung inserted humor when discussions were becoming too serious, but only when appropriate and not for the sake of being funny. He held himself strictly to Peter's questions, without expounding into a wider dimension. There was always a serious educational quality to the feel of the interview.

Peter: Jung appears to have substantially modified his doctrine of the collective unconscious since returning Home. At first he appeared to hold to a strict interpretation, implying that accessing Thomas Jefferson's past life was a random act, but later in the discussion his modification of the doctrine was significant.

When we choose to relive a past life, he says, the most important issue for us is the energetic pull of that life upon our psyche. If our need (e.g., to explain our emotional distress) is best illustrated by one of our own past lives, then that life will resonate for us more than any other, and because it is our own energy it will be easier to access. However, if there is no special energetic pull exercised by our many previous experiences, we can just as easily be led to review anyone else's appropriate life—not our own but one which energetically matches our current need. Thus we cut the coat of our past-life regression experience according to the cloth of whatever is most appropriate to access energetically. This appropriateness arises from within our psyche, he said, "because the body will have warm feelings, will have more affinity with something it perceives as being more correct, more important than something else."

In the energetic world our actual needs do the talking for us, whether it be to access a memory of our past or of someone else's. It is the energy that draws us because whichever life is accessed will have the "energy that will give us the pathway to correct something that is hindering us in the present lifetime." The force of this significant clarification by Jung of his original idea of the collective unconscious is amplified by his statement that among the souls at Home this is the common understanding of how energy works.

Often when we have been in contact with the Masters, what emerges is a new appraisal of spiritual complexities. Here is a great example. It is our own human need that calls up the relevant distant memory, and our spiritual self initiates the discovery. It is not a random access to a cosmic database of lives, but one that is dependent on the energetic pull between our self and the energy of the past life in question.

Past-life regression practitioners sometimes venture to take their clients in hypnotic trance to the celestial Akashic Library. There they have had the experience that, when the soul's own life book is accessed from the shelf or presented by the librarian, it tells its story in moving pictures. We are glimpsing the great spiritual database of lives—which includes the story of both our past and everybody else's past. Thus if we do not get an answer from our personal record, the book which the librarian hands us may well provide the common answer we are seeking for healing, and for understanding our individual need.

If Jung has modified his position on the collective unconscious, he has virtually abandoned his former doctrine of synchronicity. Rather than accepting that some external event happening to us may correspond to our state of mind, though there is no evidence of a causal connection, Jung flatly states that most likely either our subconscious mind or our higher self is the *prime cause* of the event. Our search for a source of income, a new job, a loving companion, or even a speedy end to life, is generated by our own thoughts. From time to time we may be aided from the Other Side, but each event is actually created by us, and is never an accident. "There are no accidents." Free will belongs to the soul absolutely, but the body's human ego is not free to choose the path the eternal soul has already freely decided that it must tread.

Expanding on the concept of soul choice, Jung mentioned the possibility of our deliberately choosing a life of misery or even of evil. His current view makes the normative human ethical categories of good and evil appear to stand on their head. Good can be perceived by the souls at Home in such a way that a soldier's hatred and brutality have value because they are important soul lessons. By now the reader will realize that this viewpoint is not just the opinion of Hitler's soul but the commonplace response made by the Masters and Leaders, Jung being no exception. Turning our ethical system on its head is dreadfully uncomfortable, especially with the Nazi concentration camps still fresh in our memory. This dialogue about evil cannot ever be easy. (It is like the discovery that Earth rotates around the sun.) The spirit-centered point that Jung makes forces us to realize that it is our soul, and not our human ego, that is intended to be in charge of our life. Whether or not we like what we hear, it is plain that, as souls, we do things geared to our chosen spiritual training course, far beyond our earthly control, where lessons may include being starved to death or even, conversely, being brutal to other people in the same fashion.

In the face of such a message, there is reason to believe that our most appropriate response is to go within our heart and seek enlightenment. Learning the ways of the soul is no easy task.

"Everything that has ever come into existence came from the Creator who knew only perfection. And that perfection, that completeness, is within all the energy that is a part of that presence."

Albert Einstein

1879-1955

Biographical Note

Albert Einstein was born in Ulm, Württemburg, Germany in 1879, to Herman and Pauline Einstein. His parents were secular Jews but he received a Catholic elementary education, followed by Jewish studies. Later he accepted he was Jewish but did not believe in a personal God. Yet he saw himself as "deeply religious" with an "unbounded admiration for the structure of the world so far as our science can reveal it." His God was revealed "in the orderly harmony of what exists," and not in "the fates and actions of human beings."

Moving to Munich, Einstein learned to play the violin and attended high school where, in 1891, he began studies in mathematics and calculus. When his family moved to Italy in 1894, he stayed behind at school and penned his first scientific work, *The Investigation of the State of Aether in Magnetic Fields*. Called a slow learner by his teachers, he dropped out of school, failing at the first try to gain a place in the Swiss Federal Institute of Technology in Zurich. Finally accepted, he graduated in 1900 as a physics and mathematics teacher. He was frustrated in landing only part-time teaching posts, until the father of his college friend (and future collaborator) Marcel Grossman helped him to find a position as a low-ranking technical expert in the Swiss patent office at Bern, where he worked until 1909.

In 1896 he met a Serbian student, Mileva Marić, a mathematician and the only woman in his class that year to study for the same diploma. They had a romantic relationship and a daughter, Lieserl, was born to them in 1902. The couple married a year later. Lieserl, is variously said by historians to have been given up for adoption or to have died in infancy. They later had two sons, Eduard and Hans Albert. Despite their undoubted intellectual affinity, Einstein divorced Mileva in 1919 and married his cousin Elsa four months later.

During the years in Bern, Einstein produced—in his spare time and without mentors or academic support—a wide range of theoretical physics papers. In 1905, he published four ground-breaking articles: on Brownian motion; describing the electromagnetic radiation of light; laying out a Special Theory of Relativity; and on matter and energy equivalence. In the same year, his thesis on molecular dimensions earned him a doctorate from the University of Zurich. He continued to work on quantum theory, developing the Principle of Equivalence.

In 1908 Einstein was appointed to be a lecturer at the University of Bern, but the following year saw him leave the Swiss capital for the University of Zurich to become a professor of physics. With his academic reputation as a physicist growing rapidly, he moved to Prague in 1911 for another professorial position. There he worked with Marcel Grossman on developing the General Theory of Relativity. He moved back to Zurich to another chair in physics. Then, in 1914, came a research professorship in the University of Berlin and, finally, the publication of the outstanding General Theory of Relativity.

When measurements of the 1919 eclipse powerfully confirmed his findings, Einstein achieved celebrity status. Although his theories were universally seen as creating a major scientific breakthrough, supporters of the anti-Semitic movement in Germany became highly disruptive in his seminars, and he was subjected to a Nazi campaign to discredit his theories. In 1921 he received a Nobel Prize for his work on the photoelectric effect.

Then he began to travel, to the USA, France, Palestine, and Japan. In 1924 his study of the association of waves with matter would be his last major scientific discovery.

Fund-raising for a new Hebrew University of Jerusalem, lecturing and writing, and receiving a multitude of academic awards from all over the world proved physically very demanding. In 1932 he accepted an offer to teach in the USA at Princeton University. He left Germany for the last time, just as the Nazis seized power. He settled in Princeton and worked on creating a unified field theory for the laws of physics. He supported the campaign for nuclear disarmament and the effort to fund the new Hebrew University. Having been in failing health for six years, Albert Einstein died in Princeton, NJ, in 1955, at 76 years of age.

The Dialogue

We are here to talk to Dr. Albert Einstein.

[Toni: He says he's been curious about all that has taken place and thinks what we are doing is marvelous—that we are letting voices from beyond the grave talk about their earthbound ventures, because some of them needed to be corrected. He is very happy to be a participant.]

Delighted to meet you, Albert. I'm not sure that the fourteen other people will approve, but we kept the best wine to the last.

Unfortunately, the other fourteen are listening in.

The Compass
When you were five, your father interested you in a little compass. You said it was a very important moment in your life. Why?

To know there was nothing inside but that magnetized needle, to be able to move it in any direction and have it always spring back to point north gave me the sense of the energy of the planet, the strength that came from the Earth beneath me, and in particular the pull of the poles. I began then to study the effect of gyroscopes and how their activity is of the same type of pull and effect. That one thing led to another, and it was the beginning of a fantastic journey.

That was very abstract thinking for a child of five.

I didn't think of it as abstract; I just thought of it as something living and breathing, and it intrigued me. Some five-year-olds get brought to music and it flows within them. I had had other incarnations as a scientist, so it was just a matter of tapping into some of my old memories but with new eyes.

In fact you honored that childhood experience with your very first scientific work, The Investigation of the State of Aether in Magnetic Fields, *didn't you?*

Yes, it felt like an appropriate beginning.

Was that a deliberate honoring of the experience?

I don't know that you could exactly call it "honoring." It was an acknowledgement in the same way as I acknowledged a lot of things in my academic papers. I don't see that an attempt to explain how something works is honoring the process. It is more taking that which is invisible but has a dominance in a person, and bringing it forward to explain the effect that it has on things. I saw things that others could not and I chose to share the wonder with them.

A lot of children who have the type of experience that you had—of being able to think in adult terms—find that they're not readily understood by their parents and families. Did you have that experience?

Somewhat, but I was indulged in that regard and encouraged. I was never told that I couldn't do something or shouldn't do something. I was rather left to my own devices.

In fact, as a child you made models and mechanical devices but were rather slow at lessons in school.

They bored me. I could not see the need to devote myself to elementary principles if I already understood the complex issues of science that I knew I would pursue.

The Nature of Genius

People have said that you were dyslexic, or mildly autistic, or had an unusually contoured brain. Tell me about your unusual intellectual powers. Where did they come from?

They came from a number of different sources. They came to me genetically, my having in the cells within my brain more ease of access than some other humans. Also, I did not totally sever my connections with my past lives, and I had that DNA imprint upon the energetic body that I was. I was indulged by my parents, who encouraged me not to forget what I was remembering. They did not get upset when I talked of things they had no idea about, such as discussing concepts with people who were not present, so far as they were concerned. People outside of my family considered me stupid, dyslexic, and autistic, simply because I didn't respond to the normal patterns of society. As for schoolwork, I could take a glance at an entire year's studies and know in a minute whether or not there was anything there to interest me. When there wasn't, I moved on to something that I could explore, something that I could delve into. In today's terms, you call children like me "indigos" or "crystal" children.

Or a genius?

That's the Earth term for it, yes—geniuses, prodigies, whatever you want to call us.

Is there any particular reason why you should be a prodigy?

I had chosen to experience what it was like to be totally wrapped up in my studies, in my ways of converting the workings of the universe into an account that was palatable to human beings. I also came down with my ideas and writings, to be able to spark other people to develop an entire cache of information that would enrich the planet.

Is genius usually preordained, prearranged—or can it just be an openness on the part of person who has come down?

It is prearranged, because a person creates the lessons they wish to experience. If it were possible for a person to come down in a normal body and then develop into a genius, they would not be able to fulfill the normal lessons they came down to learn— such as hate, love, abuse, abandonment. They would be totally overshadow- ed by the form of genius. The effect that genius has upon a person is to isolate them, so geniuses, in order to be able to sustain themselves, have to possess a foreknowledge of what they are doing, even though it is unconscious. In this way they do not find that the loneliness of converting ideas for human knowledge and understanding detracts from their existence. That person who is a successful genius needs to have a good contact within themselves to their soul, to feel that connection, and to feel the love from within their soul that is for themselves. In this way they do not lapse into some kind of self-destructive behavior because they are not loved or accepted by anyone, or because they are not able to interact with anyone.

Does a genius have a continuing relationship with a power base on the other side, or simply rely on his or her DNA?

It depends on the pre-designated purpose of those people having such an awareness. If they are doing it to help society in general, they maintain contact with the other side. If they are doing it in order to go through the trials and tribulations of being outside the norm of society, then they do not. It is more an unconscious thing with them than any connection with the point of origin of their intelligence and work. I maintained contact primarily because it was my purpose to come down and be that spark that ignited new endeavors and new directions for the human race.

Is maintaining contact possible for anybody, or is it only when you have a prearranged system?

That's a rather difficult question to answer. It is always possible for the human soul, while incarnate in human form, to be able to trace back to their soul inside, providing they are not totally inundated with the dramas that brought them down to learn lessons. It does not happen as frequently that way as it happens when it is preordained. However, it is not excluded if the person truly works to open up and reconnect—it is possible to do it. There is also the possibility that once a being completes the desired lessons, they move on to a soul's path. That generally entails working for the highest benefit of human society by helping individuals to access knowledge of their souls. Your channeler is an example of that type of contact.

Is it a sign of special favor to be allowed to be a genius, or just a choice?

It's just a choice. It has to do in most cases with an older soul who has experienced most of the day-to-day human lessons souls come down to learn. It has now chosen to show the way, whether in a scientific, musical, or art vein, or whatever it may be, in things which enhance the communications between the dimensions and within the dimensions.

Are there limits to one's ability to be a genius? I'm thinking, for example, of Mozart's dying young.

Mozart had a very definite pattern of things he wished to experience. One goal he had was to enable a means of musical communication beyond what was common at the time, and his music does sing, does communicate to people. He also had Earth lessons that he was learning at the same time, which had to do with overcoming obstacles, such as his hearing. Because he did not have a lot of Earth lessons to learn and was able to accomplish what he came to do within a very short period of time, he chose to come back to do something else.

So his early death was the choice of his soul?

Yes.

Marriage

In the Technical College at Zurich, you met and subsequently married Mileva Marić. Before you married, you had a daughter, Lieserl. Did the baby die, or did you give her up for adoption?

We found a loving couple who would take care of her. I knew that I was incapable of spending any time with her, and her dear mother was devoted to me. We thought it best, in an environment where Mileva's devotion was to me, and my devotion was to bringing intellectual endeavors to life, that Lieserl should not be raised in an environment that would not be healthy for her.

Did you keep in touch with her?

In the beginning. Then I became totally intertwined in my research; that was the only thing I saw, felt, breathed, ate, slept, and did.

And Mileva?

She was like my shadow.

Shortly after your marriage, with little reference material to help you, and in addition to your doctoral thesis, you wrote four amazing articles that gave the scientific community the foundation stones of modern physics. May I ask questions related to that Annus Mirabilis of 1905?

Why, of course.

How much was Mileva involved in the development of the articles you published in 1905, especially the one about electromagnetism?

She was the practical one of the pair. I was the person who, while I was bringing the material to a point where it could be used, found it too much of a bother to record meticulously what was going on. She was the historian of our travels. She was the one who could put down on paper in a concrete manner that which people could understand. I was concerned with bringing the information through, but I wasn't as concerned with having its form understandable to anyone wishing to read on the subject. She was the pencil in this relationship, the one who recorded and explained. Because she was a woman of the times, she did not receive public acknowledgment. She worshiped me, so she chose to give me the glory, but also she did not wish to be in the forefront because she was rather timid and shy.

The Source of Genius

Back again to the genius issue: How did you, without any reference material, have this amazing output? Was it indeed a miracle?

[laughs] I suppose human beings want to have a beginning and end to everything. I did appear to manifest something out of nothing, which would be considered a miracle. However, it was a matter of bringing from the universe the operation of the universe, putting it in a way that it could be seen through the eyes of a human being and understood by the brain of a human being. I was merely a translator of the energy that was there and was existing at that time. I did have help with some of the terminology and directions to make it palatable to the human mind.

Help from?

From those on the Other Side.

You were consciously translating, knowing it was coming from the Other Side?

I was, as you say today, channeling some of it.

Did you know that you were doing that?

I was aware, when I was in human form, that I had insights that just came from outside of me. Did I consciously and knowingly at that time accept the fact that it was coming from a group of others? No, I did not, because as much of a connection as I had with the other side, I did not have that knowingness. I now know that was what happened. At the time I just thought that these ideas were downloading to me, but from whence they came I did not know.

You went on to publish your General Theory of Relativity and later to begin the tasks of developing a unified field theory. Did you make any major errors in your work that you wish now that you could have corrected?

[laughs] There were some minor miscalculations, but as I look upon it, I know it was intentional, so that it would stimulate others to delve as deeply into the matter as I had done. They were nothing of significance; they were things that would just not seem right with a person who was totally into matter. And they were like clues along a pathway to a destination. You still got to your destination, but without reading the clues, you would not get the full bloom of what was going on. Things would still work without it, things were still explained without these little glitches, but it was my way of stimulating, because it was my purpose to stimulate the development of an understanding and a knowledge of the workings of the universe.

Physics Today

What has been the most successful work done since your death as Einstein, in the development of your theories and in picking up those little clues you left behind?

One of the largest things is the research that has been done in matter and antimatter, and the acknowledgement of the smaller and smaller particles, going down to the quarks and beyond.

The String Theory?
The String Theory.

How do you view that theory?
I view that they are pretty much right on—they are following the path. They are getting to the beginning of matter and the path of matter.

Can you give any clues now as to where they should be looking?
There are a number of groups that are heading in the right direction, but because of the human ego, there are matters to be considered, like Nobel Prizes and things like that. So it would not be sporting of me, so to speak, in this book to give clues to a group who might read the book, omitting those who might not.

How about clues as to where to find the information?

The information is in the universe. The information is along the path they are traveling. It is just as I followed the needle that always pointed to the north, and sought to discover and explain why it did so, that they will get exactly where they need to be.

People are searching for life in the universe. If there is life out there similar to human life, how may we most easily find it?

It will be rather difficult for a lot of people to comprehend what I am going to say now. There is life out there on other planets. However, it is not identical to human life either in form or in function. It is also not in the same linear time continuum as the planet Earth, so that if you were to go to a planet that has energy beings on it, such as the moon, you would not be able to see the occupants of that asteroid because they would be out of phase with interpretation through your eyes. It is possible for some of the inhabitants of some of the planets to lower their vibration so that they can be seen, if and when the occupants of planet Earth achieve the degree of sophistication to go and visit them.

The main fear of these other planets is the war-like nature of human beings. On Earth, it is mostly interpreted that anyone unlike themselves will have a malicious intention toward them, whether that be someone on another planet, or a lower life form, such as mosquitoes. Mosquitoes have no malicious intention, just a will to live and survive, yet man spends millions in developing products for their eradication. A mosquito is seen and immediately the attempt is made for it to be destroyed. That is the fiber that runs through humankind at this time, at least those that are thoroughly within the third dimension of existence.

Can we have a different attitude with mosquitoes so that they don't bite us?

[laughs] Well, just as the dinosaurs had to eat when they were on the planet, and when the puny little *homo erectus* came along and tried to use them as food, they turned the tables, the mosquito needs blood for its life-cycle, and since man is a larger

target than, say, a rodent, the mosquito will of course go for the mother lode.

Regarding the probes that are sent out by NASA to various parts of the solar system, can you see any purpose in this practice continuing?

Well, governments want to know if there is any resource out there that can be used by them, whether it be a life-force or some type of mineral or energy source. It's like a child at play, experimenting with the things in the play box, whether it be with stones, little toys, sand, or dirt: they need to know what is around them and what they can do with the material in order to feel that they have control of their play box. The U.S. government, NASA, and the governments of other space agencies wish to find the resources that are out there before the competition does— particularly if this is something that would, for example, enable perfect cold-fusion, which would be an extremely important power source, and also a potential source of destruction.

If life-forms on other planets are aware of the war-like nature of the planet Earth, do they have some means of knowing about Earth? Do we have a means of knowing about them? And if so, what is it?

People don't have a means of knowing about them at this time because they are oblivious to the fact that there are other energetic dimensions which they can access. Various studies now utilizing quantum physics, where unexplainable emotions affect an experiment, are starting to show the thick-headed scientists that what they can feel and see is not all that exists. The Earth is, in fact, being monitored by others to find a time when they feel it is "safe" to make contact. The one exception to this broad statement is among some of those with what you call psychic powers. They have an awareness of, and sometimes an interaction with, beings in other dimensions and upon other planets.

Other scientists may be thick-headed, but your head was tousle-haired, wasn't it?

[laughs] I never could take time to have a haircut.

Energy

Can you explain the essential difference between the energy of matter and light on the physical plane, and the energy of the spiritual world in which you now live and of which your spirit is a part on the Other Side?

The former occurs in a physical plane that is monitored or ruled by gravitational forces and thickness. The latter is the energy of all that exists, that does not have to be physical; it does not have to come together in such close order as to form a body, a chair, a table, that can be seen, sat on, and worked at. There is also the dimension of time which changes within the two paradigms. The human, and the energy within human control, is regulated by a linear time where, as it transforms, you can see the transformation from one source to another along a linear plane. Within the spiritual plane, it is the intention of the energy to be in any place at any time. It can have the intention that, as the physical is moving from a period of creation to a period of completion, the soul can choose to pop in at any place along that linear line, or to be there for the whole, whether in reverse or sideways—there is no restriction in spiritual energy fields. There is restriction based upon linear physicality in the human plane.

I note the restriction, but is there any essential difference between the energy of the universe, which you say is everywhere, and the energy that is within the physical plane? Or is it the same energy in different formats?

It's the same energy in different points of perception, whether the perception is two-dimensional, which a lot of perception has to be on the planet in order for it to be seen, or multi-dimensional as it is in its true form. All matter on the Earth plane, or any plane, is energy. On the truly spiritual plane, there is energy, but there does not have to be matter. If a spirit chooses to be made visible on the physical plane, it can order its energy into a recognizable form so as to be perceived on the physical plane.

You talk as if energy of the spiritual being has a dynamic which does not exist in the physical plane. You say that spiritual energy can have the intention of doing this or that. Is all energy intentional?

Energy is definitely intentional in the non-physical plane. Energy can be intentional on the physical plane to the degree that an incarnate being is aware of the power of directing that energy into a particular form. That has been shown in quantum physics as a way of affecting the results of pure scientific experimentation. It also has been shown to exist with energy healers who, with their intention, direct energy to a particular place or thing. There have been manifestations, within the physical plane, in the re-growth of organs and the re-blueprinting of bodies, which cannot be explained in purely physical terms.

The Nature of the Divine

Is the Divine pure intention?

[Einstein consults with the Masters before answering.]

If you consider that all energy is divinity, all souls emanated from the Creator, whom we call "Divine Energy" and "Divine Being;" so within every particle of energy there is a reflection of divinity. That reflection does what it does by the intention of the particular grouping of that energy or by the manifestation of the whole.

Is our awareness of the Divine an acceptance that the energy expressed by the Divine has a pure intent?

There is nothing but unconditional love and service in pure energy. There cannot be anything other than that which is for the highest and greatest good, because there are no polarities, no opposites in pure energy. There are only absolutes, and the absolutes are those of unconditional love and the well-being of all. Intention does not define, nor is it an explanation for divinity. Intention is the means of manifestation within the Divine. Your acceptance of your divinity allows you to manipulate the energy through the sole use of your intention.

What do you mean when you say "unconditional love"?

It is very difficult to explain to one in human incarnation because it is a state where everything is perfect, where everything belongs, everything is a part of the whole, everything is accepted. It is the ultimate experience of what the earthling yearns for and calls heaven, with all of those magnificent benefits promised by religions. But it also is much more than humanity can possibly envision. It is a state of being. It is where all energy originates and returns. Everything that has ever come into existence came from the Creator who knew only perfection. And that perfection, that completeness, is within all the energy that is a part of that presence.

So the Divine is a dynamic, cohesive, perfect form of energy?
Yes.

Albert Einstein, thank you very much for being here.
I hope I have clarified some of the points. I know that to some my thoughts or sayings at this time will be as controversial as some of my original (but not original!) work while I was on the planet.

At least you've found your Unified Theory.
Absolutely. That I am in unconditional love.

Commentary

Toni: The soul who lived as Albert Einstein has an extremely high level of energy. I felt as if I were levitating as we discussed his life. He seemed to be much more than just a single energy, and was constantly shifting intensities as he offered his explanations. When he was in his scientific persona, he was more serious—no nonsense. When he spoke on spiritual issues his energy was lighter, more ethereal, with a pleasant feeling of contentment. The whole experience was most intriguing because, although we were discussing matters of importance to the physical world, I never once felt any physical heaviness coming from Einstein. His perceived energy pattern was very like the patterns I absorb when channeling Angels and Masters.

Peter: This was about as lucid and engaging a dialogue with the great physicist as could be wished. Einstein's soul communicated with a well-tuned directness. As a non-scientist, I had been afraid the interaction would be overwhelming, and certainly, when we discussed the nature of energy, there was a neatness in his answers that shone like polished stones but took me to the edge of comprehension.

We learned a lot about Einstein the man. The nature of his genius—the continuum of connection between the mind of his incarnated soul and the energetic Source—was explained with modesty, and with cross-reference to Mozart's similar experience of genius. Einstein chose to be a genius before incarnating on Earth, so the channels within his DNA of his past incarnations as scientists (I failed to ask who he had been in previous lives) gave him the necessary structure for his writing and teaching. The content of his publications was not really his original work that he did as a human being but was knowingly downloaded from Home. No wonder he depended on his wife Mileva to ensure that his calculations were intelligible.

There was no personal pride expressed in his being a genius in the eyes of the world. There truly had been a miracle year—his *Annus Mirabilis*, as 1905 has been called—when four brilliant articles, plus his doctoral thesis, poured out of him; yet it was exactly what, before coming down, he had intended should happen. We sensed that this year had been his principal time for downloading. Intention rules the operation of energy, and most of the rest of his life seems to have been spent in consolidating and explaining his teaching, so that good scientific minds might not only understand him better but also pick up on the clues he left behind, and the little errors he puckishly claimed to have made deliberately to permit their continuing research to be fruitful.

Einstein refused to be drawn into making any new scientific statements. That would really not be kosher. Scientists are people with ambitions; in his view, it was enough to indicate that the direction physics is taking today is about right. The String Theory aims in the best direction, but physicists have to enlarge their vision to encompass forms of energy disregarded so far, if they are to get the answers right.

Talking of current space exploration, Einstein was not of the mind to think that governmental motivations were benignly scientific. The possibility of developing cold-fusion technology promises not only positive power generation, but also new deadly weapons for mankind. What was more intriguing was his simple statement about life on other planetary bodies, including Earth's moon. The moon has a life form, hidden from our sight by our lack of understanding of the dimensional nature of energy. There are also those living beings on other planets, he said, who monitor us and our planetary home, but they fear humanity's war-like nature and are waiting for a safe time to make contact with us. This confirmation by Einstein of some people's belief that our planet and its inhabitants are being monitored by extra-terrestial beings, challenges the judgment by scientists and rationalists who hold such talk to be among the more bizarre aspects of metaphysical studies.

We were hoping for some kind of definition that would help to bring physical and metaphysical studies closer. Einstein's key for a rapprochement was to be found in his reference to the concept of intention:

> Energy is definitely intentional in the non-physical plane. Energy can be intentional on the physical plane to the degree that an incarnate being is aware of the power of directing that energy into a particular form.

He illustrated his point by linking quantum physics with energy healing, and the two-dimensional planetary perception of energy with the broader, multi-dimensional form of pure energy. The dimension of time also changes within the two paradigms. Past-life regression specialists often experience this phenomenon in their work: When energetic healing or so-called "rescripting" is wrought for hypnotized clients within the framework of a specific past life, that change, newly created in that past life, can have an immediate, beneficial, and permanent effect in their clients' present-life situation.

Einstein brought us toward his understanding of the nature of the Divine. "All energy is divinity" is the basis of his definition. The Creator is pure energy, "So, within every particle of energy there is a reflection of divinity." The real issue for those within the Judeo-Christian-Islamic tradition is the concept of God as being inexpressibly "other" than us, as Rudolph Otto in *The Idea of the Holy* (1923) expressed with his concept of the numinous. For Otto and for many religious philosophers, the awe-inspiring One is both fascinating and terrifying (*mysterium tremendum et fascinans*), and also possesses force (expressed in divine wrath) and absolute inapproachability.

Not only Einstein but other Leaders and the Masters state that the truth about life is the opposite of this belief:

1. All energy in the universe has the basic quality of unconditional love.

2. All souls have been broken off by and from the Creator and each soul is an individual. At the same time, all souls are collectively the "God-Force," the unity of all energetic beings.

3. Any idea of the "otherness" of God is incorrect since we ourselves are part of the divine wholeness.

4. Our being is of the essence of the Creator, and we are separate only because we need functional individuality.

5. The need for individuality is demonstrated in self-imposed limitations and amnesia during each successive incarnation that we voluntarily undertake.

So, by pre-planning at Home, Einstein's incarnated soul remained in contact with the wisdom of universal energy that was displayed as his "genius." Now Einstein's soul has shed the restrictions of mortality and has returned to be a part of the totality of souls who are the wholeness of the God-Force. Einstein may still be seen as a great physicist, but in this radical idea of the Divine, his words equally challenge Earth's theologians. His description of the nature of energy is truly the point of contact between what has been seen until now as the two distinctly different worlds of the physical and the spiritual. For Einstein, there are different dimensions in the universe but one energy, one spiritual reality; there are many souls but one spirit body of unconditional love. And here our human quest for understanding may end, as the pure energy is metaphysically fused with the dynamic of divine love in one cosmic energetic wholeness.

"In every experience the soul has, it is learning.
It may be learning at a snail's pace, or it may be learning
at the speed of a jaguar, but nothing is for naught."

The Masters
On the Incarnated Life

We told the Masters that we had been enlightened by them and by the Leaders concerning the reincarnation cycle which each soul may choose to experience. Of special interest to us was the apparent willingness or need for individual souls, in advance of reincarnating, to choose the negative human role of an "evil" person. Leaders had explained to us that because a transparently negative role may help a soul's perception of the essential difference between negativity and perfect good, it meets a vital spiritual need in that soul's progress towards maturity. We had been told that souls who suffer at the hand of an "evil" person always do so with foreknowledge and consent, considering it a valuable and necessary lesson. Finally, the Leaders had assured us that, whatever they may have done during an incarnation, souls never lose their essential and eternal connection with and belonging to the God-Force, which is unconditional love. So with that in mind, we ventured further questions.

The Dialogue

If during an incarnation—with no prior planning—a soul exercises its free will to embrace negativity, can this decision further its growth? Or does such a soul negate the purpose of its incarnation by choosing "evil" for itself?

The soul never negates its human experience, regardless of the way in which it enters into the experience. What is drawn up prior to going into a physical form is an outline, not a step-by-step plan. If a soul wishes to learn a particular lesson, it can learn either by being in the presence of evil or by embracing evil; it is its choice which of the two ways the lesson may be assimilated. If a soul has determined to experience victimization and then gets into its lifetime but does not feel or understand what it is doing or—the opposite—it seems to be overwhelmed, it can then put the experience on hold for a subsequent lifetime, but that soul will at some time still have to go through that learning process. The pattern by which souls go through it depends entirely upon them. In every experience the soul has, it is learning. It may be learning at a snail's pace, or it may be learning at the speed of a jaguar, but nothing is for naught.

The apostle Paul struggled with this: "Shall we continue in sin, that grace may abound?" (Romans 6:1) Does this justify a young man's entering a gang because he desires to shoot, to rob, and to peddle drugs?

The reason for entering the gang is generally not a conscious desire to shoot, rob, and peddle drugs. That may possibly be a consequence of gang membership. He joins the gang for the sense of belonging, the sense of getting love from those around him (whatever he perceives to be love and acceptance), or it may be to do the shooting, robbing, and peddling because that is the only way he can get a sense of control. Every one of these elements is a lesson that he learns and carries forward with him (since his soul knows what lessons it can choose not to have to re-experience, something that it does not need to repeat). Each lesson results not in a judgment about what is done but rather in an evaluation as to the necessity and the benefit of carrying it forward within that particular lifetime.

I hear parents saying to me, "This is robbing me of the reason to say to my child, "Don't do this or that, and don't get into that sort of trouble." Surely not?

The first thing that must be realized is that nobody can affect another soul, unless that soul chooses to be affected. So it isn't robbing a physical parent of control of their child, because control of that child only exists if the child allows itself to be controlled. Each soul, regardless of its body's chronological age, makes its own decisions and determines which pathway it is going to take. The statement you just made reflects your society's impression of parents' thinking that they are totally responsible for what their child does, that they will be deemed "good" or "bad" in the eyes of society depending on how their child turns out.

Parents embrace the idea of not letting their child get under the wheels of a car, in the path of a predator, and so on. Isn't there something very important about such parenting?

There is something important about parenting in that it allows guidelines to be established. Whether the guidelines are accepted is up to the recipient, the child. If the parent does not say anything to the children about not joining the gang, of course they will do so. That would show that the parent does not have an effective interaction with the child who needs some kind of interaction, some kind of belonging. For example, in the case of a child in the ghettoes of California with a single parent who is always working, that child needs some sense of belonging which it does not get from the parent. So the child gravitates towards something where it can get its sense of belonging fulfilled. It will adopt the mores of that particular society—the gang—which has all of the negative influences (in Earth's dimension), those other than what is accepted by society. But the child is fulfilling a need it has that cannot be met otherwise. In the case of a loving family with interactive parents who tell their children not to experiment with drugs, there is consistent teaching. That may result in one of two things: The parents get through to the child that there is a negative impact, and the child may choose to say to itself, "I accept their teaching and will keep clear of drugs," or "Hey, that negative impact doesn't sound all that bad! I'm going to try it and prove that it isn't," and then they get addicted. Again, the parent cannot live the life of the other soul.

There's no reason to give up good parenting?

Absolutely not! It allows the soul to be informed of the variables in order to make a somewhat educated choice as to how it wishes to fulfill its lesson plan. The parent's soul might also want to experience being in an out-of-control situation.

Is there a benefit for the soul in what we call "tough love"?

Tough love, or not giving in and rescuing the child from every negative experience that it finds itself engrossed in, is something that helps the parents more than the child, because it allows the parents to realize that they cannot control the child. It takes the parents out of the way so that they no longer facilitate the destructive or addictive behavior of the child. A parent who constantly forgives and takes the child back actually justifies and validates the child's behavior because, even though the parent *talks* of not liking the child's behavior, their *action* in essence says, "I'll take you back, regardless of what you've done." So tough love is a way also of putting the soul of the child into a position where they must make their own decisions, instead of making it easy for them to just continue on with what they are doing.

Bearing in mind the different view of evil between souls on Earth and souls at Home, what should be the basis for human restraint or punishment for criminal acts? I am thinking of the current use of prison and of the death penalty, and also of judicial decisions regarding addicts and pedophiles, and wondering if you see gaps and faults in our judicial system that we ignore.

Everything that goes on in the construct of human society has tendrils reaching out into other parts of society. You have to balance the need to protect the masses with the lesson-learning of individual souls. This doesn't affect the soul itself, because if it comes down to a man's playing the role of pedophile, he will continue until the pattern is broken. When his soul came down it knew full well that there would be repercussions, such as prison, condemnation, being despised by people, having his freedom being taken away, just as he has taken away the freedom and the innocence of those who were his victims. Each experience is a lesson. When a person comes down to assume a role in body form, he is always aware of the possible outcomes beforehand. A murderer knows that because he offends society's laws, rules, and standards, society may ask for retribution, imprisonment, the death penalty, banishment, and so on.

On a human level there are those who must, as part of their role, be protectors for any whom they perceive to be too weak to take care of themselves, whether by reason of age or strength of character. Such is the case of the wife who is constantly abused by her husband. She is not weak because of her youth but because she doesn't know herself, and is not in touch with her worth and with her ability to manifest her own reality. With the input of society, arresting the abusive spouse and putting him into a situation where he cannot continue the activity, the woman then has the ability to tap a realization that what has gone on is not what is considered normal by society. So she has the ability to examine her feelings about the situation, and to learn the basic principles of the lesson she came down to learn—that she does not have to be a victim, and that she may grow through the experience. The realization of the lesson may only come through an intervention.

When the woman is so deeply into the experience, without an outside intervention she would not be able to get to the point of appreciating and understanding the strength she has within her. So it's not to say that any of these things interfere with the lessons; they help put the lessons into a place where individual souls can deal with them. The spouse who is taken away as an abuser has the ability to examine the fact that no one has the right to control another individual. (Of course he can't do that unless the other individual consents.) While locked up, he is in a place where he has the opportunity to examine and to choose how he wishes to deal with the lesson that he has also been learning. The world, as it exists, is perfect in all of its imperfections because it allows the individual souls to experience the various facets of every lesson in which they engage.

Some people may ask if there are better or worse ways of punishing offenders, for example in respect of the death penalty.

There are no certain effects that they have on any particular soul; it all depends on the souls themselves. Society needs its controls. Society needs to justify that it is protecting the weak. Within the controlling group that establishes the particular way of dealing with crime, various souls have differing feelings about whether they should, say, take the life of another. They may feel it is destroying a person, but it does not; it just helps the soul transition to another place. This belief about the death penalty is embroiled with physical emotions, as is the whole issue of abortion. There is no right or wrong answer, because even the feelings people have are very valuable lessons that they are learning, if they internalize them (and don't just get on a soap box and preach about their pet theories).

Accepting that those suffering may actually have chosen to experience extreme negativity (and, thereby, to raise the level of compassion in others), is people's desire to relieve such suffering, and "overcome evil by good," more important than allowing suffering to take its chosen path?

The simple answer is no. A group of people cannot modify the experience of a single soul. Restructuring what you on the planet term "good" and "evil" will only force the individual soul who wishes to learn that lesson to do so in another way. Love, hate, crime, punishment, even compassion exist only within the physical world. They have (in your terms) either beneficial effects or detrimental effects. We see them all on a par—that they have experiential effects upon the soul. If a soul wishes to experience violence it will fulfill that experience either by being the victim of what you call crime, or being in an area where there is an earthquake and they are buried under the rubble.

You speak as if there's no point in coming to their rescue! Is it just a matter of choice, not one which reflects values?

Rescue is a very difficult word to define. Rescue to you means a positive action in which you are saving the person from the whole experience. Once the experience has begun you can't save the person from the entire experience; where a person is buried in rubble they have experienced the violence of going from their bed to being crushed under rubble. But maybe just an instant, or the period of an hour until they can be, as you say, "rescued" is what their lesson is, because they have to carry into the rest of their physical life what they have learned from that. If they are not rescued they have therefore chosen to end their life at that particular time. The rescue part is allowing them to go forward with the rest of the plan that they have. They would not be in a position to be found, to be rescued, if that was not in accord with the entire plan of their earthly life. So, in that way, the rescuer who gives the sense of completion and the sense of love of another individual by performing the rescue, also allows the rescued one to take the experience of the violence and to bring it forth to fulfill and broaden his or her life. Everybody is playing a part. It is like a huge mechanism where all of the cogs must be fit into their proper place for the entire machine to work.

When I was working in hospital as a chaplain, a sixteen-year-old was brought in who had fallen out of a car, had broken his neck, and had died immediately. His mother said, "God wanted him." Are you saying to us that the boy himself wanted to die?

Not that he wanted to die—that it was a conscious physical thought on his part. His soul had made contracts with the parents so that they might experience loss, so that they could go through the questions, the blame game (should the car door have been locked that he could not have fallen out, was the turn made too sharply that allowed the door to pop open, was the door not completely closed, should he have been in a seat belt so as not to hit the door). This was a complex and intertwining series of experiences which began with the passing of that boy, but had a profound effect not only on him but upon those who discovered him, and his immediate relatives and friends. Nothing exists in a vacuum on the planet Earth.

Where is the freedom of choice in what appears to be a deterministic other world with contracts and lesson plans? Are we planned rather than free to choose?

Very much to the contrary! The fact of passing has been freely pre-determined; the method of passing is always determined with freedom of choice. He could have fallen out of the car, or climbed a tree and have fallen out of it, or slipped in the bathtub and drowned; the way chosen is where there was freedom of choice.

That freedom of choice relates back to the original plan which was made freely by that soul?

Yes.

Should we assume that incarnates who both espouse and live out the highest qualities in their daily lives are spiritually highly evolved and closer to their souls' ultimate goal of reuniting with the Source?

In most cases, yes. In an occasional circumstance, a soul will come down to experience a life of rest and relaxation. It may have experienced some extreme trauma and its entire perception of humanity is of "meat-grinder," "nuclear war," "all-that-you-consider-ultimate" negativity, and it needs to have at least one lifetime where it can experience the beauty of physical emotions. That's the exception.

Usually the soul has matured; it has dealt with the necessary basic issues, and now it is dealing with the spiritual aspects of reuniting within its consciousness the experiences of the divine with its physicality. So it is going through a spiritual evolution while in physical form, gathering up the energies of the lessons it has learned, the experiences it has had, and using all of that to live as closely as possible to the spiritual form it has at Home, thereby letting its inner energy permeate those around it on the planet.

Finally, it's not a particularly good idea to attempt to distinguish between new souls and old souls?
It serves no real purpose.

Thank you, Masters, for your teaching.
It is our pleasure.

Commentary

Peter: I chose to ask supplementary questions of the Masters because of the repeated emotional battering the Leaders had given us over the issue of souls choosing negativity—either to do evil or to endure evil. Mind you, we got their message! As Buddhist doctrine avows, life involves suffering. Spirits choose negativity in order to grapple with and to grasp, at the very deepest level, understanding of that fundamental difference between negativity within physical life and the ultimate of the positive, pure, un-polarized divine energy—the unconditional love they experience at Home, which is the nature of the Source.

We wanted to be given crumbs of comfort as we examined the virtues of concerned parenting and of brave people coming to the rescue of earthquake victims. Always the filter of the soul's free choice of how to live and how to die dominated every issue we raised. The universe turns out to be a huge machine geared to fulfill the vast multiplicity of free choices that souls make in following their path to maturity, both before incarnating and during their physicality.

There are no mistakes, no accidents. Souls may choose to follow blind paths, fail to learn lessons, even get thoroughly lost, but nothing is allowed to impede their ability to do their own thing. The fine nuances of the cosmic system are breathtaking. An earthquake strikes. Some are saved from the rubble—because *they chose* not to die. It has nothing to do with the efforts of those who dug them out. It was the survivors' souls' prior decision that caused the synchronicity of being rescued. And even that rescue might only be to enable the one saved to endure a lifetime of physical disablement or freely chosen, crushing, post-traumatic stress.

Was there to be no let-up in the intense saga of negative experiences? There was, and for us it came as a long-awaited relief. It is not wrong for us to believe that the time will finally arrive when the individual soul does achieve maturity, that it has dealt with all its experiences and lessons and is free to work on integrating its spiritual and physical aspects, living on planet Earth as close to its spiritual form as it does at Home, resonating powerfully with all around. Mahatma Gandhi appears to have achieved such a state while in the flesh, so it is fitting that we should recall the Hindu scriptures:

> *The spirit in the body does not grow old*
> *No one can kill the everlasting spirit*
> *It is pure spirit, beyond sorrow, old age and death,*
> *Beyond evil, hunger and thirst.*
> *All true love and true thought obey the spirit*
> *Those who leave this world and find their soul*
> *And that love which is truth*
> *For them there is liberty in the spirit*
> *In this world and in the worlds to come.*
>
> The Upanishads

"Copernicus and Galileo in their time turned the world upside down. Now the Masters and the Leaders are clearly willing to do the same."

Conclusions
The World Turned Upside Down

As human history has marched on, people have grappled with a disquieting series of revelations. One of the best known was the revolutionary Copernican view of planet Earth revolving around the sun, which caused ferment and hostility in the church and society of the time. More recently, Darwin's theory of evolution upset the religious community, and his views on the origin of human life are still hotly contended. For physicists, Einstein's theory of relativity was groundbreaking, but most lay people were merely intrigued, finding themselves rather out of their depth intellectually, citing his formula $E=MC^2$ often without much understanding of what it meant.

These scientific theories represent only one type of claim. Historically, emperors, monarchs, and presidents were never the gods (or the divinely inspired and anointed leaders) they claimed to be. Though they predicted that their mighty empires would last forever, in the end all were proven wrong.

On the other hand, uneducated African slaves did upset the abysmal thinking of society by proving conclusively that they were not like dumb cattle but, truly, were no less talented than their powerful masters. In many parts of the world women and men are now known to be inherently equal, despite centuries of female oppression, biased holy writings, and unjust laws.

Homosexuality occurs naturally among primates and other species, as well as among human beings, but modern society is still angrily wrestling with the question of whether it is "normal" human behavior.

We add to this gaggle of challenges, past and present, the concepts of this book. We assert sincerely that it really is true that a psychically gifted person can receive reliable information about the nature of life from guiding spirits who live at Home on the Other Side, beyond the veil of death. We will not speculate how the contents of this book may be viewed by others, but we anticipate that battle lines may well be drawn over its startling metaphysical and social comments, which we assess to be of truly enduring significance.

Over the long ages of human history, men and women have been conscious of an energetic dimension beyond the physical world, claimed to have been known by mystics, seers, shamans, and prophets, but denied to the majority of people. Many gross inconsistencies, and unnumbered charlatan psychic practitioners, have invited disbelief and derision concerning the occult. The ancient world's metaphysical knowledge has rarely mixed with the careful, painstaking method and close reasoning of science. Religion may appear to be more attuned to people's hopes and fears about life and death, but western faiths have rarely looked favorably on the occult. Theologians have largely failed to persuade scientists that faith is genuinely connected with verifiable reality.

In the past two centuries faith has been pushed by rationalists into an intellectual corner. On the one hand, liberal theologians speak about a "God of the Gaps" left by science; on the other, evangelists proclaim an intimate but unseen Savior with whom believers are in close communication, but whose intimacy is well beyond the reach of scientific verification. True, some scientists are also people of faith, but they often struggle with disconnects in their thinking, because it is hard to serve two masters, as Jesus of Nazareth pointed out in another context.

At the end of the nineteenth century there was an attempt made in Britain by three Cambridge University professors to bring reasoned academic standards to paranormal research. The Society for Psychical Research was founded in 1882 in Britain under the presidency of philosopher Henry Sidgwick. Two British Prime Ministers, W. E. Gladstone and Arthur Balfour, were early members, as were notable and respected men of science, psychology, and philosophy. Three years later, across the Atlantic, the founders of the American Society for Psychical Research included noted astronomer Simon Newcomb, former Professor of Logic and Ethics at Columbia University James H. Hyslop, and leading psychologists William James (interviewed here) and Gardner Murphy. Since that beginning, a long list of successful and well-respected scientists in every part of the world have been involved in trying to make sense of metaphysical phenomena. This speaks of a tentative awareness on their part that this frontier of human knowledge is not quite as ephemeral as it sometimes appears.

It has been difficult to convince hard-nosed skeptics that there is any merit in books concerning psychic communication with God, Jesus, Angels, Ascended and Enlightened Masters, and the discarnate spirits of the dead. Major channeled downloads from Home have included messages from the Masters, in *Many Lives, Many Masters* (1988) and sequels by psychiatrist Dr. Brian Weiss; from Jesus, in the study book *A Course in Miracles* (1975), reputedly by psychologist Helen Schucman; and from God, in several books of *Conversations with God* (1995) by PR executive Neale Donald Walsch. All have proved somewhat influential with a fast-growing but still narrow segment of the population, but there has been little credible response to these revelations in the academic and scientific community other than sheer disbelief, tinged with boredom.

Now the noise of this phenomenon of contact with spiritual beings is becoming increasingly audible, though many people (including believers) are really not sure what to make of it, or how to assess its validity. It is clear, however, that a substantial and increasing number of people, both inside and outside traditional faiths, are searching for a satisfying explanation of the meaning and purpose of their lives. This is a time in human history of major turmoil, not only in the whole global secular society but in all the major religions, and religious adherents are increasingly asking if the practice of *spirituality* can help them in their search.

Into this fray we come with our robust claim of relevance. With help from the Masters we have focused attention on fifteen individuals, the history of whose lives is well known in various circles of society. By asking them somewhat basic questions, we believe we have revealed a degree of authenticity in what they chose to say. Their individuality and unique views have illustrated the broad theme of reincarnation. In clear agreement with the comments of the Masters, these Leaders graciously answered our enquiries about their previous life and work, and how they view our world from their present vantage point in the spiritual Home. We were encouraged by this encounter. They expressed keenness to communicate, and did so in ways which seemed (despite the filter of channeling) to subtly mark their individuality. We were challenged and frequently dumbfounded by their attitudes. The information they gave concerning the life of the soul, its origin, purpose, incarnation, and Homecoming, helped us to clarify many issues.

For readers willing to listen to this evidence, they make an enormous challenge to our current way of thinking and living. Just as Copernicus and Galileo in their time turned the world upside down, so the Masters and the Leaders are clearly willing to do the same. After all, breaking new ground is what each of the Leaders has done best in the past. We are reminded of the popular song *The World Turned Upside Down*, played by the bands of the victorious forces of General Washington and General Rochambeau after the defeat of the British in 1781 at Yorktown, in the final battle of the American War of Independence:

If buttercups buzzed after the bee
If boats were on land, churches on sea
If ponies rode men and if grass ate the cows
And cats should be chased into holes by the mouse
If the mamas sold their babies

To the gypsies for half a crown
If summer were spring And the other way 'round
Then all the world would be upside down.

The Four Revolutionary Claims

Our summation of the ideas that the Masters and Leaders have given to us follows. They make four revolutionary claims which, if accepted, will surely provoke a significant renaissance in both the popular and academic life of our world society.

The first revolution in our thinking—one which the spirits indicate should be seen as being for them the most important—challenges humanity to stop thinking about God as *a person*, whether the single deity of Judaism and Islam, or Christianity's three Persons in the one *Persona* of the Trinity, or the various deities of other religious traditions.

As Bertrand Russell crisply described, the creativity of the Source is contained within a unified field of pure energy encompassing all souls, each one of whom has been "broken off" from the Creator, yet possesses both individuality and personal freedom. They told us that all human beings, without exception, have souls embedded in their human shell, with an individual life-purpose offered to and freely chosen by each soul in advance, whose goal is to achieve spiritual self-awareness and individual maturity. Our own souls are all part of this collective divinity but we may not be aware of this at all, because whenever souls incarnate on the planet they are given amnesia as to the nature and power of their spiritual essence. While incarnating, one of our final tasks on what the Masters call "the Wheel of Rebirth" is to rediscover our true self and the nature of our soul's creativity.

The second revolution in our thinking is for us to abandon the familiar concepts of Heaven and Hell as future destinations for our soul. The reality of life at Home is that *all* souls live equally in an energetic dimension quite different from that of our polarized planet. It is a realm of unconditional love, the basic energetic substance of the universe.

Hell has no part in that energetic dimension because Home is devoid of all judgment. Hell is a this-world, present state of mind which we may create within ourselves, or which may be thrust upon us while we live on the planet. In no way is Hell a dire future punitive incarceration, divinely ordained as retribution for our sins, because the Source is non-judgmental. Hell exists only within the energetic dimension of planet Earth.

Likewise, Heaven is simply a present state of mind found within our earthly experience, because Home, although suffused with unconditional love, in no way exists as a judgmental place of celestial reward for our being good and doing good. Every soul who incarnates on Earth will eventually return Home. There are no exceptions. Good and evil, as we know them in our human existence, belong solely to the ethics of our polarized planet. These concepts lose their relevance for our eternal soul when it frees itself from our human body.

The third revolution in our thinking is to grasp the manner and purpose of our soul's life on Earth.

Incarnating, we are usually programmed to be forgetful as to our origin and purpose, so that each life is a fresh adventure. Before entering a human body, we identified with our counselors at Home those types of experience we considered necessary for our personal growth toward maturity. Whatever they may be— positive or negative—these experiences are always designed to meet our personal goals. So we select our parents, talents, and environment in advance, and may also have made contracts with soul mates to provide us with challenges of various kinds during our human lifetime. If we fail to deal with the specific physical challenges that we have chosen in order to gain spiritual mastery, we are committed to face something akin to them again in a subsequent incarnation.

It is at this point that the enormous difference emerges between the thinking of the physical world and that of the spirit world. Whatever is a positive experience for the soul will not necessarily be humanly judged to have been an experience of goodness at all. Shakespeare's "All the world's a stage" is a fair description. The human experiences we have selected at Home may involve our role-playing in a way that human ethics consider profoundly negative or even downright evil. We may have agreed to be subjected to physical or psychological pain and suffering that few human minds would ever deem to be good. Before incarnating, we may have undertaken to play the negative role of a con artist, a philanderer, a murderer, even a Stalin or a Hitler. In its condemnation of such roles, the norm of human ethics totally fails to reflect the markedly different spiritual reality.

This third revolution, therefore, concerns the true basis of our physicality, which is the proving ground for the life of the soul. Earth is a place where the soul has a personal agenda to work out, which takes precedence over all other human agendas. If our agenda is to fulfill a dark mission, to understand negativity to the full, it may require that we live according to that which human beings call "evil" principles. At some point during this experience, however, our soul may fully come to terms with the nature of that negativity. We will then understand that it is an integral part of the Creator's plan to awaken our spiritual conscience, to increase the depth of our soul's compassion and, through dark experiences, finally to gain a true knowledge and wisdom of its opposite—the Source itself.

This revolution demands that we understand the process. Our soul's life at Home is one of unconditional love. The core of our self as a soul is composed of the best and highest that life can espouse—beauty, truth, goodness, love, service, and every virtue. Evil is never the working of a capricious divinity—evil in all its forms fulfills a necessity for our soul: to know the nature of darkness so that we may fully understand the magnificence of the divine Light that is the effulgence of unconditional love. Then, as we awaken to that realization, amnesia fades, and, even while still on Earth, we may apprehend our ultimate destiny.

The fourth revolution in our thinking embraces a clear understanding of our soul's place in the cosmos. Our soul never dies. In essence that is because our soul is a fragment of pure energy, searching for and eventually realizing its true identity in close harmony with the Creator.

The fact of our indestructibility affects many areas of human life and death. For example, in some respects the abortion of an unborn child is seen by those at Home as a non-issue because the aborted fetus's soul (rarely present) is not adversely involved in the destruction of fetal tissue, and simply returns Home well in advance of the abortion procedure. You cannot kill the soul. Yet, at the same time, abortion can be a very real and agonizing spiritual issue for the mother and father who have chosen not to keep their baby, and for the larger society.

Likewise, the spirits insist, euthanasia and life-support issues are challenges which everybody involved with the patient must face, yet the patient may be involved least of all, because the patient's soul has already substantially detached from the shell of the body and is usually only nominally connected until the body dies. On the other hand, suicide may represent a spiritual failure with karmic consequences for terminating an incarnation too soon out of weakness.

So our place in the cosmos as human beings provides the means for our spiritual self to learn its experiential lessons. Our egos and our body shells are designed simply as vehicles for this spiritual work, and we will use them until that moment when our mature soul can say in joy, "I know, even as also I am known."

"Test the Spirits"

There is much more to be gleaned by further analysis of the dialogues we held with the Masters and Leaders, which we hope other people will undertake. Revolutions of this kind are costly because they force us out of our comfortable habits and treasured beliefs. But, looking back, humanity has benefited greatly from new ideas—from the cosmic view of Copernicus to the societal movement for women's liberation.

Our spiritual mentors have made it clear to us and to other spiritual writers that the progress of human life is faulty. Our world society is in severe chaos, and presumably, short of slowing or stopping the practice of incarnation on planet Earth altogether, something must be done about it. It is our belief that the current wave of messages from Home, of which this book is only one reflection, has washed on our shores in order to help us to stay our hand from producing even more chaos among the nations and wreaking irreparable damage on planet Earth herself.

We take seriously the wise biblical injunction: *"Beloved, believe not every spirit, but test the spirits whether they are of God."* (1 John 4:1) We have now spent years working with this large group of spirits who identify themselves to us as Ascended Masters, and whose enlightened membership has included mature souls and angels. We have witnessed their genuine concern, reliability, warmth, and loving good humor—not only to us but to all who come for their help. So we have put aside our hesitations of going public and, fully believing these spirits to be divine, have published these dialogues for them, and with their *imprimatur.* We hope that the messages they have given will help to save us all from a chaotic world. Otherwise, quite soon, even the toughest spirits may no longer wish to incarnate on planet Earth.

The wise words of our ascended friends renew within us the sense of adventure, so that we may all come to know ourselves for what and who we truly are. So, eventually we will all return to our spiritual Home, the dimension of unconditional love, whose Builder and Maker is the creative Source of all life, and of whom we are each a small but integral and beloved part.

The Authors

Toni Ann Winninger, JD, CH, is well established as a psychic channeler in practice with individuals, and with groups large and small. A Reiki master, she specializes in spirit release and teaches metaphysical subjects and Light Language. Previously she worked for 27 years as a criminal prosecutor in the Chicago area. Toni is the President of Celestial Voices, Inc. which promotes the Masters' messages. She channeled for all the books listed here:

Peter Watson Jenkins, MA (Cantab.), MH, is a master hypnotist working in past-life regression and spirit release. In the 1960s he studied theology at Cambridge University, England, and served for 21 years in parish ministry. He is the C.E.O. of Celestial Voices, Inc., a spiritual publisher based in the USA. He interviewed souls and compiled the books listed here:

Talking with Leaders of the Past
Talking with Twentieth-Century Women
Talking with Twentieth-Century Men
How I Died (and what I did next)
Spirit World Wisdom
The Masters' Reincarnation Handbook: Journey of the Soul
Healing with the Universe, Meditation, and Prayer
Exploring Reincarnation (May 2011)

Our websites

MastersoftheSpiritWorld.com

CelestialVoicesInc.com

Facebook: Reincarnation Guide

Lightning Source UK Ltd.
Milton Keynes UK
UKOW06f0329190716

278666UK00001B/14/P